G000160780

The Fascination of
BIRDS
From the Albatross to the Yellowthroat

William Young

DOVER PUBLICATIONS, INC.
Mineola, New York

Bibliographical Note

The Fascination of Birds: From the Albatross to the Yellowthroat is a new work, first published by Dover Publications, Inc., in 2014.

Library of Congress Cataloging-in-Publication Data

Young, William, 1952– author.
The fascination of birds : from the albatross to the yellowthroat / William Young.
    pages cm
Includes bibliographical references and index.
ISBN-13: 978-0-486-49278-0 (alk. paper)
ISBN-10: 0-486-49278-8 (alk. paper)
1. Birds—Miscellanea. I. Title.
QL699.Y68 2014
598—dc23

2013050361

Manufactured in the United States by Courier Corporation
49278801   2014
www.doverpublications.com

Dedicated to

Gemma Radko

CONTENTS

INTRODUCTION ix

1. Albatross Birds and Superstition 1
2. Anhinga Waterbirds Who Are Not Waterproof 4
3. Ani Communitarian Birds 6
4. Avocet Birds and Sexual Attachment 8
5. Bee-Eater Birds in Unpleasant Places 11
6. Bird of Paradise Birds as Theater 13
7. Blackbird Birds Who Inspire Crimes 17
8. Bluebird Birds as Symbols of Happiness 20
9. Bowerbird Birds Who Are Master Builders 23
10. Bunting Sexual Attitudes toward Birds 26
11. Bustard Bird Fatalities 29
12. Cardinal Feeder Birds 32
13. Cassowary Dangerous Birds 36
14. Catbird Birds Who Sound Like Other Animals 39
15. Chickadee Bird Names That Are Puns 42
16. Chicken Domesticated Birds 45
17. Cockatoo The Importance of Details about Birds 50
18. Coot Birds with Image Problems 54
19. Cormorant The Eyes of Birds 57
20. Crane Birds Who Dance 60
21. Crow Birds as Political Symbols 64
22. Cuckoo Birds as Symbols of Marital Infidelity 68
23. Dipper Walking Birds 72
24. Dove Birds as Symbols of Peace 75
25. Duck Bird Stamps 81
26. Eagle Unnoticed Birds 87
27. Egret Birds as Symbols of Conservation 91
28. Emu Exploring the World to Look for Birds 94

Contents

29. Fairy-Wren	Birds with Intense Colors	97
30. Falcon	Birds as Corporate Symbols	100
31. Finch	Birds as Measuring Devices	105
32. Flicker	Birds and Space Travel	110
33. Flycatcher	Uncertainty in Identifying Birds	113
34. Frogmouth	Invisible Birds	117
35. Gannet	The Symmetry of Birds	120
36. Gnatcatcher	Bird Nests	123
37. Goose	Migratory Birds	127
38. Grackle	Gangs of Birds	133
39. Grebe	Bird Reproduction	136
40. Gull	Birds and Balls	140
41. Hawk	Changing Attitudes toward Bird Conservation	144
42. Heron	The Liberating Quality of Bird Romance	148
43. Honeycreeper	Birds with Multipurpose Bills	151
44. Honeyeater	Birds Who Don't Sound Like Birds	154
45. Hornbill	The Sound of Bird Wings	156
46. Hummingbird	Jewel-like Birds	159
47. Ibis	Sacred Birds	166
48. Jay	A Bird in the Hand	168
49. Kingfisher	Birds and Mythology	172
50. Kite	Birds and Snake Venom	175
51. Loon	Heavy Birds	178
52. Lyrebird	Birds Who Mimic and Mock	181
53. Manakin	Improbable Birds	184
54. Merganser	Birds and Hunters	187
55. Mockingbird	Birds Who Sing All Night	189
56. Nightingale	Birds Who Inspire Human Emotions	193
57. Nightjar	Birds with Rude Names	196
58. Nuthatch	Nonconformist Birds	199
59. Oriole	Confusing Bird Names	201
60. Osprey	Birds with a Worldwide Distribution	204

Contents

61. Owl	Mean Birds	207
62. Parrot	Bird Names That Are Verbs	214
63. Peafowl	Birds and the Visual Arts	219
64. Pelican	Birders with Bird Names	222
65. Penguin	Birds and Paperback Books	225
66. Plover	Birds Who Deceive	228
67. Puffin	Birds Near the Maelstrom	231
68. Quetzal	A Life Devoted to Birds	236
69. Rail	Trying to Catch a Wild Bird	243
70. Raven	Birds as Religious Messengers	247
71. Roadrunner	Birds in Cartoons	251
72. Robin	Violent Birds	253
73. Sandpiper	Birds at the Beach	256
74. Shearwater	Dreams about Flying Like a Bird	261
75. Skua	Bully Birds	264
76. Skylark	Bubbly Birds	266
77. Snipe	Birds and Practical Jokes	269
78. Sparrow	Bird Wars	271
79. Spoonbill	Charismatic Birds	275
80. Starling	Birds and the Bard	277
81. Stork	Birds and Babies	279
82. Storm-Petrel	Out-of-place Birds	282
83. Swallow	Birds as Seasonal Harbingers	285
84. Swan	Monochrome Birds	287
85. Swift	Bird Spit	291
86. Tanager	Overwhelming Birds	293
87. Tern	Birds and Daylight	296
88. Thick-Knee	Birds in Obscure Literary References	299
89. Thrasher	Birding on a Moonscape	301
90. Thrush	Bird Music	303
91. Tropicbird	Watching Birds in the Nude	306
92. Turkey	Birds and Holidays	308

Contents

93. Vireo   Monotonous Birds   312
94. Vulture   Birds as Symbols of Death   314
95. Warbler   Birds and Espionage   319
96. Woodcock   Birds Who Fly Slowly   325
97. Woodpecker   Headbanger Birds   328
98. Wren   Girl Birds and Boy Birds   334
99. Yellowthroat The Poetry of Birds   337

INTRODUCTION

I'm probably the only person to own a birding magazine signed by the noted sex therapist Dr. Ruth Westheimer. In 1996, I went to the National Gallery of Art in Washington and noticed Dr. Ruth waiting in line to enter an exhibition of the paintings of Johannes Vermeer. I thought it would be fun to get her autograph, but all I had for her to sign was the birding magazine I had brought to read on the subway. Dr. Ruth was as pleasant and gracious in real life as she was on television. When I handed her the magazine, she asked what it was. I told her about my love for birds, and she signed the title page "Dr. Ruth Westheimer," with a squiggle underneath. I thanked her, and as I was leaving, she said in her wonderful manner that stresses every word, "KEEP WATCHING BIRDS!"

Birds have been much loved throughout human history and have been prominent in culture, folklore, and literature. The ancient Romans tried to predict the future by looking for omens in the flight patterns and feeding habits of birds. A person entrusted with reading such omens was called an auspex (or auspice), which is derived from *avis*, meaning "bird," and *specere*, meaning "to look at." The omens seen by the auspex were called auspices, a word used today to suggest protection or support, as in the expression "under the auspices of." The Romans felt confident about pursuing activities under positive auspices. In *Coined by Shakespeare*, Jeffrey McQuain and Stanley Malless point out that in Shakespeare's poem "The Rape of Lucrece," the word "auspicious" was used for the first time. Shakespeare made positive auspices into an adjective meaning "favorable."

Birds fascinate people for many reasons. While the ability of birds to fly is not unique in the animal world, humans consider bird flight more beautiful and inspiring than the flight of insects or bats. Some birds have beautiful plumage. Some behave in entertaining ways. Some sing beautifully—many bird hobbyists prefer to be called birders rather than birdwatchers, in part because the activity involves listening to birdsong as well as looking at plumage. Birds provide links with people in other countries and other eras. An Osprey or Peregrine Falcon I see in the United States is the same species people see in Europe, Asia, and Australia. The jealous swan mentioned in a Chaucer poem from the fourteenth century is probably the same species that I have seen in twenty-first-century America.

Many millions of people in the United States and other parts of the world have a recreational interest in birds. The level of interest ranges from beginners who hang feeders in their yard to enthusiasts who buy expensive optical equipment and take expeditions to remote corners of the planet to seek unusual birds. Since grade school, I have devoted a substantial portion of my life to trying to understand the behavior of birds, their role in nature, and their relationship to humans. I spend many hours studying the birdlife near my home in Northern Virginia, just across the Potomac River from Washington, DC. Birds also have drawn me to many far-flung places throughout North America and other continents.

When studying birds, the sky is the limit, both literally and figuratively. You can discover connections between birds and an almost limitless range of subjects, such as biology, ecology, literature, music, history, politics, economics, religion, geography, physics, chemistry, linguistics, the visual arts, the performing arts, sports, and comedy. For instance, you can learn how cuckoos have a link with marital infidelity, your tailbone, and the "hook 'em Horns" gesture used by fans of the University of Texas football team. You can find out why terms such as "cocker spaniel" and "sniper" are connected to people who hunt birds. You can develop a better understanding of the countless bird references that appear in literature. And you might come across surprising bits of musical information, such as the unpleasant meaning of the lyrics to the French song "Alouette" or how the Beatles song "Blackbird" is thought to have been an inspiration for the murders committed by Charles Manson.

The illustrations in this book come from *The Birds of America* by John James Audubon, who lived from 1785 to 1851. Audubon is America's most famous wildlife artist and is now considered to be the patron saint of American birds. Not all of the birds I mention in the following essays are seen in America or have an accompanying illustration. For those not illustrated, you can find many photographs for almost every species on the Internet.

Unlike bird books that are designed to be carried into the field to aid in identification, *The Fascination of Birds* is written to be enjoyed at home. The essays are arranged in alphabetical order by type of bird, from the albatross to the yellowthroat, and each essay has a subtitle about a context in which the bird is discussed. No previous knowledge of birds is necessary to understand the text. The book might help beginners to better understand the birds they see and the avian references they encounter. It might help experienced birders to learn more about many ornithological and nonornithological aspects of birds.

The Fascination of Birds will help all types of readers learn something about the wonders and variety of the birds with whom we share the planet. I hope that what I have written will cause people to develop a stronger love for these remarkable creatures and to understand why so many people have been fascinated by them. Dr. Ruth, who knows a lot about love relationships, has offered sound advice—KEEP WATCHING BIRDS! If you do what Dr. Ruth suggests, the results could be auspicious.

1. ALBATROSS
Birds and Superstition

In a 1970 skit on *Monty Python's Flying Circus*, John Cleese dresses as an ice cream lady in a cinema and tries to sell a huge seabird to the filmgoers. He walks down the aisle yelling, "Albatross!" When asked what flavor it is, he replies, "It's a bloody sea bird. . . . It's not any bloody flavor."

A more famous albatross appears in Samuel Taylor Coleridge's poem "The Rime of the Ancient Mariner." The mariner tells a long story to a wedding guest, causing both of them to miss the wedding. Sailors considered the albatross a good omen, and the mariner caused an uproar on his ship when he shot one. Shortly after the shooting, the wind stopped, stranding the ship at sea. Coleridge then wrote the famous line: "Water, water everywhere, nor any drop to drink." The superstitious crew blamed the mariner for the bad luck, and he utters the lines that led to the expression about "having an albatross around your neck":

> Ah wel-a-day! what evil looks
> Had I from old and young!
> Instead of the cross, the Albatross
> About my neck was hung.

Albatrosses are found in the Northern and Southern Hemispheres, but because they spend most of their time at sea, most humans have never seen one and never will. Unless you go to their nesting grounds during breeding season, you usually can see them only by taking a pelagic trip, which involves a boat ride far into the ocean. On their breeding grounds, pairs of albatrosses engage in affectionate courtship displays to strengthen their pair bond.

Albatrosses are among the longest-living birds in the world. In 2013 on Midway Atoll in the Pacific Ocean, a female Laysan Albatross named Wisdom, who in 1956 had an identification band put around her leg by the ornithologist Chandler Robbins, was located with a chick. Wisdom was thought to be sixty-two years old (having been about five years old when banded), making her the oldest documented wild bird in the Northern Hemisphere.

The Wandering Albatross has one of the longest wingspans of any bird in the world—more than eleven feet—and its hefty body can weigh up to twenty pounds. I saw Wandering Albatrosses on a pelagic trip from Australia, and one who flew near our boat seemed as big as a pterodactyl. Large albatrosses usually are found only in the Southern Hemisphere, which is where the first albatrosses are thought to have evolved. To fly from southern oceans to northern ones, a seabird must cross an area of calm winds near the equator called the doldrums; the expression "to be in the doldrums" comes from the problem sailors encountered when there was not adequate wind in this area to propel their boats. Smaller albatrosses can achieve adequate lift to take off from the water surface in calm winds, so they were able to make it through the doldrums and north of the equator. The term "smaller" is relative, because small albatrosses are quite large compared to most other seabirds.

In Bernard Shaw's 1934 play *The Simpleton of the Unexpected Isles*, one of the characters makes a pun about an "albatrocity." Ornithologist Carl Safina uses the same pun in a more serious context to describe why most of the world's albatross species now are threatened with extinction. In his 2002 book *Eye of the Albatross*, Safina explains how during the twentieth century, Pacific seabird colonies were ravaged to collect feathers (for bedding, pen quills, hats, and clothing), bird droppings (for fertilizer), and eggs (for photographic albumen prints). Modern society has introduced environmental regulations to reduce some of this ruthlessness, but twenty-first-century albatrosses are encountering different problems. There are no ocean equivalents of wilderness areas in which albatrosses can be protected, because all areas of the ocean are now accessible to large commercial fishing boats. Longline fishing is killing adult birds at sea and destroying their food sources. Miles of fishing line with tens of thousands of baited hooks stretch through the ocean. While the lines are being set, albatrosses and other seabirds dive for the bait. Some albatrosses swallow the hooks and are drowned when yanked underwater by the lines. Another albatrocity is caused by plastic and other trash. Safina describes a mother albatross trying to regurgitate food for a chick and revealing a toothbrush stuck in her throat. He says it is unlikely that any living albatross chick is free of plastic.

The name "albatross" is based on a pun. It comes from *alcatraz*, which is a Spanish word for a water container. *Alcatraz* also became a word to describe a pelican, because a pelican's bill resembles such a container. In previous centuries, people who coined bird names were not as precise as modern ornithologists in differentiating among similar-looking species. A big white pelican looked pretty much like a big white albatross or any other big white seabird. Some punster changed the "alca" part to "alba," which means "white." So when Burt Lancaster starred as a bird-loving convict in the 1962 film *The Birdman of Alcatraz*, he portrayed a murderer who was imprisoned on an island named after pelicans who gave their name to the albatross.

2. ANHINGA
Waterbirds Who Are Not Waterproof

If you visit swampy areas in the southeastern United States, you might see large birds who look as if they are being crucified. They perch with outstretched wings, waiting for their feathers to dry. They are called Anhingas, and they have long dark bodies, long snaking necks, and dagger-like bills, which they use to spear fish. They also will eat snakes and baby alligators. Anhingas swim low in the water, sometimes with only their neck showing above the surface. This behavior, rather than their taste for snakes, has led to the nickname "snake bird." The Anhinga's tail is long and wide like a turkey's, which has led to another nickname—the "water turkey." Anhingas dive for fish, but their feathers are not waterproof. Waterproof feathers would make them more buoyant, inhibiting their ability to swim underwater. Water-soaked feathers serve a similar purpose to a scuba diver's weight belt. When the birds leave the water, they must stand or perch somewhere in a cruciform pose to allow their wings to dry.

A soaring Anhinga resembles a giant plus sign suspended in the air. Its long tail sticks out behind its wings, and its long neck sticks out in front. An adult Anhinga has a lot of white feathering on its back and wings. The white feathers on the black body create an illusion that the bird has been snowed upon. The comparison to snow might be wishful thinking when observing Anhingas in a hot, humid Florida swamp.

There are four anhinga species in the world. The species in the Americas is called simply the Anhinga. In the United States, it is found most commonly in the states around the Gulf of Mexico. Its scientific name is *Anhinga anhinga*, making it the only bird in the world whose genus, species, and common names are all the same.[1] In scientific

---

1. Living things are grouped into various categories. All birds are in the kingdom *Animalia* (they are animals), the phylum *Chordata* (they have a spine), and the class *Aves* (they are birds). The

names, the first name is the genus, or general grouping, and it is capitalized; the second identifies the species, or specific entity, and it is not capitalized. The other three species in the genus *Anhinga* are called darters because of the way they dart at fish with their long, pointed bill. The American species does this also.

Near the eastern entrance to Everglades National Park in Florida is the Anhinga Trail. It runs less than half a mile through a sawgrass marsh. In 2003, visitors to this trail witnessed a daylong battle between an alligator and an invasive snake species called the Burmese Python. The fight ended in a draw. In another section of the Everglades, I heard a ranger tell a story about a more successful alligator. The alligator was in the water a few feet below a perched Anhinga. The gator curled its tail so that the tip was wiggling just at the surface of the water. The Anhinga saw the movement and thinking it was a fish, dove after it. That was the Anhinga's final dive ever.

---

class is divided into various orders, the orders into families, the families into genera (the plural of genus), and the genera into species. There are also further divisions of species into races and subspecies. Biologists have developed many mnemonics to remember the Kingdom-Phylum-Class-Order-Family-Genus-Species progression, such as "Kids Prefer Candy Over Fresh Green Spinach" and some not-so-clean ones about the exploits of King Phillip.

3. ANI
Communitarian Birds

An ani is a black cuckoo with a thick, curved bill and a long tail that it moves back and forth. Its name is not pronounced the same way as the Annie from the theater—the A is pronounced like the A in father. And unlike the tuneful red-haired moppet, anis have limited musical talent. There are three ani species, and all live in the American tropics and subtropics. Two species normally can be seen in the United States: the Smooth-billed Ani, mainly in southern Florida; and the Groove-billed Ani, mainly in southern Texas. The Greater Ani is substantially larger than the other two. People in the United States are more likely to know about the ani as an answer to the crossword puzzle clue "cuckoo" than from a personal encounter.

Many cuckoo species lay their eggs in the nests of other species and let the foster parents raise the young—but not the anis. They are communitarians, with groups of anis roosting together and building communal nests. Often, multiple females will lay eggs in the same nest. The males help with incubation. The ornithologist Alexander Skutch includes a chapter about anis in his pioneering 1987 book *Helpers at Birds' Nests*, which examines the phenomenon of birds giving assistance at the nest to others who are not their mate or their young—and in some instances, not even of the same species. Skutch describes anis as highly social and affectionate birds who live in great amity with group members. I have seen two Smooth-billed Anis perched so close to each other on a wire that their bodies and bills seemed to form a heart silhouette. However, Skutch notes that female anis sometimes eject eggs already in a nest.

Communal nesting by anis might have similar advantages to some types of communal living by humans. Imagine that you live in a multi-unit structure with three other households. You might establish a system in which each household does chores every fourth day, such as

6

cooking, cleaning, and laundry. You would need only one set of appliances instead of four. The tradeoff of losing independence might be offset by having three other households do some of your work. The same principle applies to anis. Individual pairs lose some control over their individual eggs or offspring, but all the anis might benefit by allowing each parent bird to spend less time sitting on eggs and more time looking for food. Should a parent die while eggs or young are in the nest, its genes are more likely to be passed on, because the other anis will assume responsibility.

Because of its black plumage, the Smooth-billed Ani is sometimes called the "death-bird." How that plumage became black is the subject of a Mayan folktale, which Anne Lebastille related in a 1997 issue of *International Wildlife* magazine. A proud mother ani with pretty pink plumage was best friends with a female hawk, whom she told to avoid ani chicks when hunting. The hawk asked for a description of the youngsters, and the female ani described them as the most beautiful of any birds. Later, the hawk went hunting and saw a nest with a half-dozen scrawny and ugly chicks with gaping mouths, and proceeded to eat them. When the mother ani returned with food for her young, she found the nest empty. She became furious and immediately went to find the hawk. The hawk told the ani that she had kept her word and had eaten only six little black runts who could not have been the beautiful ani chicks. The distraught ani realized how her exaggerations had resulted in the death of her children, so she put on her black mourning garb. This is why anis have all-black feathers and twitch their tails in grief. It is also why you should be careful not to brag too much about your children.

4. AVOCET
Birds and Sexual Attachment

Aldous Huxley's 1932 novel *Brave New World* describes a society in which human sexual activity is frequent and involves no emotional attachment. Seven years earlier, his brother Julian, a famous biologist, described similar circumstances within the society of shorebirds called avocets. He claimed that the Pied Avocet has no courtship and that the males do not engage in any special sexual displays, vocalizations, or ceremonies.

Just as some critics have questioned whether Aldous was correct about trends in human sexuality, critics have questioned Julian about avocet sexuality. The French website "Oiseaux-Birds" features photos of the elaborate courtship rituals and breeding behavior of the Pied Avocet. The breeding of avocets has been a subject of great interest in parts of Europe. The Royal Society for the Protection of Birds chose the Pied Avocet as its symbol when avocets bred on society reserves after World War II—the first known successful avocet nesting in Britain in roughly a hundred years. The population of British avocets had crashed in the 1800s because of hunting, habitat loss, and hobbyists collecting avocet eggs from nests.

Avocets are in the same family as stilts, and both types of birds have long, spindly legs. Avocets have a delicate and elegant appearance. Unlike many shorebirds whose bills are straight or curve downward, an avocet's long bill curves upward. The technical term for such a bill is recurved, while downward-curving bills are decurved. A British nickname for the avocet is "cobbler's awl," because the bill looks like a tool used by shoemakers. In many avocet photographs, the bill appears to bend to one side rather than upward, but this is an optical illusion. The Wry-bill, a small New Zealand plover, is the only bird in the world whose bill hooks to one side.

There are four avocet species in the world. Red-necked Avocets are found in Australia, while the Andean Avocet is found in South

America. The Pied Avocet has the widest range and is found in Europe, Africa, and Asia. The American Avocet is found in North and Central America and the Caribbean. In North America, it is more commonly seen in the West than the East. The American Avocet is a mostly black-and-white bird in nonbreeding plumage. In breeding season, its head and neck are a lovely russet. One often sees avocets in ponds or along the coast, sometimes in large flocks. The female's bill is shorter than the male's but has a stronger upward curve.

Stilts look like they are wearing micro-miniskirts, because their legs are extremely long in proportion to their body size. John James Audubon painted one bending over so that the bottom half of the painting would not show only its spindly legs. In flight, their legs stick out far behind their tail. Stilts have the appearance of being delicate both on the ground and in the air. Unlike avocets, they have a thin, straight bill. There are about a half-dozen species of stilts in the world, and one who lives in New Zealand is among the rarest shorebirds in the world. Most stilt species have black-and-white plumage, and their legs are red or pink. Only the Banded Stilt in Australia deviates from a monochrome feather scheme by having a chestnut band across the breast.

The suitability of a particular bill shape depends on the preferred food and habitat of the species. What works well for one species might not work for another. Avocets feed by swinging their bill back and forth in sand, mud, or shallow water, stirring up small crustaceans and insects with the curved portion and grabbing any edible morsel that pops up. To understand why this technique is effective, imagine that you have lost something at the beach an inch or so below the surface of the sand. You would have a better chance of finding it if you sifted through the sand with the curved top of a coat hanger than if you repeatedly jabbed a straight piece of wire into the sand. But if you were looking for something visible at or near the surface of the sand, it might be more efficient to impale it with a straight piece of wire. Stilts and most other shorebirds have straight bills and use the equivalent of the straight piece of wire, while avocets use the equivalent of the coat hanger.

In 1842, the Austrian physicist Christian Doppler developed a theory about how the frequency of a sound changes when either the observer or the source of the sound is moving. Doppler's work has been applied in many fields, including weather forecasting (Doppler radar), echocardiograms, submarine sonar systems, speed guns for baseball and tennis, and the detection of speeding automobiles. Long before Doppler came along, avocets were using the principle behind his theory to fool predators. They utter a series of notes that change in pitch, making the approach of the sound seem faster than it actually is. But avocets have never been used by the police to nab speeding motorists.

5. BEE-EATER
Birds in Unpleasant Places

Birding can create strong mental associations with particular places. The places can be as close as your kitchen window or as far away as the other side of the Earth. These places become infused with memories and significance from the birds you associate with them.

Not all of the special places are pleasant, and one would never visit many of them were it not for the birds. Some birds are found in mucky and insect-infested swamps and marshes. In Arizona, birders often hike through areas that contain shin daggers—pointy bits of vegetation that penetrate socks and stab your ankles. Parts of the rain forest floor in Australia are covered with lawyer vine, named for its nasty stickers that are hard to shake off once they get hold of you. Garbage dumps can be excellent places to look for birds. Someone gave me a shirt with "BROWNSVILLE DUMP" written below the image of a crow. This dump is a refuse site in south Texas that used to be the most reliable place in the United States to see the Tamaulipas Crow, a species typically not seen north of the Mexican border. Also in south Texas, I went to odiferous chicken farms that dump chicken innards into adjoining fields, attracting large numbers of hawks, caracaras (who are in the falcon family), and vultures.

Sewage lagoons attract many birds, who do not mind the smells as much as people do. I have visited sewage lagoons in the United States and Trinidad, as well as in Australia (in both Brisbane and Cairns), where they are sometimes called poo pits. In the Cairns poo pits in northeastern Australia, I set up a telescope at close range to look at a stunning bird called a Rainbow Bee-eater. He was perched at eye level in perfect light. These birds eat bees, removing the stinger before swallowing, and their iridescent feathers reflect the colors of the rainbow. Each color blends seamlessly into its adjacent color. Two feathers tipped with little racquets extend about an inch beyond the edge of the tail. The bird at the poo pits was silent, but Rainbow Bee-eaters have a call that sounds like a referee blowing a whistle at a water polo match. They do not make nests, but instead excavate holes in mud banks or in the ground to create an area for laying eggs. Some males lose their tail racquets when digging the nest burrows.

There are more than two dozen species of bee-eaters in the world, and most of them are beautiful. Bee-eater species are found primarily in Africa and Asia. The Rainbow Bee-eater is the only bee-eater in Australia, and a few bee-eater species can be seen in Europe. In 2012, a species called the European Bee-eater became the subject of an international incident when a dead one was found by a Turkish farmer. The bird had an aluminum band around its leg that said "Israel," and because the bird had one nostril that looked bigger than the other, Turkish authorities thought that Mossad, the Israeli intelligence agency, might have implanted surveillance equipment in the bird's bill. Though the dead bee-eater was ultimately exonerated, the incident reflected the deterioration of relations between Turkey and Israel. A similar incident occurred later in the year involving a vulture found in Sudan who was accused of spying for Israel because it was wearing a tracking device placed there by bird researchers.

No bee-eaters are found in the Americas. However, birds in the American tropics called motmots look somewhat similar. The name motmot (which is "tomtom" backwards) comes from its call. Most of the ten species of motmots have beautiful iridescent coloration and tails with racquet tips. The ornithologist Alexander Skutch said the Guatemalans sometimes call the motmot by a Spanish name that means "stupid bird" because of its habit of sitting in the same spot for long periods while looking for prey. I won't tell you this Spanish name, because I don't want you to use it on family and friends.

6. BIRD OF PARADISE
Birds as Theater

Kabuki is a stylized form of Japanese theater that originated a few centuries ago. It features elaborate costumes, some of which have droopy sleeves that resemble the wings of a bird when the actors wave their arms. Australia has three species of birds of paradise called riflebirds whose mating rituals resemble Kabuki. From a distance, a male riflebird looks like a small crow with a long, curved bill. On closer inspection, he shows gorgeous black iridescent plumage, and his breast feathers reflect blue-green light.

My first encounter with a riflebird was in 1995 on the first day of my first trip to Australia. I flew into Cairns at midday and went to a lodge called Cassowary House in nearby Kuranda. Cassowary House is in a rain forest, about a thousand feet above sea level. I ate lunch on a veranda surrounded by bird feeders, and the birds around the veranda did not act afraid of humans. I did not finish my piece of dessert cake, and as I stood up to leave, a male Victoria's Riflebird hopped onto the table to eat the cake from my plate. The bird was so close that I could hear his wingbeats, which sounded like the swishing of taffeta. When I returned to Cassowary House the following year, I saw a male riflebird in a tree about ten feet from the doorway to the kitchen. As he was pecking at some food, I observed his feathers at close range. They appeared to have little raised knobs, which might account for the taffeta sound.

Before a foreign birding trip, you can study a field guide that shows how birds look and describes how they behave. But even if you see a foreign bird, learning useful information about it usually requires seeing its behavior in its preferred habitat. I made wrong assumptions about riflebirds based on my first encounter. They typically are not tame feeder birds who hop onto tables to snatch the remnants of your dessert. They usually perch in thick, leafy trees, and you are less likely

13

to see them than to hear a periodic vocalization—two Australian rifle-bird species squawk and one whistles.

The display perch where a male riflebird does his Kabuki perfor-mance usually is a bare horizontal branch from which he can be seen and heard. A male trying to attract a female performs a slow, stylized dance, raising his wings over his head to make them resemble a dark cape. With wings upraised, he alternately dips each shoulder, gradu-ally increasing the speed of his dance and wing movements. With each shoulder dip, there is a clapping noise. Meanwhile, what appeared to be a black iridescent breast with a blue-green tinge becomes a glis-tening blue-green breastplate and throat. When he opens his bill, he reveals a bright-yellow throat lining. If an interested female comes to the perch, he approaches her and ends the performance by mating. The fertilized female, whose plumage is drab brown, is responsible for building a nest and raising the young with no help from him. He stays at his perch, trying to lure more females with his Kabuki. In 1999, I saw a species called the Magnificent Riflebird do the wing-clapping Kabuki display in the Cape York region of northeastern Australia. No female was attracted by his effort, but a young male riflebird came to the perch, perhaps to pick up pointers on technique. The older riflebird's sexual display to the young male would not be unusual in a Kabuki theater, where female roles have been played by male actors.

David Attenborough featured the Kabuki dance of a riflebird in his *Trials of Life* series. Attenborough adores birds of paradise, and they were the subject of his film *Attenborough in Paradise*. After glimpsing birds of paradise in New Guinea in 1957, he dreamt of returning to make a film about these remarkable birds, which he did four decades later. New Guinea has about forty bird of paradise species. Were you to give LSD to a group of art students and ask them to design plum-age for birds, they would not be likely to come up with anything as bizarre and colorful as the New Guinea birds of paradise. Many of the species have large, colorful tail plumes; the Ribbon-tailed Astrapia has tail streamers that are more than a yard long. The King of Saxony Bird of Paradise (the only bird in the world with a six-word name) has two 16-inch feathers that form a V in the back of his head. Some birds of paradise have a bunch of racquet-tipped wire feathers sticking out of the back of their head, like the deely-bobber contraption people put on when trying to look like a Martian. A couple of bird of paradise species have a pair of large curlicues sticking out at their back end. The King Bird of Paradise has two long wires coming out the end of his tail, tipped with little green doodads that resemble emeralds. The Superb Bird of Paradise has a green breast shield that can be lifted to become a giant cravat. Some species can puff out their plumage to resemble a starched skirt. The Black Sicklebill has two large epaulettes that become part of a long black vampire cape.

For most bird of paradise species, the plumage of the males is part of an elaborate display to attract females. Some of the males hop or dance. Some swing from perches. And some do Kabuki. David Attenborough's 1996 film captures examples of many of the incredible sexual displays. He describes the colors of one of the New Guinea birds of paradise as "incandescent." Because the plumage of birds of paradise is so beautiful, it has been highly sought after by hunters and collectors, and some tribes in New Guinea have used the feathers for currency. A silhouette of the Raggiana Bird of Paradise appears on the flag of Papua New Guinea, and the national airline of Papua New Guinea has a bird of paradise as its logo.

The name "bird of paradise" resulted from the way the birds were seen 500 years ago. The first skins of some of the New Guinea species were brought back to Europe in the 1520s by survivors of the crew of Ferdinand Magellan's fatal voyage. The specimens, whose feet and wings had been removed, were a gift from a king in the Spice Islands. The people of the Spice Islands, where the birds do not live, did not know how these beautiful birds could function if they could neither walk nor fly minus their wings and feet, and they contrived a story about the birds floating down from heaven. Magellan's crew members repeated the story when they returned to Europe. To this day, the Greater Bird of Paradise has the scientific species name *apoda*, which means "without feet."

7. BLACKBIRD
Birds Who Inspire Crimes

A blackbird is the subject of song lyrics that are thought to have contributed to a terrible crime. Vincent Bugliosi, the lead prosecutor of Charles Manson for the 1969 Tate-LaBianca murders in Southern California, entitled his book about the case *Helter Skelter*, because Manson was deeply influenced by a song with that name from the Beatles' *White Album*. The words "helter skelter" were written in blood on a refrigerator door at the site of the murders. Elsewhere at the site, the word "rise" was written in blood. Based on interviews with Manson's followers, Bugliosi believed that this word was inspired by the song "Blackbird," also on the *White Album*. The song repeats the line, "All your life you were only waiting for this moment to arise."

The species in the Beatles song is a black Eurasian bird who is not related to the blackbirds in the Americas. The Eurasian Blackbird is a thrush closely related to the American Robin. It looks and behaves like a robin whose body has been dipped into black ink. Just like American Robins, Eurasian Blackbirds are common garden birds who eat earthworms and berries. Their song and presence cheer the lives of many people. English settlers introduced them to Australia, where they now are common garden birds in some parts of the country.

In a well-known British nursery rhyme, four-and-twenty blackbirds were baked in a pie. Some people in the medieval period used to make such pies, which involved baking a pie crust and then inserting live birds—not necessarily two dozen—before serving it. Sometimes the birds were tied together inside the pie, while at other times they were allowed to escape and fly around the room when the pie was cut open, to the delight or consternation of guests.

The blackbirds of the Americas are in a diverse family that includes orioles, meadowlarks, cowbirds, grackles, caciques, oropendolas, and others. Sometimes, enormous mixed flocks of blackbirds congregate. These flocks might include European Starlings, who look like American blackbirds but are not related to them or to the Eurasian Blackbird. In some areas where the huge flocks are considered agricultural pests or a public nuisance, drastic measures have been taken. Blackbirds in the United States are protected by federal law, but they may be killed when found "committing or about to commit depredations upon ornamental or shade trees, agricultural crops, livestock, or wildlife, or when concentrated in such numbers and manner as to constitute a health hazard or other nuisance." The methods of killing blackbirds include poisoning them or spraying them with chemicals to reduce the insulating qualities of their feathers, causing the birds to die of hypothermia. The "blackbirds falling dead from the sky" phenomenon that has been reported in Arkansas, New Jersey, and other places was caused by the ingestion of pesticides applied by farmers for the purpose of preventing crops from being eaten by birds.

The Yellow-headed Blackbird, common in the western United States, has a song that sounds like someone being strangled. But some American blackbirds are excellent singers. A Central American species is called the Melodious Blackbird. The *conk-a-ree* call of the Red-winged Blackbird is a familiar sound in marshes in the United States. The Bobolink, named for its long and bubbly flight song, was the subject of a famous 1855 poem by William Cullen Bryant entitled "Robert of Lincoln" (as in Bob-o'-Linc).[2] Male Bobolinks are handsome. The nape of their neck is gold, and they have white on their rump and wings to accent their black body. The female is colored like a streaky-brown

---

2. The *Oxford English Dictionary* lists John Adams, before he was elected president, as the earliest written source of the word Bobolink. In 1774, Adams made the following excessively avian entry into his diary: "Young Ned Rutledge is a perfect Bob-o-Lincoln—a swallow, a sparrow, a peacock; excessively vain, excessively weak, and excessively variable and unsteady; jejune, inane, and puerile." The Bobolink must have been commonly known by this name before 1774. Rutledge, who was from South Carolina, was the youngest signer of the Declaration of Independence.

sparrow. Bryant's poem about the loud, showy male and his "Quaker wife" has verses such as:

> Modest and shy as a nun is she;
> One weak chirp is her only note.
> Braggart and prince of braggarts is he,
> Pouring boasts from his little throat:
> Bob-o'-link, bob-o'-link,
> Spink, spank, spink.

Flocks of Bobolinks often fatten up in rice fields. Bobolinks used to be called butter birds by hunters who killed the fat birds for meat, especially in the Caribbean. The Bobolink's scientific name is *Dolichonyx oryzivorus*, with "oryzivorus" meaning rice-eating. The next time you visit a Chinese restaurant, try saying that you are in an oryzivorus mood, and see how people respond.

8. BLUEBIRD
Birds as Symbols of Happiness

In my youth, I frequently heard about a mysterious bluebird of happiness who was part of humorous wishes toward other people, such as, "May the bluebird of happiness fly up your nose." Sometimes, people wished the bluebird of happiness would defecate on someone else's person or possessions. Gary Larson drew a *Far Side* cartoon with the caption, "*The Bluebird of Happiness long absent from his life, Ned is visited by the Chicken of Depression.*"

The original bluebird of happiness was a product of the Great Depression. A song with that title was written in 1934, and a rendition sung by Jan Peerce became a hit. It begins, "The beggar man and his mighty king are only different in name." It ends with the uplifting verse, "We are in a world that's just begun, and you must sing his song, as you go along, when you find the bluebird of happiness." The bluebird in the song is a symbol for the happiness people seek during difficult times. The song creates a more specific image of hope than Emily Dickinson's poem "'Hope' is the thing with feathers," even though the vocalizations of the Eastern Bluebird do little to inspire either hope or happiness. The Cornell Laboratory of Ornithology website describes the call of the Eastern Bluebird as "querulous."

The happiness from the bluebird is inspired more by its color than its song. Certain colors are associated with specific feelings and emotions. In the United States, the three species of bluebirds (who are in the thrush family) have light-blue backs that resemble the color of the sky on a sunny day. In 1852, Henry David Thoreau wrote in his journal that the "bluebird carries the sky on his back." Bluebirds are not a dark blue that might induce Duke Ellington's "Mood Indigo." In the 1946 Disney movie *Song of the South*, Uncle Remus sings a happy song called "Zip-a-Dee-Doo-Dah," in which he has Mister Bluebird on his shoulder; the bluebird is a symbol for the beauty of the day and how wonderful Uncle Remus feels. The lyrics of Irving Berlin's 1927 song about "blue skies smiling at me" includes the lyric, *"Bluebirds singing a song, nothing but bluebirds all day long."* The corresponding symbol for dark moods is the blackbird. "Bye, Bye, Blackbird" was written around the same time as Berlin's blue skies song, and it has been performed by many artists who play popular music, rock and roll, and jazz. Its lyrics begin, "Pack up all my cares and woes, feeling low, here I go, bye bye blackbird." Black is the color of the rain clouds that cause bleak moods, so by saying good-bye to a bird of that color, one is hoping to say good-bye to unhappiness.

Conservationists in the twentieth century could have written a depressing song entitled "Bye, Bye, Bluebird." Bluebirds are cavity nesters who typically nest in holes in dead trees. They are not capable of making the holes, but they used to be able to find ample nest sites, mostly in holes created by woodpeckers, who evolved earlier. When European settlers came to North America and cleared land for agriculture, bluebirds flourished. A lot of farm fields were surrounded by wooden fence posts, which could be used for nesting. Unfortunately, the good times did not last. Europeans introduced aggressive invasive species such as House Sparrows and European Starlings who outcompeted bluebirds for nest holes. Wooden fence posts were replaced with metal ones, which are of no use to nesting bluebirds. And a lot of old or dead trees with suitable nest holes were removed. Around the time Irving Berlin and others were writing songs about these feathered symbols of hope, bluebird populations were plummeting.

As early as the 1930s, people began to address the problem by creating bluebird trails—areas with wooden bluebird houses (which serve as artificial tree cavities) spaced over a distance based on the birds' territorial requirements. Interest in the effort intensified in the 1950s and 1960s in the United States and Canada. Lawrence Zeleny, who in 1978 created the North American Bluebird Society, inspired a significant increase in the number of bluebird trails and local bluebird societies.

The work of Zeleny and countless volunteers has made a tremendous difference in helping bluebirds to survive. The people who put up the boxes also monitor them to ensure that they are not commandeered by House Sparrows, European Starlings, or other species. The monitoring of these boxes is taken very seriously. Lola Oberman, who has published two books of delightful birding and natural history articles, wrote an article about bluebirds in which she describes how she killed House Sparrows she found in bluebird boxes. She called the sparrows "terrorists" who kill hatchlings and adult bluebirds.

A drug called *Cialis* is prescribed to men who have trouble reproducing because of erectile dysfunction. By coincidence, the scientific species name for the Eastern Bluebird, who has had trouble reproducing because of the twin problems of invasive species and habitat loss, is *sialis*.

9. BOWERBIRD
Birds Who Are Master Builders

Not many people enjoy encounters with broken glass. If you try to pick it up, you can cut your hand. If you step on it, you can cut your foot. If you bike or drive over it, you can puncture a tire. If a piece gets into your food, you can suffer internal injuries. A sign of urban decay is the presence of a lot of broken glass on the streets. Yet on my first trip to Australia, I was enchanted by the sight of broken glass. I encountered a woven tube of sticks on the ground; it was a couple of feet long and about a foot high. The two sides of the tube did not meet at the top. In front of the structure was a pile of broken glass from bottles, both green and white. More broken glass was strewn inside the tube. Pieces of red plastic from broken automobile taillights were interspersed.

This structure is called a bower, and it was built by a species called the Great Bowerbird. While male birds of paradise try to impress females with showy plumage and eye-catching movements, male bowerbirds believe that the best babe magnets involve architecture. A male Great Bowerbird takes meticulous care of his bower and waits for females to come along to check it out. Should a female be interested in walking through the glass-strewn avenue, he follows her, mates with her, and sends her along to build a nest and raise the young by herself while he waits for another female. The female builds a simple cup-shaped nest that is not nearly as elaborate as the male's bower.

Male Great Bowerbirds are grayish and about a foot long, and they were building bowers long before they had access to broken glass. They are attracted to the glass for its color and texture. Some of their bowers have bleached snail shells, which probably were the decoration of choice before the advent of the throwaway culture. The male Satin Bowerbird, whose entire body becomes a deep satiny blue when he reaches adulthood at age seven, decorates his tube of sticks with blue objects. In an Australian rain forest, I saw one of these bowers that had a blue comb, blue bottle caps, pieces of blue plastic, and blue feathers from other species. Should another bird or animal knock down a bower, the male bowerbird rebuilds it immediately. Sometimes, male bowerbirds knock down the bowers of other males and steal the decorations. Captive male Satin Bowerbirds have killed birds with blue feathers and used the corpses for bower decorations. While the bower is a very important sexual attractant, female Satin Bowerbirds are also influenced by other factors when choosing a mate. A 1986 study by University of Maryland researchers Christopher Loffredo and Gerald Borgia found that the choices of female Satin Bowerbirds are affected by the length and quality of male courtship vocalizations.

The tube-like structures described above are called avenue bowers. Other types of bowers are either much less elaborate or substantially more complex. The Tooth-billed Bowerbird stays in two dimensions, clearing an area and spreading large, flat leaves on the ground. But the male Golden Bowerbird, a lovely ten-inch bird who is brown and gold, builds an incredibly elaborate structure. I saw one of these bowers in an area featuring two nearby thin trees with a horizontal log in between. Each thin tree supported a tepee of sticks. In between was a connecting weave of sticks, decorated with lichens. This type of structure is called a maypole bower. Unlike the Great Bowerbird, whose male is likely to build a new bower annually, male golden bowerbirds add to their existing bower each year.

There are about twenty species of bowerbirds in the world, all in Australia and New Guinea. The most artistic builder of the bunch is a New Guinea species called the Vogelkop Bowerbird. The Vogelkop's bower is a roofed shelter with an opening in the front. Inside are piles of berries, flower petals, insect parts, and other colorful treasures. It looks like a forest doll-house, with the complexity of a human structure but too small for a human to occupy. The word "Vogelkop" is Dutch for "bird's head" and is the name of the peninsula (which was thought to resemble a bird's head on the map) in West Papua where the bowerbird resides.

Some male bowerbirds are drab, but others have brilliantly colored plumage. The Regent Bowerbird, the symbol for O'Reilly's Rain Forest Lodge in Australia, is jet black with bright-golden wings, a golden head, and golden eyes. During one of my stays at O'Reilly's, there was a simple avenue bower of a Regent Bowerbird in the bushes right outside my room. This is one of the species of bowerbirds that is known to use tools to decorate his bower. The male Regent Bowerbird uses a wad of leaves to apply a paint-like mixture, made mostly from his own saliva, to the walls of the bower. Other bowerbird species use reeds as brushes to apply a similar type of decorative paint. The Regent Bowerbird males are not shy, and they hang around the feeding area at O'Reilly's. Once when I was in the feeding area, some males perched on my hands and arms as I fed them raisins (or sultanas, as they are called in Australia). The intense golden color on the head appears orange when the bird is right under your nose. Being able to see a color that intense at such close range was well worth the many claw marks the birds left on my arm.

Shortly after I had had the Regent Bowerbirds on my arm, I went back to my room to get something. In the O'Reilly's lobby was a German film crew with about a ton of equipment. I asked what they were planning to film, and they said they hoped to get some footage of the elusive Regent Bowerbird.

10. BUNTING
Sexual Attitudes toward Birds

Are birders sexist in their attitudes about birds? A lot of birders have a strong preference for male birds and sometimes don't feel they have "seen" a particular species unless they see a male. Ornithologists use the term "sexual dimorphism" to describe the condition of the male and female of a species having different plumage. The plumage differences can be significant, usually between a colorful male and a drab female. As with humans, female birds typically bear much or all of the burden of raising the young, and conspicuous plumage at a nest can make both the female and the nestlings more vulnerable to predators. Females are much safer wearing drab plumage.

The Indigo Bunting, a small finch who nests in the eastern United States, is a species whose male and female have significantly different plumage. The male is a rich indigo when he returns from his wintering ground in Central America or the Caribbean. The indigo can appear intense in bright sunlight, especially when he is singing from a tree or exposed wire. The female's plumage is altogether different. From a distance, she appears to be dull brown with hardly any distinguishing field marks. The three other bunting species regularly found in the United States have significant plumage differences between males and females. The male Painted Bunting, found in the southern United States, is one of the gaudiest birds in North America, with a blue head, red breast, and chartreuse back. The female is a plain bird who is olive above and slightly lighter below. Birders are inclined to look much longer at a male Painted Bunting than at a female, and seeing only the female might be regarded as disappointing.

I once saw a female Indigo Bunting in the hand. Rather than being a dull uniform brown, some of her feathers had subtle blue edges. These small embellishments would be noticeable to a nearby male but not so showy that they would draw the attention of predators. This lovely

detailing tends not to be mentioned in field guides, because it is virtually impossible for birders to see on a female perched in a tree. The
females of many bird species other than buntings are not nearly as
drab as some people might think. From a distance, the female Mallard
appears to be a solid-brown duck, but if you focus a telescope on her
at close range, her feathers reveal a beautifully complex design. Also,
birds have ultraviolet vision, and some of their plumage features might
be visible only under ultraviolet light. That means that a birder in the
field would not see certain characteristics of a bird, but a bird of the
same species might see them during a courtship display. It also means
that the males and females of a species who are indistinguishable to
humans will look different to each other. Birds such as kestrels, who
are small falcons, use ultraviolet vision to see the urine of mice and
voles and more easily catch these animals. The mice and voles also
have ultraviolet vision, which helps them to communicate among their
own kind with urinary messages.

The Indigo, Painted, and a few other American Buntings are in the
same family as the Northern Cardinal, but they are not related to the
buntings found in Eurasia and Africa. The Eurasian and African buntings are related to the American sparrows and an American species
called the Lark Bunting, who is the state bird of Colorado. I discovered
why it is the state bird when I was driving through an agricultural area
in Colorado on a June morning and saw a Lark Bunting on about every
fifth fencepost.

The Ortolan Bunting in Europe has become the subject of controversy in the gastronomic world. The French government has passed a
law prohibiting the eating, selling, or hunting of Ortolans. But some
prominent French chefs consider Ortolans to be a great delicacy and
continue to kill the birds, in violation of the law. The birds are sometimes captured and then fattened for a few weeks by methods similar to
what is done to geese to make foie gras. Chefs kill them, cook them, and
serve them to be eaten—bones, guts, and all. Former French president

François Mitterrand chose to eat an Ortolan as one of his final meals when he was on his deathbed, and the chef Anthony Bourdain calls the written account of Mitterrand's meal one of the most lushly descriptive works of food porn ever committed to paper. There are three species of unrelated African finches called cordon-bleus, but French chefs do not kill and bake these birds as they do with the Ortolans.

In Britain, a slang term for women is "birds." On a visit to London, I bought a button that reads, "The reason why women are called birds is because of the worms they pick up." Setting aside the battle of the human sexes, male and female birders should take a closer look at female birds, or as the British might call them, bird birds. As is the case with buntings, they can be far prettier than you might think.

11. BUSTARD
Bird Fatalities

I used to help a friend who did bird banding, which involves setting up nets in which to trap birds, measuring and recording data about each bird caught, and affixing a numbered aluminum band to its leg so the individual can be identified should it be trapped again or found dead. John James Audubon was the first person known to band birds in the United States when in the early 1800s he attached light silver thread to the leg of a migratory Eastern Phoebe to determine whether the same individual would return to his farm the following year (which it did). On one of my banding trips, a thunderstorm blew in quickly and unexpectedly. My friend and I hurried around the banding circuit to close all ten nets. When we arrived at the tenth net, we found a dead rain-soaked White-breasted Nuthatch. Just as humans can die of hypothermia after relatively brief exposure to cold, birds can die quickly if severely chilled.

I was involved in the death of a much larger bird in Australia in 2003. On the final day of a three-week trip that covered more than 3,200 miles, our minibus was riding through an arid area. Suddenly, two Australian Bustards flew out of a gully and in front of the bus. Bustards look like long-legged turkeys and are among the heaviest flying birds in the world. I saw one of the bustards veer away while the other was hit by the front of the bus. The incident featured one of those horrible moments that seemed to freeze time as life was draining from the large, broken bird. The event reminded me of an essay I had read in *Harper's Magazine* in 1990 by the environmental writer Barry Lopez, which discussed animals who are hit by vehicles. Lopez wondered, "Who are these animals we kill?"

My other memories of bustards are more positive. There are about two dozen species of bustards, but none are found in the Americas. They range in size from the big ones who weigh more than forty

29

pounds to a species called the Little Brown Bustard (found in Ethiopia and Somalia), who weighs less than two pounds. The "tard" part of bustard comes from a Latin word meaning "slow," even though bustards can run quickly. The Australian Bustard is a big, haughty-looking bird, slowly strutting with its beak pointing upward at a forty-five-degree angle. The male has a black cap that extends behind the back of his head, resembling a bad toupee. The male also has a breast sac that hangs almost to the ground when inflated for sexual and territorial displays. In 1999, I saw two male bustards with their breast sacs blown up. Because no female bustards were present, the display probably was territorial. Graham Pizzey, in his *Field Guide to the Birds of Australia*, compares the call of a displaying male Australian Bustard to the roar of a distant lion.

The Great Bustard was reintroduced into England in 2004 after being eliminated by hunting during the nineteenth century. A golden representation of the species is on the flag of the English county of Wiltshire. Some species of bustards can be found in Africa, and they sometimes walk near zebras and other large grazing animals. The walking of hoofed animals causes insects and other small creatures to jump, at which time they are snapped up by the bustards. This is an example of what ecologists call commensalism, in which one species benefits from the actions of another without causing it any harm. Herons, cranes, and other types of birds use this same feeding strategy.

Precise figures for preventable bird fatalities are impossible to determine, but the estimates are staggering. A 2013 peer-reviewed study by the Smithsonian Conservation Biology Institute and the U.S. Fish and Wildlife Service estimates that cats in the United States kill from 1.4 to 3.7 billion birds annually, with the majority of the fatalities caused by free-roaming cats, especially from programs that neuter them and turn them loose back into the environment. Another leading cause is window collisions; an estimate from 2006 on the American Bird Conservancy website is of fatalities from a hundred million to a billion per year. Even birds who seem to survive the initial window impact might die a short time later from internal injuries. Collisions with electric power lines and motorized vehicles cause large numbers of bird deaths. The latest major threat is wind turbines, which unfortunately seem to provide the most power when placed in windy areas that birds use as migration routes. Among other major causes of preventable bird fatalities are hunting, commercial fishing, and pesticide poisoning.

On the trip when the bustard was killed, someone showed me a bustard feather found near one of our campsites. This large feather featured intricate patterns you cannot see when viewing the bird from a distance. The feather patterns have developed over many millennia to help the species be camouflaged in its natural habitat, thereby enhancing its chances of survival. Over the same millennia, bustards and other birds never had reason to evolve survival strategies to elude anything as large, fast, and powerful as motorized vehicles. The bustard hit by our minibus no longer remembers the moment of impact, but I still can see it clearly.

12. CARDINAL
Feeder Birds

Millions of Americans feed birds, both to enjoy watching the birds eat and to provide nourishment for the birds. Some people do it only during the winter when other food sources might be scarce or inaccessible, but many do it throughout the year. Feeding birds can affect the range of their population. For instance, the Northern Cardinal, one of the most popular feeder birds in the United States, has not always been a northern species. In the 1700s, cardinals were mostly southern birds. Their range has now extended through most of New England. Bird species can expand their range if they find suitable habitat and food. The popularity of bird feeding in nineteenth-century America provided the food, and many cardinals followed the bird feeders. The Evening Grosbeak, who like the cardinal has a large bill for eating seeds, was primarily a western species at the beginning of the 1800s, but it also might have followed the feeders to expand its range into New England and eastern Canada.

There are about a half-dozen other species in the Americas called cardinals, but none are as popular as the well-loved "redbird," as it is called by many people. The males are bright red with a crest and a black mask. The females are olive brown. The cardinal's song is a loud, rich whistle that sounds like *purty purty purty*. During the spring of 2004, I went to a reception at the French Embassy in Washington attended by about 500 people. At one point, the embassy's cultural attaché, who was a friend of mine, led me away from the crowd to show me a hedgerow on the embassy grounds that contained a cardinal nest. He whistled, and a cardinal whistled back. Cardinals are not found in France, where the attaché was from, but he quickly became enamored with them when he came to Washington. He hung numerous feeders outside his office window to attract cardinals and other species. He also sent embassy Christmas cards featuring a cardinal perched in a holiday tree.

Cardinal

The Northern Cardinal is closely related to the American grosbeaks and buntings. Bird banders must be careful when handling cardinals, because the same powerful bill that grinds seeds can damage a bander's fingers. Young cardinals have a dark-gray bill, while adults have a red bill. On a banding outing one summer, a friend and I caught a very young cardinal. Protruding from the area where its bill attached to its face were bits of yellow skin, resembling tiny lips. These lips are called flanges—the same word used by the construction industry for the rim of a pipe or beam. For many bird species, the inside of the mouth (or gape) of baby birds is a bright color that is the target at which adult birds stuff food. After young cardinals grow up and become independent, the lips disappear.

The distinctive crest of the cardinal sometimes can be attacked by feather mites. At a park in Virginia, I saw a male cardinal who had lost all his head feathers. Rather than a red crest, this cardinal had a bald black head. I saw the bird for three consecutive springs, so he apparently was otherwise healthy. During one of these springs, he was accompanied by a female, who seemed to go for the skinhead look.

At the same park during the spring of 2012, I shot video footage of a female cardinal with a rare plumage abnormality. Her feathers were deficient in a pigment called phaeomelanin. Instead of being a warm-brown color, she was gray. In humans, phaeomelanin is the primary determinant of skin color, and red-haired people have a high level of it. I made a video about the aberrant cardinal called "Gray Girl" and posted it on YouTube. The strangest color aberration I have ever seen in a bird is in photos of gynandromorph cardinals: half of the bird is brown like a female and the other half is red like a male. The bird looks like one of the half man–half woman attractions in a circus sideshow. This very rare condition occurs when the sex chromosomes do not split properly in the egg.

The word "cardinal" is derived from a word that means the hinge of a door. The hinge was something on which other things turned, which is why "cardinal" now is used to describe things that are deemed important. The cardinal points on a compass are north, south, east, and west. The cardinal numbers are used in basic arithmetic, as opposed to the ordinal numbers that designate a place value; for instance, two is a cardinal number, but second is an ordinal. There are cardinal sins and cardinal virtues; the four cardinal virtues are prudence, justice, temperance, and fortitude. In the Catholic Church, cardinals are the important officials just below the pope and are elected to be part of the College of Cardinals. The red bird was named because of the red robes worn by Catholic cardinals.

The Northern Cardinal is the favorite choice as a state bird, representing seven states: Illinois, Indiana, Kentucky, North Carolina, Ohio, Virginia, and West Virginia. (Six states have chosen the Western Meadowlark, and five have chosen the Northern Mockingbird.) St.

Cardinal

Louis used to call both its baseball and football teams the Cardinals. However, the football team moved to Arizona, where it is still known as the Cardinals. There is a southwestern race of the bird called the Arizona Cardinal. A closely related species in Arizona is the Pyrrhuloxia, a crested bird who is mostly gray with a few splashes of red, but fans would have difficulty warming to a team called the Arizona Pyrrhuloxias.

13. CASSOWARY
Dangerous Birds

Rarely have I feared for my safety because of a bird, but I had a frightening close encounter of the bird kind during my first visit to Cassowary House in Australia. The place was named before the owners, John and Rita Squire, knew there were Southern Cassowaries on the property. Cassowaries are large, flightless birds found only in Australia and New Guinea. My room at Cassowary House was across the garden from the kitchen. One or more cassowaries generally showed up during the day to be fed, and I asked Rita to call me if one came. As I was washing my hands one morning, Rita called, "Bill, the cassowary is here." I quickly left my room and was walking toward the house when I saw an adult female cassowary walking toward me. She was about five feet tall and more than a hundred pounds, and she apparently thought I would be providing the food. No matter how adventurous a life you have lived, you are unlikely to be able to draw on any experience that will help you decide what to do when eye-to-eye with a bird who is almost as big as you are. Fortunately, Rita quickly appeared from the kitchen with a tray of bananas and apples.

During that visit to Cassowary House, I held a tray to feed both the adult female (six years old) and a youngster (eleven months). In addition to apples and bananas, they ate meat and dog biscuits. The adult and juvenile never came to be fed at the same time. The female cassowary had a bare blue neck that was red on the back and had red wattles (droopy pieces of skin). The youngster, who was smaller and paler, was more skittish; once when a plane flew over, it went into the bushes and sat down. The Squires had wormed the adult but thought the youngster would not survive, because the adult female did not want it around.

When I returned to Cassowary House the following year, the adult female and the youngster were gone, replaced by an adult male with two chicks who were probably about a month old. The sex roles of cassowaries are atypical. After cassowaries copulate, the female lays eggs and leaves the male to incubate the eggs and raise the young. The male cassowary is smaller than the female. The cassowary's esophagus is on the side of the throat, and I watched pieces of food make their way down his long neck, similar to the way long-necked birds swallow something large in animated cartoons. All three of the birds liked bananas the best. Rita said the female would eat tomatoes, but the male didn't like them. Each of the chicks had a tawny head and a striped body. Both were small, but one was a bit larger and more aggressive than the other. Sometimes, they picked up pieces of chicken that were bigger than they could swallow. Their most amusing visit occurred late one afternoon. They became tired and sat on the lawn outside the kitchen. Their eyelids drooped as if they were about to fall asleep. While they rested, their father vigorously preened himself.

Cassowaries have small vestiges of wings that you can see if you are close to the bird. Their body is covered with feathers that resemble hair, and their rear end looks bushy. Flight feathers on most bird species have a central shaft (called a rachis) with barbs coming out of each side. Coming out of the barbs are appendages called barbules, which have tiny hooks to hold the barbs together. A cassowary feather has two shafts that meet at the bottom. Because cassowaries don't fly, their feathers do not need barbules. The primary functions of cassowary feathers are to maintain body temperature and protect skin. Some species of flying birds have plume-like feathers for sexual displays, but their flight feathers have the conventional central shaft, barbs, and barbules.

The head of a cassowary has a horny structure called a casque, which resembles a battle helmet. One purpose of this helmet might be to allow the bird to move through thick brush without damaging the top of its head. Military imagery would be more appropriate for their feet, which have three toes. John Squire showed me a weapon from New Guinea made from the middle toe of a cassowary. The middle toe has a long, hard nail, and cassowaries can leap and deliver a potent downward kick that can disembowel a dog or other adversary. So my momentary fear during the eye-to-eye encounter with the female cassowary might have been justified.

14. CATBIRD
Birds Who Sound Like Other Animals

Birds often are named for their vocalizations. Some names are based on a representation of what the bird says, such as curlew, towhee, pipit, phoebe, and pewee. Some bird names describe the quality of the vocalization rather than representing the actual sound. Babblers are named for their babbling, trillers for their trilling, whistlers for their whistling, and screamers for their screaming. In some names, the representation of the sound is achieved with an adjective, such as the Laughing Gull, Whistling Kite, Piping Plover, Chipping Sparrow, Plaintive Cuckoo, and Dark Chanting-Goshawk. Some nouns of assemblage are based on bird vocalizations, such as a chattering of choughs. (The word "jargon" comes from a French word that means a chattering of birds, but not necessarily choughs.[3])

In a few instances, the names of birds are based on the similarity of their vocalizations to the sounds of other animals. The Barking Owl in Australia sounds like a barking dog. The call of the Gray Catbird in the United States sounds like a mewing cat, while the unrelated catbirds in Australia, who are in the bowerbird family, sound like alley cats in heat. One of the Australian catbird species sounds as if it is uttering a loud, ungrammatical *Here I arrrrrre*.

In his 1893 book *Our Common Birds and How to Know Them*, John B. Grant wrote about the catbird: "The bird is really a handsome one, but owing to its skulking habits, and the unsocial manner with which it resents inspection, scarcely a favorite." Contrary to what Grant wrote, I have found the Gray Catbird to be a friendly, confiding species. When I was very young, my grandmother would tap on the railing of the deck at my aunt's house, and a catbird she had named Bickie would appear. Bickie ate raisins and other treats offered by my grandmother

---

3. Chough is pronounced as if it were spelled *chuff*.

for about seven years. Catbirds are not fussy eaters; in addition to raisins and other fruit, they will eat cheese, fish, meat, and various table scraps. The Gray Catbird has a gray body, a black skullcap, and a rufous patch under the tail, and it is common in many parts of the United States during the nesting season. It is closely related to the Northern Mockingbird, and it mimics the songs of other species. The mockingbird repeats the songs of other species numerous times, while the catbird generally sings each song only once. The sound that resembles the mewing of a cat often punctuates the renditions of the other songs.

The animal that the catbird sounds like is killing a great many of them. Scientists from the Smithsonian Institution's Migratory Bird Center and Towson University in Maryland studied mortality of nesting catbirds in suburban areas. In 2011, they reported that roughly four out of five of the baby catbirds fell victim to predation, and of these, almost half fell victim to cats. Predation rates were highest shortly after the baby birds left the nest, when they tend to be noisy and try to get the attention of adult catbirds.

The catbird is probably best known in the United States from the expression "in the catbird seat," which means to be in a commanding position. Some people have suggested that the origin comes from the catbird having a good view of his surroundings from a lofty perch. In fact, catbirds tend not to be found on lofty perches and are usually seen at eye level or below. The term is often attributed to the late baseball announcer Red Barber, but he said he did not originate it. In Paul Dickson's *Baseball Dictionary* (Third Edition), Barber is quoted as saying that he first heard the term in a poker game when one of his opponents had a pair of aces and won a pot after a number of raises. Upon showing the aces, his opponent said that he had been in the catbird seat from the start of the hand. Barber said he had never before heard the term, but he could tell from the context exactly what it meant. He added that because he had paid for it by losing the hand, he felt he could use the expression. James Thurber heard Barber say the phrase on the radio and subsequently used it as a title for a story in the *New Yorker*.

Dickson says that when Barber later tried to write a column entitled "The Catbird Seat," he was told that he could not do so because of the now well-known story that Thurber had written. Barber was upset about this and wrote to Thurber, saying "that was getting the goose a little far away from the gander." Because I don't feel like explaining any more Southern bird expressions, I am going to stop the discussion here.

15. CHICKADEE
Bird Names That Are Puns

The late Jeff Swinebroad, who taught birding classes at the Smithsonian in Washington, used to give some of his students a take-home quiz with 150 questions. Each answer was a pun on the name of a bird. Among the questions were: What bird describes a crime? (robin); What bird supports trains? (rail); What bird is a nocturnal windstorm? (nightingale); What bird is an expense for tableware? (spoonbill); etc. Other questions involved species rather than types of birds: What bird is a Russian political organization? (Common Tern); What bird describes the straightening of a large nose? (Evening Grosbeak); and so on.

Some bird puns that are not quite as forced as the ones on Jeff Swinebroad's quiz involve the families of birds that include chickadees, titmice, and tits. The avian tits include Great Tits, Dusky Tits, Varied Tits, Fire-capped Tits, Stripe-breasted Tits (which seems redundant), Sombre Tits, and Elegant Tits, to name a few. The penduline-tits are in a different family, as is the Tit Berrypecker and a funny little bird sometimes called the Bearded Tit. This latter is a Eurasian species more commonly called the Bearded Reedling, and the male looks like a tit trying to disguise himself with a ridiculously large fake Fu Manchu moustache. The name "tit" comes from the Icelandic *titr*, meaning small, and it has nothing to do with the word for breast that makes a lot of people titter. Likewise, the name for seabirds called "boobies" has nothing to do with breasts or boobs. It is a derogatory name based on how stupid the birds look and act, just as one human might insult another by calling him a boob or booby.

The Blue Tit, a common species in much of Europe, raised issues about whether birds can transmit learned behaviors from one to another. In Britain at the beginning of the twentieth century, people had milk delivered to their door in bottles without tops. The milk was not homogenized, so each bottle had a layer of cream floating on top. Blue Tits learned to perch on the bottles and drink the nutrient-rich cream. After World War I, milk was delivered in bottles covered by a thin layer of aluminum foil. The Blue Tits figured out how to punch a hole in the foil so they could continue to drink the cream. By the 1950s, the knowledge had spread through the Blue Tit community so that most of them knew how to get at the cream. The homogenization of milk, the replacement of bottles with cartons, and the end of home milk delivery ended the cream bonanza for the Blue Tits. In his book *The Ape and the Sushi Master*, Frans de Waal suggests that humans are not the only species capable of culturally transmitted learning. The behavior of the Blue Tits would be an example of such learning if each tit learned to do it by watching others rather than learning it individually.

Chickadees are small, round birds with a tiny bill, a cap, and a bib. Their name comes from their call. Chickadees became media celebrities as a result of the 1940 movie *My Little Chickadee*, starring W.C. Fields and Mae West. The title probably was chosen because of the way the bird's name rolled off the tongue of W.C. Fields and because of the "chick" reference. I know of no evidence that Fields or West chose it because the bird is in the same family as tits. A similar-looking bird on the other side of the Atlantic is the Willow Tit, which is best known for being the subject of a sad song near the end of *The Mikado* by Gilbert and Sullivan. Allan Sherman sang a

parody of the *Mikado* song entitled "The Bronx Bird Watcher" on his *My Son the Celebrity* album.

Chickadees are friendly little birds who often are seen in mixed flocks with other species. When I was in the mountains near San Diego, a woman birder I encountered threw some birdseed very close to my feet, and Mountain Chickadees and other species immediately came down and started to feed on it. Chickadees are among the birds you can, with patience, train to eat out of your hand. Titmice behave in a similar manner to chickadees. The "mouse" part of their name has nothing to do with rodents; it is a variant of an old German word for bird, so titmouse simply means "small bird." There are five titmouse species in the United States, and all are small gray birds with crests. The most common is the Tufted Titmouse, and it is most prevalent in the Southeast. Its song is a distinctively rich whistle that sounds like *peter peter peter*. Titmice also utter harsh, scolding notes. They tend to be active and easy to see.

Tufted Titmice make nests in tree cavities and often line them with fur or hair. Arthur Cleveland Bent, an amateur ornithologist who during the first half of the twentieth century compiled a twenty-six-volume series of the life histories of North American birds, recounts incidents involving a titmouse landing on a person's head (one man and one woman) and trying to yank out hair. Another incident involved a titmouse yanking out hair while perched on the back of a woodchuck. Titmice do not seem to be deterred if the hair they are gathering is still being used by its owner.

16. CHICKEN
Domesticated Birds

If you ask people in the United States to name the type of bird with whom they have the most contact in their daily lives, some would mention a wild bird they see outdoors. Some might mention a pet bird. But few outside of rural areas would mention chickens. Admittedly, the chickens most people see are likely to be plucked and prepared for eating, bearing little resemblance to live birds. Gary Larson made fun of this in a *Far Side* cartoon featuring limp birds at a boneless chicken ranch. Worldwide, tens of billions of chickens are raised each year to produce meat and eggs for human consumption. At a time when the populations of many bird species are dwindling, chickens have through human intervention become the most plentiful birds on our planet.

Domestic chickens are descended from an Asian pheasant called the Red Junglefowl, whom I saw in the wild in Thailand. The male looks like a large barnyard cock with a long tail. He has a bright-red comb, and his call is a loud *cock-a-doodle-doo*. Chickens who are bred to provide eggs keep laying them because they are one of numerous bird species who are indeterminate layers. This means that a hen will not start trying to hatch the eggs until she has produced a full complement of them, known as a clutch. When people remove eggs from the nest, the hen will continue to lay, trying to get the clutch to the requisite size.

Over the years, chicken breeders have created hundreds of breeds, many of whom do not look at all like the original species. One of the more bizarre ones is called a Showgirl. It has a naked neck and upper breast, and the rest of its body appears to be wearing a coat made of fluffy white fur; its otherwise-naked head sports a matching white fur hat. The Showgirl is a cross between two other odd-looking breeds called the Silkie and the Naked Neck. A breed in Japan has tail feathers that grow to be twenty feet long. Both Delaware and Rhode Island have

45

named a breed of chicken as their state bird: the Delaware Blue Hen and the Rhode Island Red.

The scientific name for the Red Junglefowl is *Gallus gallus*, which repeats the Latin word for cock. I say cock instead of rooster, because the word "rooster" has been around only since the late 1700s. According to Hugh Rawson, who has written a book about euphemisms, rooster was created by Americans who felt uncomfortable saying cock. Rawson notes that the origin of cock to mean "penis" is unclear. The reason the King James Bible refers to cocks rather than roosters is that the word "rooster" was not in use when the King James translation was done. Cocks are absent from the Old Testament, because they had not yet been domesticated in the Holy Land.

"Rooster" is not the only euphemism connected with chickens. The terms "white meat" (or light meat) and "dark meat" were coined by Americans who were too embarrassed to say "breast" and "leg" at the dinner table.[4] Wild birds who both walk and fly a lot, such as ducks and geese, have a high level of a protein called myoglobin in their legs and breast. In vertebrates, myoglobin plays a similar role for muscles that the protein hemoglobin plays in the blood. Domestic fowl who mostly walk but rarely fly need a lot of myoglobin in their leg muscles but not much in the breast muscles involved in wing flapping. That is why the breast meat on domestic turkeys and chickens is white but the leg meat is dark.

The comedian George Carlin said he sniggered as a youth when he discovered the word "cock" in the Bible. The story to which he refers involves Jesus at the Last Supper foretelling the denial by his disciple Peter. In Matthew 26:34, Jesus says to Peter, "That this night, before the cock crow, thou shalt deny me thrice." In Mark 14:30, Jesus says, "That

---

4. According to a possibly apocryphal anecdote, Winston Churchill was reprimanded by a woman at a dinner in the United States for asking for some chicken breast meat. When he asked the woman what he should have requested, she said, "White meat." The next day, Churchill allegedly sent the woman a corsage with a note that told her she could pin it on her white meat.

this day, even in this night, before the cock crow twice, thou shalt deny me thrice."

In many cultures, cocks play an important role in regulating the schedules of people's lives. There is no need for alarm clocks if you have alarm cocks crowing at first light to tell you to arise. In modern cities, many people raise chickens for eggs and meat. The production of chickens on huge industrial farms is a recent phenomenon. In addition to the cruelty involved in this type of farming, huge factory farms pose an increasing risk to human health because of the possible spread of viral epidemics that could kill millions of people around the world. Fear of avian influenza already has resulted in the slaughter of hundreds of millions of chickens. When huge numbers of birds are confined in close proximity, any viruses they carry have the potential to spread and mutate rapidly. Should a particular virus jump from chickens to humans, make humans sick, and then spread from person to person, an epidemic could occur. Because of the speed with which a virus can mutate and move through a human population, public health officials can have difficulty developing an effective vaccine, producing it in large quantities, and inoculating everyone in a timely manner.

An extensive amount of the blood sport of cockfighting still occurs in many places throughout the world. While the term "chicken" is often used to imply cowardice, fighting cocks certainly cannot be called chicken. The birds are bred for aggressiveness and then pitted against each other, usually with knives or other sharp objects tied to their legs so that they can inflict a greater amount of damage. In 2011, a man in California died after being stabbed by a knife attached to the leg of a fighting cock. Cockfighting probably originated in the same part of the world where cocks were first domesticated, and it was practiced by the ancient Greeks and Persians. The sport is legal in the US territories of Guam, American Samoa, the Virgin Islands, and Puerto Rico. It is illegal in all fifty of the United States, but in about a dozen states it is only a misdemeanor rather than a felony. In some states, cockfighting is illegal but owning a fighting cock, owning cockfighting implements, and attending cockfights are all legal. In California, where cockfighting is a felony, a 2007 police raid in San Diego found more than five thousand fighting cocks at two locations, but the fifty people caught were charged with misdemeanors because the birds were not engaged in fights during the raid. Cockfighting remains legal in many countries throughout the world, especially in Asia. It is also legal in parts of France and Spain.

Cockfighting is not the only blood sport in which chickens and other fowl have been used. Until the late 1700s, people in England engaged in cock throwing. A cock was tied to a post, and people threw weighted sticks at it until the bird died. This activity was especially popular on the Christian holiday of Shrove Tuesday, which is the day before Lent begins. Another popular Shrove Tuesday activity was goose pulling, which was practiced into the 1800s in England and other European countries, as well as in parts of North America. A frame resembling a soccer goal was assembled, and a live goose with a greased head was hung from the crossbar. Men on horses would gallop quickly through the frame and try to yank the greased head off the live bird. Anyone who succeeded was considered a hero. A variation on goose pulling continues to be part of Shrove Tuesday celebrations in parts of Germany, Belgium, and the Netherlands in the twenty-first century, using a dead goose rather than a live one. Sideshow geeks, who were similarly known for separating the heads from the bodies of fowl, were not highly esteemed like the successful goose pullers. Before "geeks" became a term for people with expertise about computers, they were people in circus acts who chased live chickens around a ring and bit off and swallowed the heads of the chickens they caught.

Through most of human history, almost anything that had feathers was considered a source of protein, and people have long sought ways to preserve bird meat by keeping it cold. In 1626, the author and scientist Francis Bacon caught pneumonia and died after trying to preserve a chicken by stuffing it with snow. In the United States during the eighteenth and nineteenth centuries and at least the first part of the twentieth century, an enormous number of birds were hunted and then sold freshly killed in markets prior to the widespread availability of refrigeration. For instance, during the late nineteenth century in Washington, DC, one could find thousands of dead robins for sale in a local market. Wild birds in American markets have now been replaced by chickens and other domesticated birds in the butcher shop or supermarket meat department, but there are still many countries where the slaughter of wild birds continues, and not only in the Third World. When I was in Thailand in 2001, I went through villages where people put out lime-sticks, which are covered with a glue-like substance to trap birds. In 2010, the author Jonathan Franzen wrote a long article for the *New Yorker* about the continuing widespread slaughter of songbirds in Cyprus.

While more chickens have existed on the Earth than any other type of bird, it is also true that more chickens have been slaughtered than any other type of bird. One could argue that they have died so that other birds might live. So the next time you see a frozen chicken in an American grocery store, try to appreciate the sacrifices it is making to promote avian diversity.

17. COCKATOO
The Importance of Details about Birds

In the eighth chapter of Oscar Wilde's novel *The Picture of Dorian Gray*, Lord Henry Wotton says: "One should absorb the colour of life, but one should never remember its details. Details are always vulgar." In another work, called "The Decay of Lying," Wilde wrote: "What Art really reveals to us is Nature's lack of design, her curious crudities, her extraordinary monotony, her absolutely unfinished condition. Nature has good intentions, of course, but, as Aristotle once said, she cannot carry them out. When I look at a landscape I cannot help seeing all its defects."

Oscar Wilde was a witty writer who made perceptive observations about society and art, but he was totally out of his depth when talking about nature. Wilde was too busy drinking at parties in grimy Victorian London to notice the beauty and subtlety of nature. Unfortunately, he was a precursor to the modern art movements of today that not only fail to understand nature, but also are actively hostile toward it. Precisely because of nature's remarkable details, it exudes a greater level of richness than any human could ever create or understand. Nature is anything but monotonous.

Much of my pleasure from the study of birds comes from noticing details or learning something surprising about a particular species. For example, there are about twenty species of parrots in a family called the cockatoos, and I have seen about half of them on my trips to Australia. They are in the same order with the other parrots of the world, but in a separate family. This small group of birds has provided a wealth of wonderful memories for me. Cockatoos are loud, inquisitive birds who sometimes gather in large flocks. They are a noticeable presence in the lives of Australians the way crows might be a noticeable presence in the lives of North Americans.

The most common cockatoo in Australia is a pink-and-gray species called the Galah. It is extremely adaptable and can survive even in deserts. In some towns, Galahs rather than pigeons are the most common birds in public parks. When they land, they raise their wings in a V over their head, as if to steady themselves. An Australian couple told me about a Galah who arrived at the doorstep of a particular house in their neighborhood every day around dusk. The people who lived in the house would put the bird into a cage with food and water. The next morning, the people let the bird go so it could fly around the neighborhood all day.

While I was on a trip to an Australian desert in 2003 with the naturalist John Young, he found a tree that contained the nest hole of a Galah. We observed a female Galah rubbing oil from her preen gland on an area near the hole that she had stripped of bark. Preening is the process by which birds keep their feathers clean and in good working order for flight and the maintenance of body temperature. Oil from the preen gland assists in this process. By rubbing the preen oil on the debarked section of the tree, the Galah makes the surface smooth and slippery, which can inhibit predators from climbing near the hole. When we saw the female Galah fly off, our group approached the hole. The wood had a smooth feel as well as a faint musky smell that John said helps to repel large monitor lizards. John, who is one of Australia's foremost authorities on bird nests, is not aware of any other species in Australia who tries to repel nest predators by chewing bark and polishing the exposed tree areas with preen oil. He said a non-parrot species called the Spangled Drongo sometimes smears fruit on a section of a tree near its nest to repel ants.

The Sulphur-crested Cockatoo is found in all of the most populated areas of Australia. It is large (about eighteen inches), white (with subtle lemon touches under the wings), and extremely loud. I once heard one calling from more than a mile away on the other side of a gorge. Sulphur-crested Cockatoos can be inquisitive, mischievous, and destructive. Someone told me about a parking lot at an apartment complex where one morning the residents discovered that cockatoos had removed all the windshield wiper blades from the parked cars. Someone else told me about cockatoos who had figured out how to undo siding screws on houses. Such stories are amusing unless the car or house belongs to you. In captivity, these cockatoos can survive more than fifty years. A captive Sulphur-crested Cockatoo named Snowball created a YouTube sensation by moving in time to the rhythm of recordings by Lady Gaga and the Backstreet Boys, among others. While humans have a sense of rhythm, dogs, cats, and other primate species do not seem to have one.

The Sulphur-crested Cockatoo gets its name from its large yellow crest, which sticks up like a mohawk. If you observe one of these birds face on, you will see that it actually has two crests that lean together to meet in the middle of its head. When the bird lands, the crests momentarily separate before closing. The Major Mitchell's Cockatoo, a slightly smaller pink-and-white bird, has a crest that looks like an American Indian headdress, with alternating layers of white, red, yellow, red, and white. When the bird lands, its crest rises to its full height as soon as its feet make contact with a perch. The Major Mitchell's Cockatoo is one of the most beautiful bird species in the world.

Australia has seven cockatoo species who are mostly black or dark gray. The smallest is the owlish-looking Gang-gang Cockatoo, whose call sounds like a creaky hinge. While I was staying with a friend in New South Wales, I heard the creaky hinge while I was hanging laundry. When I went into the street to try to determine where the sound was coming from, a woman in one of the nearby houses asked what I was doing. I told her about the cockatoos, and she said, "They are in a tree in my yard. Go back and look at them." A male (who has a red head and a dark gray body) and a female (who lacks the red on the head) were placidly nibbling on nuts about fifteen feet up in the tree. A less common species who is larger and darker than the Gang-gang is the Glossy Black-Cockatoo. It eats casuarina nuts, which are extremely difficult for humans or any other creatures to open, but its powerful bill is capable of getting to the nut meat. The first Glossy Blacks I saw were perched in a tree, and I could hear the soft sound of their bills working on the shells of the nuts.

Flocks of Yellow-tailed Black-Cockatoos or Red-tailed Black-Cockatoos can be seen in some parts of Australia. The wings and body of these large black species are longer than those of crows, and their wingbeat is slower and more majestic. The Palm Cockatoo is one of the largest parrots in Australia. It is all black, except for two big red cheeks. I have seen a pair of Palm Cockatoos in the National Zoo in Washington, but the cheeks of the captive birds were the color of liver. The ones I saw in the wild had bright-red cheeks under their unruly black crest. The zoo birds apparently were not eating a proper diet to maintain the redness of their cheeks.

The above information about the various species of cockatoos represents some of the details I have enjoyed about a small group of birds found halfway around the world from where I live. You could argue that none of these details are important. Yet anyone who subscribes to Oscar Wilde's belief in art for art's sake should not dismiss people who believe in nature for nature's sake. The world would be a poorer place without art. Without nature, both art and all forms of life would cease to exist. Failing to understand the beauty and importance of nature is not so much vulgar as it is ignorant and shortsighted.

18. COOT
Birds with Image Problems

Some types of birds have a bad image, and their names are used to disparage people. Calling someone a turkey suggests that the person is stupid or inept. Calling someone a loon questions the person's sanity. Also in this derogatory group are birds called coots. Calling someone a coot implies foolishness. The term is typically used to disparage older people—one is more likely to be called an old coot than a young coot.

Coots are in the rail family, but they sometimes swim with ducks and geese, to whom they are not related. Adult coots are about a foot long, which is smaller than most American waterfowl. Their feet are lobed rather than webbed, so instead of paddling around with the effortless grace of a duck, coots pump their heads forward and look as if they are working hard to achieve forward momentum. The head pumping also might help them to judge distance. Coots are all black with a white or light-colored bill and a fleshy extension of the upper bill that forms a facial shield. For some species, the facial shield is a different color than the bill.

The American Coot is the only coot species regularly found in the United States. I once was at a park in Virginia looking at ducks, and far in the distance was a raft of a couple thousand coots. With the naked eye, they looked like a mat of aquatic plants. In my telescope, they looked like a shimmering kinetic sculpture, with the white from the bills and facial shields acting as little points of light among the mass of black bodies. While coots sometimes congregate in large groups, I have also seen solitary coots or a small group of them, sometimes swimming with other waterfowl.

Many features of coots are hidden when they are swimming. It is a bit like when television newscasters sit at desks so that you can see them only from the waist up. You cannot tell whether their clothing from the waist down matches what they are wearing on top or if they are wearing jeans and flip-flops. The American Coot has enormous feet, and when the bird is on dry land rather than in the water, it looks as if it is wearing clown shoes. The toes have no webbing between them, but they do feature nails, which coots use when fighting. When an American Coot dives, you sometimes can see the edging of white feathers on the underside of the tail, which becomes important when the bird needs to communicate information to other coots about the presence of a predator. The Horned Coot of South America has developed a unique way to discourage predation. It constructs an island of stones in the shallow water of a lake and builds its nest of vegetation upon it. A land-based predator has to cross the water to reach the nest. Some of these coot-made islands contain more than a ton of pebbles.

A group of coots is called a cover or covert. There are about a dozen coot species in the world, including a South American species called the Red-gartered Coot. The garters at the tops of its legs are usually hidden underwater, just as the tops of the legs of a modest woman wearing red garters usually cannot be seen. Still, the name is one of the most colorful among the roughly ten thousand bird species in the world. Other contenders include: Croaking Cisticola; Imperial Shag; Cryptic Forest-Falcon; Strange Weaver; Sad Flycatcher; Melancholy Woodpecker; Tambourine Dove; Tropical Boubou; Mustached Babbler; Curve-billed Reedhaunter; Henna-hooded Foliage-gleaner; Scaly-throated Leaftosser; Black-girdled Barbet; Rusty-breasted Nunlet; Zigzag Heron; Oleaginous Hemispingus; Lacrimose Mountain-Tanager; Spectacled Prickletail; and Bare-faced Go-away-bird.

Gallinules are in the same family as coots, but are not quite as somber looking. The word "gallinule" comes from the Latin word *gallus*, for cock, but gallinules are not related to chickens. The Common Gallinule in the United States was lumped with the European Common Moorhen in the 1980s and called the Common Moorhen. A few decades later, ornithological groups in the Americas re-split the species, once again calling it the Common Gallinule. The Common Gallinule is black like a coot, but it has a yellow-tipped red bill rather than a white bill. The Purple Gallinule, found in Florida and along the Gulf Coast to Texas, is a lovely purple and blue; it has never been called a moorhen. I took video footage in Panama of a male Purple Gallinule who repeatedly jerked his wings upward every ten seconds or so as if he were being zapped with an electric shock. In Australia, there is a flightless gallinule called the Tasmanian Native-hen.

Young American Coots have a bald red head and a fringe of orange feathers that runs in a circle below the bill and eyes to the back of the head. Adults might determine the priorities for feeding the hatchlings, who might number between five and ten, based on the intensity of these head and neck colors, and they might even kill some of the chicks if food is scarce. Young Eurasian Coots are not treated any better. If a chick begs too aggressively for food, a parent might attack it and drive it away, causing the chick to starve to death. As with American Coots, this behavior becomes more likely with the scarcer availability of food. The behavior of the adult Eurasian Coots is difficult to understand, because from an evolutionary standpoint, it would seem that the more aggressive chicks would have a greater chance of succeeding on their own. Nonetheless, the end result is that a lot of young coots do not survive to become old coots.

19. CORMORANT
The Eyes of Birds

I attended a presentation by an accomplished nature photographer who said that the most important part of any bird photograph is the bird's eye. Ever since, I have paid more attention to bird eyes. I once focused a telescope on the eye of a pelican who was standing about twenty feet away. Pelicans are large birds with large eyes, and this particular eye filled almost the entire telescope field. Some bird eyes can be beautiful but difficult to see. An example is the lovely turquoise eye of the Double-crested Cormorant, the most common cormorant species in North America. Getting near enough to the bird to get a good look at the eye can be a challenge.

Cormorants are waterbirds who specialize in pursuing fish and other sea creatures underwater. Swimming after prey requires more energy than flying after it, so cormorants burn more energy and have to eat more food than predatory birds who pursue their prey through the air. The name "cormorant" means sea crow, because many cormorant species are all black, although some are black and white. Like the Anhingas described previously, cormorants do not have waterproof feathers, so they frequently perch with their soaked wings outstretched to dry. This soaking of cormorant feathers was known to the ancient Greeks, as reflected in a passage from the *Odyssey* in which Homer describes the god Mercury: ". . . he swooped down through the firmament till he reached the level of the sea, whose waves he skimmed like a cormorant that flies fishing every hole and corner of the ocean, and drenching its thick plumage in the spray."

Some cormorants roost in huge colonies. Off the coasts of Africa and South America, the areas containing these colonies accumulate large amounts of cormorant guano (excrement). In the James Bond novel *Dr. No*, the title character is a Chinese operator of a guano mine, and Bond manages to kill him by burying him in guano. Guano is harvested because it is rich in nitrogen and can be used as fertilizer. However, it is not prized everywhere; in the United States, the guano from cormorant colonies has been blamed for killing trees and vegetation that are important for other species.

Flocks of Double-crested Cormorants sometimes fly in a V formation like geese. The flying birds have a lead-butt appearance, with their rear end lower than their head. While geese often honk in flight, cormorants are silent. The silence of cormorants is the subject of an American Indian tale recounted in Ernest Ingersoll's *Birds in Legend, Fable and Folklore*. The raven, who was one of the chief gods, invited a cormorant to go fishing. The cormorant caught many fish, while the raven caught none. The jealous raven told the cormorant to stick out his tongue because there was something on it. The raven grabbed the cormorant's tongue and pulled it out, which is why the cormorant is silent. In real life, cormorants can vocalize, but one seldom hears them. Ingersoll also relates an Arawak Indian legend about how a cormorant dove into the water to catch a brightly colored water snake from whom the other birds got their colorful plumage. Because the cormorant was

modest, he kept only the snake's black head for himself, which is the reason the cormorant's feathers are mostly black.

Cormorants are long-suffering birds. The Chinese and Japanese traditionally have used cormorants to catch fish, fitting their necks with a ring so that when they catch a fish, they cannot swallow it. Cormorants often appear on the news after an oil spill, coated with black goo. And in 1998, a group of men was arrested for slaughtering more than a thousand Double-crested Cormorants in the New York portion of Lake Ontario. The men believed that cormorants were responsible for a decline in the number of fish in sport-fishing areas. Fishermen in Texas call cormorants "sky rats" and "fire ants with wings." Both the federal government and some state governments have yielded to pressure by fishermen to limit the growth of cormorant populations. In some instances, nests, eggs, and even adult birds have been destroyed with government sanction.

Some species in the cormorant family are known as shags, a name that comes from the feathers that stick out from the back of their head. The British singer Robyn Hitchcock wrote a song called "Bass" that has a line, "It's not a cormorant, it's not a shag, it's only something in a plastic bag." The word "bass" is a heteronym, which means there are at least two pronunciations and meanings for words that are spelled the same. In the Hitchcock song, the bass refers to the fish rather than the musical instrument. There is a bird name that is a heteronym, as demonstrated in the sentence "The dove dove."

20. CRANE
Birds Who Dance

Cranes are magical birds. They are tall and stately, with long necks, long legs, and hefty bodies. And they are great dancers. There are fifteen crane species in the world, but unfortunately, more than half of them have been categorized as vulnerable, endangered, or critically endangered.[5] The species of the fifteen with the largest population is the Sandhill Crane, who is one of the two species found in the United States. There are different races of the Sandhill Crane, ranging in size from the Greater Sandhill Crane (about four feet tall) to the Lesser Sandhill Crane (about three feet tall). The adults of all races of the Sandhill Crane are mostly bluish-gray, with a patch of bare red skin above the bill. Like the bare skin on a human forehead, it can be slightly raised in times of excitement. At rest, some of their wing feathers form what looks like a bustle toward the back of the bird.

In 1997, I went to Nebraska to witness one of the most breathtaking nature spectacles in North America—hundreds of thousands of migrating Sandhill Cranes along the Platte River. There are a few scattered populations of Sandhill Cranes that live year-round in Florida and other places, but most of the others migrate through Nebraska each March. The Platte River area is attractive to the cranes for a number of reasons. A lot of corn is grown in the region, and the birds can eat what is left in the fields from the previous growing season as well as dig for insects and grubs in the same area. Also, the Platte River offers a degree of safety from predators. Most rivers are shallow by the shore and deep in the middle. The Platte is deep by the shore (with a fast current) and shallow in the middle. As such, flightless predators have

---

5. Vulnerable means that the species faces a high risk of extinction in the medium term. Endangered means that it faces a very high risk of extinction in the near future. Critically endangered means that it faces an extremely high risk of extinction in the immediate future.

trouble reaching the cranes. The cranes stand in the river through the night and take off at daybreak to feed in the fields. If you go to the fields in the morning, you can see flocks of cranes gently parachuting down. The cranes tend to be less wary when feeding early in the morning than they are later in the day.

As night approaches, hundreds of thousands of Sandhill Cranes leave the fields and head for the river. While young birds have a soft piping call, the adult's call is a loud bugling that carries a long way. The distinctiveness of the bugling is created in part by the crane's unusually long trachea (windpipe). Hearing a huge flock of cranes bugling at the same time is awe inspiring. One night, I watched from a blind as the birds gradually descended into the river. There was a full moon, which made the water shimmer like mercury as the birds approached. Another night just before sunset, I watched as flock after flock crossed in front of a beautiful sunset. At one point, after huge numbers of birds had settled in the river, something made them fly—perhaps a hawk or a loud noise. The enormous mass lifted into the air all at once. I also watched the cranes take off before dawn. On some days, they would all take off at once. On other days, they departed the river gradually as the sun rose—still an impressive sight. Slightly before dawn and after dusk, you can see the unmistakable silhouettes of the standing and flying birds. As the sun rose and the light changed, the color of the birds went from whitish to bluish gray.

When cranes are nervous, they often dance. This involves opening their wings and hopping vertically about two feet. Their spread wings tend to slow the descent a bit. Sometimes, the dance includes picking up a clod of dirt and trying to throw it forward while leaping. The dancing is also part of their courtship behavior. In preparation for mating, these tall, elegant birds jump like ballet dancers. In Charles Mountford's book *The Dawn of Time*, there is an Aboriginal legend about the dancing of the Brolga, an Australian crane species who looks like the Sandhill Crane. An evil magician wanted to marry Brolga, a beautiful girl known for her dancing, but he was told by the old men in her tribe that she could never become his wife. The magician said that if he could not have Brolga, he would change her into some other creature. One day, when he saw her dancing by herself, he enveloped her in a cloud of dust. When the dust cleared, Brolga had changed into a tall, graceful crane who danced the same way as when she was a girl.

The International Crane Foundation in Baraboo, Wisconsin, has worked since 1973 to conserve cranes and their habitat. George Archibald, the organization's founder, is internationally renowned for his tireless work in crane conservation. Among the species he has helped to save is the Whooping Crane, the tallest bird in North America. Unlike the bluish-gray Sandhill Crane, the adult Whooping Crane is white. During the 1930s, the population of the species dropped to fewer than twenty. Because of concerted conservation efforts and captive-breeding programs, the number in the wild now is at the three-digit level, but still perilously low. I saw a couple of Whoopers mixed in with the Sandhill Cranes during my visit to Nebraska. I had previously seen Whooping Cranes by taking a trip to their southern Texas wintering grounds. In 2011, two people in Indiana pleaded guilty and were sentenced for shooting a Whooping Crane in 2009. Later in 2011, another Whooping Crane was found shot in Indiana. These were not isolated incidents; Whooping Cranes have also been illegally shot and killed in Louisiana, Georgia, and Florida. Sandhill Cranes can still be hunted legally in some states, and there are recipes on the Internet for cooking them.

Cranes who have not been killed and eaten have provided a great deal of inspiration for people from all walks of life. A Grey Crowned-Crane is on the flag of Uganda. Construction cranes are named for their resemblance to the long-necked birds. Cranberries used to be called "craneberries," and one explanation for why they were so named is that the open flower of the plant resembles the head of a crane. Another explanation is that cranes liked to eat the berries. Ernest

Crane

Choate's *Dictionary of American Bird Names* says that the word "crane" is based on the bird's cry, and he points out other crane-related words. The Greek word for crane is *geranos,* and geraniums get their name from the resemblance of their seed pods to a crane's bill. All but five species of the world's cranes are in the genus *Grus,* which is the Latin word for crane. The word "pedigree" comes from a French phrase meaning foot of the crane, because the lines on a family tree resemble a crane's foot. So if you are a Ugandan, a construction worker, a diner at a Thanksgiving dinner, someone looking for your historical roots, or someone planting flowers in your window box, you are among the many people who have a connection with a crane.

21. CROW
Birds as Political Symbols

The crow became a symbol for one of the ugliest chapters in American history. In an 1830s minstrel show, a white comedian in blackface created a character named Jim Crow. The name of the bird with black feathers was given to people with black skin. Jim Crow became the symbol for legalized segregation in the United States, which lasted past the middle of the twentieth century. Native Americans, another group that has been the target of widespread discrimination, have a tribe in Montana called the Crow Nation, who adopted Barack Obama as a member in 2008 when he became the first presidential candidate ever to visit them.

Crows are in a family called the Corvidae and are closely related to jays, magpies, and ravens. Members of this much-maligned family, who are sometimes called corvids, are very intelligent. The New Caledonian Crow of the South Pacific uses tools made of leaves to extract insects from crevices and passes information about how to do it to subsequent generations. Crows also tend to be garrulous, gregarious, and mischievous. A friend once asked what she could do to rid her yard of crows. She was annoyed because when her husband left expensive steaks unguarded on an outdoor grill, crows came and pecked at them. Corvids will eat just about anything and have no special preferences for expensive cuts of beef. There is an eating disorder called pica in which people will eat dirt, excrement, chalk, paper, and various other items that are not generally considered food, or will eat raw rice, flour, or other items that are food ingredients rather than a finished food product. *Pica* is the Latin word for magpie, and the disorder was called this because magpies are thought to eat anything they can get their beaks on.

Crows often gather in the thousands at roosting sites. A group of crows is called a "murder." Murder has become somewhat easier for them as the woodlands in the United States have shrunk and the landscape has become increasingly suburbanized. Reduced woodland area has resulted in more forest edges, giving crows and other predators better access to the nests of small songbirds. Crows especially like to snack on the eggs and young of other bird species. Sometimes, a group of crows will start to caw loudly for no apparent reason. A possible motive for this is to try to induce songbirds to leave their nests to investigate the commotion, thereby allowing the crows to see the locations of eggs and/or nestlings. Small songbirds often fly at crows, trying to drive them away. Crows, in turn, attack hawks and owls, who sometimes rob crow nests of young and eggs. If crows detect a hawk or owl nearby, they usually will mob it, flying around and cawing loudly.

The extent of damage that crows do to agricultural fields is open to question. They eat crops, but they also consume significant numbers of pests who damage crops. Despite efforts to scare them, poison them, and shoot them, crows remain plentiful in many areas. A much bigger threat to crows has been West Nile virus, which has taken a heavy toll on some crow populations. Each year, the National Audubon Society sponsors a Christmas Bird Count to monitor winter bird populations throughout the Americas. I began to report data for a section along the Potomac River in 1991. The number of crows recorded on the count dropped from more than 125 in 2001 to fewer than 20 in four of the seven counts from 2002 to 2008, with West Nile virus being the probable cause. (There is a rock group called Counting Crows, but to my knowledge, they do not participate in Christmas Bird Counts.)

There are more than two dozen species called crows in the world. Not all of them are solid black. In Moscow in 1975, I saw Hooded Crows, who are mostly gray with black on their head and wings. I commented to a Russian tour guide that in the United States, the crows are all black. She replied, "In the United States, everything is all black." (The Cold War was still in progress.) In 2012, I saw a YouTube video showing a Hooded Crow in Russia using a round disk to "snowboard" down a roof, apparently just for the fun of it.

The United States has four crow species. One of them can be seen only from the northwest corner of Washington State to southern Alaska. Another is found only in a small area of southern Texas, and it is uncommon there. The two most common crow species in the United States are the American Crow and the Fish Crow. The American Crow is found pretty much all over the United States and Canada, while the Fish Crow is found mostly along the East Coast and in southeastern states. The two are virtually indistinguishable except by call; the Fish Crow's call is more nasal.

The Rook is a Eurasian crow species, and a group of them is called a building of rooks. They roost in large numbers, and such a roosting place is called a rookery, a term also used for the roosting or breeding places of herons, penguins, seals, and certain other creatures. Rooks look a bit different from other crow species, because the base of their bill is gray, and they have loose feathers around their thighs. Their

plumage is solid black, which is a reason the Rook plays the role of the parson at the funeral in the poem "Who Killed Cock Robin?" The word "rook" also means to steal or swindle, which comes from the habits of the bird, especially with respect to agricultural crops.

In his 1897 travel book *Following the Equator*, Mark Twain praised the Indian Crow as the "Bird of Birds." The species he saw in India is today called the House Crow. Twain talked about the bird's many different characteristics, comparing them to Hindu incarnations in "a sublime march to ultimate perfection." Someone else must have really admired this bird, because the scientific species name is *splendens*, which means splendid. The crow features prominently in the work of the twentieth-century English poet Ted Hughes. The Ted Hughes Society, which is dedicated to the study of his work, uses a crow silhouette as its symbol.

The crow's feet around people's eyes were so named because the pattern of wrinkles resembles the foot of the bird. While crows do not always hop when moving on foot, "crow hop" is a term used in a variety of contexts, including the action of a horse trying to throw its rider, the movement of a baseball player preparing to make a throw, and a construction joint that is out of alignment. The verb "to crow" can mean to boast or to make a joyful sound, such as by an infant. In all likelihood, the linking of crowing to boasting is derived more from the behavior of crowing cocks than crowing crows. Cocks strut and are not afraid to be seen, while crows tend to act in a more wary manner, as if concerned about being caught at whatever they are doing.

Even though crows tend not to crow, they do have the ability to mimic. They can repeat simple words and imitate a man's laughter. If you change the spacing and punctuation of "man's laughter," you can spell "manslaughter," which would seem an appropriate activity for a murder of crows.

22. CUCKOO
Birds as Symbols of Marital Infidelity

If you are seated while reading this, you are sitting on something named for a bird's bill. I do not mean the piece of furniture on which your butt is resting. I mean your coccyx, or tailbone—the end of the line for your vertebral column. *Coccyx* is the Greek word for cuckoo. Long ago, an anatomist with ornithological interests noticed after cutting open a cadaver that the human tailbone resembles the bill of a cuckoo.

Cuckoos have been referred to frequently throughout history when making people the butt of jokes. More than 2,400 years ago, Aristophanes wrote a satirical play called *The Birds* (which has a totally different plot from the Alfred Hitchcock film with the same name) in which characters try to intercept smoke from sacrifices to the gods to create their own heavenly city called Cloud-Cuckoo-Land. The effort fails miserably, and cloud-cuckoo-land now is a metaphor for a crazy unrealistic scheme. *Cloudcuckooland* was also the name of the 1989 debut album by the rock band The Lightning Seeds.

Cuckoos have become a powerful symbol in literary and social history because of their reproductive practices. The majority of the more than one hundred cuckoo species in the world are parasitic nesters, which means they lay their eggs in the nests of other species and place the burden of protecting the eggs and raising the young on foster parents. As such, they are symbols of sexual activity without subsequent responsibility. The term "cuckold," which describes a man whose wife is sexually involved with another man, is derived from the behavior of cuckoos, even though cuckoos do not engage in cuckoldry. A better analogy for cuckoo behavior would be two lovers who leave their progeny (or more accurately, potential progeny) on someone else's doorstep. However, there are many other species of birds previously thought to be monogamous who through DNA testing have been found to regularly engage in cuckoldry.

Cuckoo

The University of Texas athletic teams are nicknamed the Longhorns, and their fans frequently use the "hook 'em Horns" hand signal, which involves holding up the forefinger and pinky to resemble the horns of a steer. The same gesture has been used for many centuries to mock cuckolds. A chapter in Desmond Morris's 1979 book *Gestures* discusses fourteen theories for the origin of this signal. The sarcasm theory, castrated bull theory, and mad bull theory are based on portraying the horns of a bull as the University of Texas students do. Similarly, the promiscuous cow theory suggests that the cuckold's wife is as promiscuous as a cow. Some theories suggest that the gesture represents two penises, a woman's spread legs, or the horns of a stag or the devil.

The six cuckoo species in the United States, including the roadrunner, build their own nests, even though some of them occasionally lay their eggs in the nests of other birds. As such, the American cuckoos are not associated with marital infidelity. However, their image is far from positive, because the word "cuckoo" is associated with insanity and clouded thinking. Sometimes in cartoons, when a character is hit hard during a violent encounter, little birds fly in a circle around his head and say, "Cuckoo, cuckoo," imitating a cuckoo clock. (Cuckoo clocks were first made in the 1600s in the Black Forest region of Germany, and the sound imitates the familiar call of the cuckoos in that region.) The gesture of pointing one's forefinger toward one's head and making circles suggests that someone is cuckoo or crazy. In Thailand, I saw and heard a species called the Large Hawk-Cuckoo, whose call is a crazed, relentless *brain fee-ver, brain fee-ver, brain fee-ver*; the vocalization is consistent with the insanity image.

In Australia, I saw a cuckoo species called the Common Koel, named for its loud and persistent call. The male, who is about seventeen inches, is solid black with red eyes. A male koel flew over a car in which I was riding, and when he spread his tail, he looked like the eagle on the German coat of arms. On a nature walk in 1996, my Australian friend Diane told me that before she became a serious birder, she used to hear a bird she called the "storm bird," because it would return to her neighborhood each year around the beginning of the rainy season. For a few years, she never could see the bird. When she finally did, it turned out to be a koel. Someone who overheard Diane's story said that where he comes from, koels are called bugger birds, because the buggers sing at 3 a.m. Right after Diane told this story, I walked a short distance up a hill near where a koel was singing. Suddenly, a lot of bulls and cows approached me. John Young, the Australian naturalist who was leading the walk, ran up the hill, got down in a three-point stance like a University of Texas football lineman, and started scratching at the ground and making threatening noises as if ready to charge the herd. The cattle turned around and ran in the other direction. That's a good trick for a city boy like me to know. I ended up not seeing the koel.

Cuckoos sometimes are blamed for things they don't do. English gardeners use the term "cuckoospit" to describe a frothy substance produced by the larvae of insects called froghoppers. Cuckoos are not known to spit on garden plants or anything else. The word "cuckoospit" appears in one of the many impenetrable sections of *Finnegan's Wake* by James Joyce. In *Ulysses*, Joyce created the character Leopold Bloom, who is one of the most famous cuckolds in twentieth-century literature.

The cuckoos of the world are extremely diverse. Some are as small as sparrows, while others are as large as pheasants. Some are plain, while others have gorgeous iridescent plumage. Some spend most of their time in trees, while others stay on the ground. Some build nests and have complex cooperative breeding arrangements, while others lay their eggs in the nests of other species. Some of the American species of cuckoos are not easy to see. Even though they do not have to be surreptitious like their parasitic brothers and sisters, some of them tend to perch high in trees and occasionally call, and finding one in a leafy treetop can be difficult.

Reproducing by parasitizing other species is much more common (and sometimes gruesome) among insects, such as wasps, than among birds. Parasitic nesting by birds is a remarkable evolutionary accomplishment when one considers all of its complex elements. After two parasitic cuckoos have mated, the female must find an unguarded nest of another species at precisely the time she wants to lay an egg. She sometimes removes existing eggs from the nest. Her egg must be accepted and incubated by the host species. The timing of the hatching of the egg must allow the young cuckoo to outcompete the other nestlings when the host parents return with food. With some cuckoo species, the chicks have the instinct to lift the eggs of the host species over the side of the nest to reduce the competition for food. When there are young birds of the host species in the nest, the baby cuckoo must know what sounds to make to elicit the proper feeding responses from the host parents. Despite negative traits such as cuckoldry and insanity that humans associate with them, cuckoos are amazing birds.

23. DIPPER
Walking Birds

In 1970, Jack Blanchard and Misty Morgan recorded a hit novelty song called "Tennessee Bird Walk." The lyrics begin with the removal of trees, wings, birdbaths, feathers, and common sense from birds, and end with the birds "walking southward in their dirty underwear." The song has little value for anyone wishing to learn ornithology, but it calls attention to the fact that birds use their legs as well as their wings to move from place to place.

Just as not all birds can fly, not all of them can walk. Loons, who spend most of their lives on water, have legs that help with swimming and diving but are positioned so far back on the bird's body as to be virtually useless for walking. Swifts, who spend most of their waking hours in the air, use their weak feet to hang onto a wall or tree when roosting, but their legs have not evolved for walking. Lacking the ability to walk is much less common among birds than lacking the ability to fly. Yet flightlessness has some advantages. Being flightless allows a species to become heavier and stronger without having to worry about lugging around the extra weight in the air, but it also inhibits the ability to escape quickly from land-based predators. Some bird species evolved to become flightless because they did not have the need to escape from such predators. But when humans and human-introduced mammals entered their habitats, these flightless species had no natural defenses, and many became extinct.

Sandpipers and other wading birds tend to walk as humans do: one foot forward, then the other. Some bird species hop with both feet. Large flightless birds such as ostriches and emus use their long powerful legs for running. Pheasants, quails, and chickens are poor flyers, and most of their movement involves walking; they use flight primarily to escape danger. Roadrunners (beep-beep) fly well, but prefer to walk or run. Birds in the American tropics called antpittas and antthrushes spend most of their time on the ground, preferring walking to flight. One of my favorites is a strange species I saw in Panama called the Streak-chested Antpitta. It looks like a thrush with long legs and a very short tail. When it stands on a log and sings, it puffs out its entire body as if it has swallowed a balloon that repeatedly inflates.

The walk of the American Dipper is especially fun to watch. This plump little gray bird (seven to eight inches) has a short tail that appears to have been lopped in half. Dippers follow the advice from the title of the 1979 Blondie album *Eat to the Beat*. They constantly bob their body rhythmically while looking for food (such as fly larvae) in fast-rushing streams, and this behavior is the basis for their name. The five dipper species in the world are the only aquatic songbirds. Some sandpipers teeter in a similar manner when searching for food, but they do not dive totally underwater as dippers often do. If you get close to a dipper, you might see it swimming/flying underwater. They are reputed to be able not only to enter the water flying but also to come out flying.

Most birds have a gland that secretes oil for feather maintenance. The oil gland of the dipper is about ten times larger than for most songbirds, because more oil is needed to waterproof feathers. Dippers have flaps over their nostrils to keep out water while they swim. As with other bird species, they also have a special translucent third eyelid called a nictitating membrane, which is responsible for the cloudy appearance of the eyes of some sleeping birds. For dippers and species who dive into water, this membrane provides added protection while they are submerged. Humans have a remnant of a nictitating membrane in the corner of the eye near the bridge of the nose.

Exactly a hundred years before I saw my first dipper in Yosemite in 1994, John Muir wrote affectionately about the dippers he saw there. He called them Water Ouzels, which is a colloquial name for them in America and Europe. In describing a dipper's nest, Muir wrote: "The Ouzel's nest is one of the most extraordinary pieces of bird architecture

I ever saw, odd and novel in design, perfectly fresh and beautiful, and in every way worthy of the genius of the little builder. It is about a foot in diameter, round and bossy in outline, with a neatly arched opening near the bottom, somewhat like an old-fashioned brick oven or Hottentot's hut."

Walking seems to be the topic of the vocalizations of three birds of the Australian rain forest. The Wonga Pigeon says, "*Walk-walk-walk-walk-walk.*" The Brown Cuckoo-Dove asks, "*Didja walk? Didja walk?*" And the Noisy Pitta uses his loud voice to say, "*Walk to work! Walk to work!*"

24. DOVE
Birds as Symbols of Peace

The word "dove" makes people think of peace and love, as in lovey-dovey. The word "pigeon" makes people think of urban birds who are a nuisance. In fact, doves are pigeons, and pigeons are doves. If you look in an old bird field guide, the name given to the feral pigeons found in cities used to be Rock Dove. The name in newer guides is Rock Pigeon. Some people believe that the last name of Christopher Columbus comes from the Latin word for dove, as does the name of the former television detective Columbo. The name Jonah is the Hebrew word for dove, and his name is symbolic in the Biblical story about his adventures inside the whale. In the 2006 best-selling novel *The Elegance of the Hedgehog*, one of the lead characters is a twelve-year-old girl named Paloma, which is the Spanish word for dove, and her older sister is named Columbe, which is the French word for dove.

In the Bible, the dove is an important part of the story of Noah and the flood. According to Genesis 8:8–11: "Also he sent forth a dove from him, to see if the waters were abated from off the face of the ground; But the dove found no rest for the sole of her foot, and she returned unto him into the ark, for the waters were on the face of the whole earth: then he put forth his hand, and took her, and pulled her in unto him into the ark. And he stayed yet other seven days; and again he sent forth the dove out of the ark; And the dove came in to him in the evening; and lo, in her mouth was an olive leaf pluckt off: so Noah knew that the waters were abated from off the earth." From this early time, the dove was associated with the olive branch, which is a symbol of peace. Doves also appear in the New Testament. In Matthew 10:16, Jesus tells his disciples: "Behold, I send you forth as sheep in the midst of wolves: be ye therefore wise as serpents and harmless as doves."

Anyone who has read *King Solomon's Ring* by the Austrian naturalist Konrad Lorenz might question why the dove is considered a harmless symbol of peace. Lorenz put a home-reared male turtle-dove and a female ring-dove in a roomy cage. When he returned the following day, he found the turtle-dove on the floor of the cage with most of the feathers on his head, neck, and back ripped out. The turtle-dove was still alive, but the ring-dove continued to peck at him mercilessly. Lorenz wrote: "Only in two other instances have I seen similar horrible lacerations inflicted on their own kind by vertebrates: once, as an observer of the embittered fights of cichlid fishes who sometimes actually skin each other, and again as a field surgeon, in the late war, where the highest of all vertebrates perpetrated mass mutilation on members of his own species."

Lorenz, who in 1973 won the first Nobel Prize awarded for studying animal behavior (with Niko Tinbergen and Karl von Frisch), theorized a reason for this gruesome dove behavior. Many animals have a submission response to signal surrender to an opponent. A wolf losing a fight with another wolf might expose its neck to the attacker. This signal makes the attacking wolf stop fighting so that the vanquished wolf can leave without further injury. Doves do not possess a submission signal. In such situations, the losing dove usually flies away. If flight is not possible, such as when two birds are in a cage, the more powerful dove recognizes no signal to stop the attack and might kill the weaker bird. Outside of cages, doves tend to be peaceful and mostly vegetarian, eating low on the food chain. The gentle behavior of doves seems to reflect feminine rather than masculine qualities. The passage from Genesis about the great flood uses feminine pronouns for the dove.

There are more than 320 species of doves and pigeons in the world, and they come in many shapes, colors, and sizes. Unlike most birds, doves and pigeons are suction drinkers, which means they can bend over and drink without having to raise their head to allow water to go down their throat. They also have an unusual way of feeding young. The young bird sticks its bill down the throat of the parent, who regurgitates a meal consisting of a milky-looking mixture rich in fat and protein. When the chicks are newly born, they are fed exclusively on this milk, which is produced by both parents. The production of this milky substance is stimulated by prolactin, the same hormone that stimulates lactation in a nursing human mother. The pigeon chicks gradually are weaned from the milk as their diet begins to include other food.

Some of the most unusual and attractive pigeon and dove species live in New Guinea and Australia. The crowned pigeons of New Guinea are the largest pigeons in the world, measuring between twenty-six and thirty inches. The crest on their head looks like a grayish Afro. The Topknot Pigeon, an eighteen-inch Australian species, is mostly gray and looks as if it is wearing an improperly fitted hairpiece. The call of the Wompoo Fruit-Dove is a deep, rich *Wom-poooo* that sounds as if it is being uttered by a person in the trees. Wompoo Pigeons measure up to twenty inches, and their lovely plumage is green, gold, gray, yellow, and burgundy.

The most common native dove species in North America is the Mourning Dove, named for its mournful cooing. The male and female share nesting responsibilities; the male incubates from morning until evening and the female from evening until morning. I once discovered an active Mourning Dove nest in a thin, bare tree on a busy corner in downtown Washington. It was a flimsy structure—most pigeons and doves build simple nests—and this pair of Mourning Doves abandoned it after a week. Unlike many species whose numbers have declined with the cutting of North American forests, Mourning Doves have bene-fited by the increased amount of open area. The hunting of Mourning Doves is permitted in many states. Dove hunters in the Middle Atlantic region are allowed to kill twelve doves each day of the hunting season, which starts in September and runs through November, December, or January (depending on the state). In 1984, Indiana lifted a hunting ban on Mourning Doves that had been in place for more than a century. In previous eras, people commonly participated in contests to shoot live pigeons released from a trap. Eventually, such "trap shooting" contests substituted clay disks for live pigeons, which is why the disks are called clay pigeons.

Hunting was a major cause of the extinction of a North American species called the Passenger Pigeon. At one time, Passenger Pigeons numbered in the billions. The flocks darkened the skies, sometimes taking days to pass over. In *Vanishing Birds*, Tim Halliday recounts their demise. They nested in huge colonies and sought roosts with an adequate food supply. Hunters went into roosting and nesting areas and killed enormous numbers of the birds. One method of trapping was to bait a small area of ground with grain. To attract the birds, a live pigeon whose eyes had been sewn shut was tethered to a nearby perch. This perch was called a stool, from which we get the expression "stool pigeon" for someone who is a spy for the police. Improvements in transportation and communications allowed trapping to become more sophisticated, and the dead birds could be sent to market more quickly. By the 1880s, the Passenger Pigeon was in serious decline.

One theory for why the population crashed so quickly is that the birds relied on large numbers for breeding success. Once the population dropped below a certain level, flocks became too small to maintain the viability of the species. The last known individual, a female named Martha, died in the Cincinnati Zoo in 1914, the same place the last Carolina Parakeet died four years later. After only three centuries of American settlement by Europeans, one of the most abundant bird species on Earth had become extinct. Previously, the Dodo had been another member of the pigeon family driven to extinction by humans, mainly sailors looking for food. This flightless bird from the island of Mauritius was more than three feet tall and weighed more than forty pounds—larger than any pigeon species living today. By 1700, all of them had been wiped out.

Rock Pigeons, a Eurasian species, have adapted well to cities throughout the world. They originally nested on rocky cliff faces, and buildings with ledges suit their needs just as well. They are among the smartest, most diverse, most versatile, and most adaptable birds in the world, but many people think of them as flying rats. Tom Lehrer got laughs with his song "Poisoning Pigeons in the Park." Even in Assisi, the home of Saint Francis, an ordinance was passed to prohibit the feeding of pigeons. City pigeons sometimes end up on people's dinner tables. A friend from Italy told me that when her grandmother did not have meat to cook for dinner, she opened her kitchen window and sprinkled bread crumbs on the sill. When a pigeon came to eat the crumbs, Grandma conked it with an iron skillet, plucked it, and cooked it.

The homing ability of pigeons has been known for thousands of years. Pigeons were used by the ancient Greeks to transmit messages. They have been used extensively to send messages in times of war, up through World War II. In 2011, a pigeon was caught trying to carry marijuana and crack-cocaine to prisoners incarcerated in a prison in Colombia.

Because of the intelligence of pigeons, many scientists have studied them. The psychologist B.F. Skinner developed some of his theories about behaviorism from his experiments with pigeons. Donald Blough, a psychologist at Brown University, taught pigeons to recognize all the letters of the alphabet. The vision of pigeons has been the subject of many experiments, with scientists discovering that pigeons can see in slow motion and have the ability to detect a far greater range of colors than humans can. Charles Darwin was a pigeon enthusiast and based some of his theories about sexual selection on the study of his own pigeons. Former heavyweight boxing champion Mike Tyson became an avid pigeon fancier as a young boy in Brooklyn and maintained his interest through adulthood. In 2002, the *New York Times* ran a story about pigeons who seemed smart enough to ride the subway; in fact, they were entering the cars to look for food and exiting when they were done rather than using the trains to ride from one specific station to another.

In 2004, I was quoted in a story about pigeons in the *Washington City Paper*. I had parked in the National Mall area one afternoon, and when I returned to my car, it was covered with pigeons as well as a lot of food they had recently excreted. As I was trying to figure out why this happened, a young reporter approached and asked what I thought of the situation. I was not pleased about the mess, but I took time to give him background information about pigeons, much of which he misquoted. When his story appeared the following week, I understood why the pigeons were there. A man who lived nearby showed up late each afternoon to feed the pigeons in the area where I parked, so they learned to wait for the food. B.F. Skinner would call this operant conditioning. I won't say what I called it.

25. DUCK
Bird Stamps

When my friends travel to foreign countries and ask if they can bring back anything for me, I suggest bird postage stamps, which are easy to transport and relatively inexpensive. I have collected more than 2,500 postage stamps depicting birds from around the world. The depictions include photographs, artwork, and cartoons, and they often reflect a country's attitude toward birds. In some instances, the featured birds are chosen for decorative purposes and not found in the countries issuing the stamps. In 2009, I gave an hour-long presentation to a local bird club about bird stamps, featuring more than three hundred images.

My bird stamp collection also includes nonpostage stamps. In 1934, the United States Postal Service created Federal Migratory Bird Hunting and Conservation Stamps for the United States Fish and Wildlife Service. They are known as duck stamps, because they originally served as licenses for hunting migratory waterfowl. They now also are purchased by nonhunters to gain admission to National Wildlife Refuges. A new federal duck stamp is issued annually, and proceeds from the sales are used to purchase and lease wetland habitat for waterfowl and other animals. States issue similar stamps to raise money for state refuges.

I buy a federal duck stamp every year, both to contribute to wetland conservation and because I like the artwork. Ducks are among my favorite birds. My home is filled with ducks—ceramic ducks, rubber ducks, duck paintings, hand-sewn ducks, duck cups, duck refrigerator magnets, and other duck items. Ducks seem calm, regardless of where they are. Sea ducks can sit in a choppy ocean and look as placid as ducks sitting on a still pond. Watching ducks tends to be easier and more relaxing than many other types of birding. Ducks are large and generally stationary. Usually, there is adequate time to set up a telescope and have a leisurely look, albeit sometimes at a long distance and in poor light. One of the challenges of duck watching can be seeing too many birds, for they often congregate in large flocks. If you know that an uncommon duck species is visiting an area, you might have to scan a lot of ducks to find it.

Ducks are in the same family as geese and swans. When they land from a considerable height, they work their way into the descent through a process called whiffling, which involves tilting from side to side to decrease the momentum from the drop. The word "whiffle" means to flutter, which is the basis for the name of the whiffle balls that children play with. Some duck species get food by dabbling, which means reaching down into the water without diving below the surface. Other ducks dive completely below the surface for animal or plant food. Many dabbling ducks have black butts. Dabblers are vulnerable to predators from above when their head is below the water and their butt is sticking up. Against the dark surface of the water, a black butt will be more difficult for a predator to see than a light butt.

Some dabbling ducks dive when confronted with danger. I once saw a small dabbling duck called a Green-winged Teal dive when a Peregrine Falcon tried to grab it and "take it home for dinner." The Peregrine eventually flew away without the teal meal. There are more than fifteen teal species in the world. Nonbirders know the color "teal" as a blue green. It is supposed to be the color of the wing of a European species of teal (best seen when the bird flies). But it seems to apply to a variety of bluish-green shades, some of which do not resemble the color on any teal wing I have ever seen.

The Mallard, the most common of the dabbling ducks world-wide, is thought to be the ancestor of most breeds of domestic ducks. Sometimes, Mallards interbreed with domestic ducks, creating strange-looking hybrids. As with chickens, ducks are intentionally bred to pro-duce unusual new breeds. In the United States, the number of ducks bred each year, mostly for meat and eggs, is in the tens of millions. One

odd breed from Indonesia is called the Runner Duck, because it stands erect and runs rather than waddles. A very small breed is the Call Duck, which was used by hunters in Europe as a live decoy to attract (call in) ducks in the wild. Wild Mallards are closely related to many species of wild ducks found in various parts of the world. They evolved in the Northern Hemisphere, but they have been introduced into the Southern Hemisphere. They were taken to Australia from England in the 1860s and now are causing problems for the closely related Pacific Black Duck. The Mallards and black ducks are interbreeding, diluting the bloodline of the black ducks.

Some American ducks are not bothered by human presence, while others fly quickly when they detect humans. The Wood Duck is one of the most skittish as well as one of the most gorgeous. Seeing Wood Ducks in breeding plumage is one of my great joys of springtime. Often, at the slightest human approach to a pair, they fly off, with the female squealing like a puppy whose foot has been stepped on. Wood Ducks nest in tree cavities or nest boxes, and I sometimes saw them perched in trees on the White House grounds when citizens were still allowed to walk near the White House grounds. After the eggs hatch, the ducklings sometimes must jump from a considerable height to get to the ground. They are very light and amazingly tough, so almost all of them make it safely. A female Wood Duck sometimes will lay eggs in the nest of another female, producing what is called a dump nest. Some of these dump nests, often in nest boxes, contain many more eggs than a single female can successfully incubate.

The American Wigeon is one of the most aggressive of the dabblers. Its colloquial name is Baldpate; "bald" means "white," and this duck has a white cap. Baldpates like to eat wild celery that grows underwater, but they are not adept at getting it. They often hang around with skilled diving ducks and steal celery and other food from them. Baldpates can see the diving ducks coming up through the water and will try to snatch the food as soon as the other ducks surface.

Some diving ducks, including the eiders, spend much of their time at sea. Eiders have been prized because of their soft feathers. Eiderdown is soft and does not conduct heat well, so it is highly sought as a lining for blankets, coats, and pillows.[6] Before substitute products were developed, the demand for the feathers resulted in the slaughter of huge numbers of eiders on their nesting grounds. Some people raise eiders on farms to obtain the down. There are four eider species in the world, and three are big and bulky. The male Common Eider is black and white, with a wash of green on his head. The male King Eider, one of the most beautiful ducks in the world, has an orange face shield, reddish bill, gray cap, and a subtle pink wash on his breast to complement his black-and-white body. The scientific name for the King Eider is *Somateria spectabilis*, with the genus name meaning "body wool" (because of the eiderdown) and the species name meaning "showy" because of the coloration of the male's plumage. The females of both Common and King Eiders are mostly brown.

The Dutch naturalist Niko Tinbergen, who shared the 1973 Nobel Prize for medicine with Konrad Lorenz and Karl von Frisch, devoted

---

6. The French name for the Common Eider is *Eider à duvet*, which, roughly translated, means "eider with the down." The duvets on beds originally were soft quilts stuffed with eiderdown, but most now are stuffed with synthetic fibers.

a chapter in his book *Curious Naturalists* to the behavior of Common Eiders. The female eiders Tinbergen observed were so devoted to their incubation that they starved for the month they sat on eggs. They left every second or third day for ten to fifteen minutes, but only to drink. The ducklings clean themselves shortly after hatching to prepare to walk with their mother to the sea. Sometimes "aunt" eiders assist with the journey from the nest to the sea.

Among my favorite bird species is the Musk Duck, the Darth Vader of waterfowl. This Australian species is mostly dark gray. Some dark ducks have velvety plumage. Musk Ducks look as if they have swum through an oil slick. They swim low in the water and dive frequently, rolling below the surface like a frogman. The male has a large disk of skin hanging from his chin, and he makes it larger during mating displays that involve kicks, splashes, and other hijinks. Musk Ducks get their name from the musky odor of the male, which serves as an effective deterrent to being hunted. On a voyage to Australia, the explorer George Vancouver, after whom the Canadian city and island were named, complained that a Musk Duck shot by his men had stunk up his ship. No other ducks in the world are similar enough to the Musk Duck to be in the same genus. The name of the genus for this bizarre bird is *Biziura*. The entry about Musk Ducks in the Steve Madge and Hilary Burn guide to the waterfowl of the world begins, "A large and

bizarre Australian duck, one of the oddest of all waterfowl." The first line of Graham Pizzey's entry about them in his 1980 field guide is, "A decidedly strange duck."

The British comic Eddie Izzard has done a routine about Noah and the flood in which a pair of ducks refuses to come onto the ark. When Noah warns about the impending great flood that will cover the entire Earth with water, the ducks respond: "So? What's the big problem?" Izzard's ducks might have shown more concern about more recent problems. The populations of many waterfowl species declined sharply in the second half of the twentieth century, primarily because of habitat loss. North America was duck heaven before Europeans arrived. The land was filled with grassy wetlands that concealed ducks from predators and offered ample food for adults and nestlings. But vast expanses of wetlands have been drained, destroying a great deal of waterfowl habitat. For some species of ducks, the female determines where nesting will occur, probably because it is important for her to know the area since she takes the responsibility for raising the young. A male might select a mate on their wintering grounds, after which they will often fly to breed in the area where she was hatched rather than the one where he was, provided that it is still there. Hunting and pollution have also contributed to declining waterfowl numbers.

Ducks, like cows, are one of the few groups of animals for whom the term used for the female is also used to describe the whole group. A male duck is a drake. To further confuse sex roles, the word "Mallard" comes from the same root as "male," so a Mallard duck suggests a male female. Male and female ducks vocalize differently, and not all ducks quack. The expression "if it walks like a duck and quacks like a duck, it's a duck" does not take into account the converse: that it could still be a duck even if it does not quack. Of those species who quack, the female makes a louder quacking sound. And contrary to the claim made on many Internet lists of amazing facts, a duck's quack will echo.

26. EAGLE
Unnoticed Birds

Many people travel through life without noticing the wondrous creatures around them. When I go into the backyards of friends, they are often amazed when I point out bird species they never knew were there. In the winter, I occasionally go birding in an area along the Potomac River in Virginia to look at the Bald Eagles who gather on the mudflats at low tide. This section of the river is next to a path used for running, hiking, and biking. If I am looking at the eagles through my telescope, I sometimes ask passers-by if they want to see one. Representations of Bald Eagles appear on the back of one-dollar bills and on countless insignias and graphics, but many people act shocked to see a live eagle in a place they frequently visit. They probably have gone up and down this path often but have never taken the time to look closely at the river.

Bald Eagles live mostly on fish, but they also eat carrion, small birds, and small mammals. They do not always catch the fish they eat. Ospreys, who are hawks about two-thirds the size of Bald Eagles, are more adept at catching fish. An Osprey carrying a fish might be forced to drop it when harassed by a much larger eagle. The eagle grabs the fish out of the air and flies off. The scientific term for this practice is kleptoparasitism, which means parasitism by theft.

Bald Eagles now are regularly seen around the nation's capital. On New Year's Day in 2005, I saw an adult Bald Eagle fly in front of the Capitol Dome—a photo opportunity many photographers would die for. But in the 1960s, the survival of Bald Eagles was imperiled, primarily because of pesticides such as DDT. In 1963, only about four hundred nesting pairs remained in the lower forty-eight states, although there were a lot more in Alaska. The population in the lower forty-eight has rebounded somewhat, with the number of nesting pairs now in the thousands—still a low number, but better than it had been. In addition to the Bald Eagle, the only other regularly occurring eagle species in North America is the Golden Eagle, which is more likely to be seen in the West than the East. While the Bald Eagle prefers habitats near water, the Golden Eagle stays inland in the ever-dwindling wide-open spaces.

Eagle populations worldwide have been affected by pesticides, habitat loss, and deliberate poisoning and shooting. Bounties used to be paid to hunters to kill the birds, who were considered a threat to livestock. John Vandenbeld's 1988 book *Nature of Australia* features a photo of a fence with a dead Wedge-tailed Eagle hung between each pair of posts. Some farmers saw Wedge-tailed Eagles feeding on dead livestock and assumed the eagles had done the killing. In fact, their primary food is rabbits, who are agricultural pests. Although most eagle killings by farmers have stopped, I was with a group in Australia in 2003 who discovered the remains of a shot Wedge-tailed Eagle. Included was a foot of the bird, which looked like a grappling hook, with three forward-pointing toes and one pointing back.

In 2011, the British tabloid newspaper *The Daily Mail* tried to stir up public passions by running two grainy photos that purported to show a Golden Eagle carrying a lamb in its talons. The accompanying story called the bird a "swooping assassin" with "razor-sharp talons" that

was "confirming farmers' worst fears for their flocks." The photos were allegedly taken by a birder in Scotland who did not want to give his name. In 2012, *The Guardian*, one of Britain's more respectable newspapers, was one of numerous news outlets whose website ran links to a video that purported to show a Golden Eagle snatching a toddler in a Montreal Park. The video was a fake that had been produced by students at a French Canadian computer graphics school. Such pranks exacerbate people's unwarranted fear of large and powerful birds.

Both the Wedge-tailed Eagle and the Golden Eagle are in the genus *Aquila*, which is the Latin word for eagle. An aquiline nose on a human is large and curved, resembling the beak of an eagle. Wedge-tailed Eagles build enormous nests in trees, usually not very high off the ground. The area at the base of the tree typically is littered with skulls, vertebrae, and other remains from meals. The nests are made of sticks and branches, some of which are so large that you wonder how a bird could carry them. The eagles sometimes use nests built in previous nesting seasons, rotating from year to year. Some species of small songbirds build nests among the bottom sticks of the eagle nests. The eagles have no interest in attacking little birds, and predators of the songbirds are reluctant to approach the eagles. The eagle nests are not deep, and active ones are lined with a fresh layer of leaves. Wedge-tailed Eagles lay one to three eggs per nest, and if there is not enough food to feed the young, older nestlings might kill the younger ones.

One of the most fearsome eagles in the world is the Harpy Eagle. This rare Central and South America species stands more than three feet tall and is strong enough to kill and carry off mammals as large as monkeys and sloths. It is named after unpleasant creatures from mythology called Harpies, who had a woman's head and the body of a rapacious bird. The Harpies were instruments of the divine vengeance of Zeus, and they enjoyed snatching food from hungry men. Among their most noted victims were a group led by Aeneas, who led the Trojans when they fell for the wooden horse trick. One can imagine how the mythological Harpies might have come to the mind of an ornithologist who saw a Harpy Eagle snatching a monkey from the top of a tree.

While the name for the Harpy Eagle was inspired by an ancient myth, some mythological figures had direct confrontations with eagles. One of the best known involved the Titan Prometheus, who was the brother of Atlas (the guy who is usually portrayed with the Earth resting on his shoulders and whose name was given to books of maps). Prometheus was a cheeky guy who stole fire from the gods to give to mortals, which really ticked off Zeus. As a punishment, Prometheus was tied to a rock, and an eagle came every day to peck at his liver. The eaten portion of the liver would grow back each evening, only to be eaten again the next day by the eagle. The liver is unique among human organs in being able to regenerate itself, but it is doubtful that the ancient Greeks knew this. In another Greek myth, Zeus turned himself into an eagle and abducted a handsome young prince from Troy named Ganymede. He took Ganymede to Olympus to be a servant and boy toy; centuries later, similar abductions would be called white slavery. Eagles have also been important symbols in Islamic culture. The Egyptian flag features the eagle of Saladin, who was a twelfth-century Muslim sultan.

Because the eagle is one of the symbols of the United States, it has been appropriated many times for use in popular culture. One of the most popular rock bands of all time was called the Eagles, and another less popular one was called Eagles of Death Metal. When I was growing up in the Philadelphia area, the eagles I heard the most about were the Philadelphia Eagles, the city's professional football team. It was the first team with a bird name to play in the Super Bowl. The team's effort in that game was as ill fated as the venue at which the game was played—the New Orleans Superdome. If you go to the Philadelphia area and want to sound like a local, pronounce the football team as if it were "Iggles."

27. EGRET
Birds as Symbols of Conservation

The Great Egret is the symbol of the National Audubon Society. Egrets became conservation poster birds because, like Marilyn Monroe, they were victims of their own beauty. During the late 1800s and early 1900s, egrets and other birds with pretty feathers were almost wiped out by hunters who sought to provide plumes for women's hats. Egrets were called "aigrettes" in the 1500s, and the same word was used to describe the long breeding plumes of the adult birds. A few centuries later, these plumes, which are twelve to eighteen inches, were in great demand by hat makers. Plume hunters did not want to shoot wading birds in wetlands, because the feathers would be of little value if they became stained with blood or fell into the water or mud. The most effective hunting strategy was to enter a breeding colony to kill egrets on nests. Egrets often nest in large colonies as a protection against certain types of predators. This behavior made them easy prey for human predators.

The killing of adult egrets on breeding grounds not only decreased the number of adult birds, but it also meant that eggs did not hatch and nestlings were not fed. A similar carnage was wreaked on other types of birds, including gulls, terns, shorebirds, and songbirds. According to Robin Doughty's book *Feather Fashions and Bird Preservation*, an estimated two hundred million birds were killed annually for their feathers at the beginning of the twentieth century. The slaughter was widespread throughout the United States, Europe, Asia, and Australia.

As with Marilyn Monroe, egrets became associated with an American president, albeit with more positive results. Theodore Roosevelt acted to protect birds on their breeding grounds. During his administration at the beginning of the 1900s, the federal government established more than fifty bird refuges where hunting was prohibited. Roosevelt's efforts, along with intensive campaigns by the Audubon

Society in the United States and the Royal Society for the Protection of Birds in Britain, were important in raising public awareness about the plight of egrets and other species. Eventually, women's hat styles changed, decreasing the demand for the plumes.

Most people think of egrets as beautiful white herons. While egrets are beautiful herons, not all of them are white. The genus *Egretta* has about a dozen species, including the lovely Snowy Egret. But it also includes the Reddish Egret (of the southern United States and Central America) and the Slaty Egret and Black Heron (both of Sub-Saharan Africa). The Great Egret is not in the genus *Egretta*. It is in the genus *Ardea*, the same genus that contains the Great Blue Heron. There is a white form of the Great Blue Heron that lives in Florida and the West Indies, and it can be confused with a Great Egret.

The Great Egret has a long, sinuous neck. It hunts by slowly stalking in shallow water and quickly stabbing at prey with its long, pointed bill. The Snowy Egret is smaller and looks more delicate. When it lifts its feet, you sometimes can see its beautiful golden slippers that contrast with its black legs. The Reddish Egret has the colloquial name "Jesus bird" because of its animated hunting style. It spreads its wings and appears to walk quickly over the surface of the water, stirring up prey. The spread wings create shadow and reduce glare, allowing the bird to better see prey in shallow water.

The Great Egret is also found in Australia, along with the Little Egret and the Intermediate Egret. You won't win a prize for figuring out which one was named third.

28. EMU
Exploring the World to Look for Birds

When I visited London in 1984, the British pound was worth only $1.20, so merchandise in stores seemed inexpensive by United States standards. I spent a lot of time in bookstores and shipped many books home, including Graham Pizzey's *Field Guide to the Birds of Australia*. After paging through the book, I dreamt of someday visiting Australia to look for these birds. An opportunity arose when I heard I would be attending a meeting in Hawaii in 1995. Hawaii is about a third of the way to Australia, so I thought I might as well go the rest of the way.

While I was planning the three-week trip, a birder friend suggested that I stay part of the time at Cassowary House in the northeastern part of the continent. I wrote to Cassowary House, said I wanted to stay there a week, and asked for suggestions of places to visit during the other two weeks. One of the owners of Cassowary House suggested that I stay with Graham Pizzey for part of the time. I wrote to Graham, and he wrote back with a suggested itinerary for my entire trip. The last leg was a five-day stay at his home. He lived in a nature reserve he created in Dunkeld in the Grampian Mountains, a few hours by car west of Melbourne.

Graham was waiting to pick me up the evening I arrived at the small bus stop in Dunkeld. He asked what I had seen already on my trip and wanted to know if there were any birds I especially wanted to see. I told him I still had not seen an Emu. He smiled and said I wouldn't have to worry about that. The next morning, I awoke at six o'clock. My bed was next to a window, and when I opened my eyes, I saw three large figures moving through the bushes. They were Emus heading toward a cherry tree. To reach the cherries, the Emus leapt straight into the air like clumsy ballerinas. The birds seemed wary and would stop eating and look around if they heard a noise. At times, they acted aggressively toward each other, perhaps because it was the mating season. Emus are about six feet tall, with wide bodies. When they move quickly, their rump feathers flounce, and they look as if they are wearing a hoop skirt. Later during my stay at Graham's house, I watched a comical pair of Emus bathing in a pond. They knelt down in the water, stood up, and shimmied their hoop skirt feathers to dry off. A few times, I heard female Emus making a noise that sounded like someone repeatedly hitting a bass drum.

Emus, ostriches, rheas, kiwis, and cassowaries are all in separate families, but they are lumped into a category of large flightless birds called ratites. They have vestiges of wings that hang as two little limp flaps at the front of their body, having shrunk from disuse over countless generations. Ratites are skilled swimmers, because as flightless birds, they would have no other way to traverse a body of water. Ratites are the most primitive birds in the world, in the sense that they are thought to have evolved to their current state before all other bird species. The two ostrich species, both native to Africa, are the most primitive of the ratites and the only birds in the world with two toes on each foot; other ratites have three. On a hike through an arid area of central Australia, I was with a friend who found the remains of an Emu leg, which allowed me to look closely at the leathery foot with three toes. In the same area, we saw three-toed Emu tracks in the sandy soil. You also can track Emus by looking for their excrement, which is a big flat blob of greenish runny mess.

Ratites have unconventional sex roles for the rearing of young. The male makes the nest, and sometimes several females lay eggs in it. In his book *Watching Birds*, Roger Pasquier says that rheas, who are South American ratites, lay green eggs that turn successively yellow, blue, and finally white at the time of hatching. The clutch of eggs can reach thirty. The male broods the eggs and raises the young without help from the females. In Australia, the male Emu plays a similar role in raising young. He stays with young birds six to eighteen months after they hatch. One often sees groups of Emus that have one adult male and a dozen or so youngsters. Very young Emus are tan with dark stripes.

Rheas, birds of the grasslands, have characteristics similar to both ostriches and Emus. They are mostly vegetarian but will occasionally eat insects and small animals. Like other ratites, they have a better-developed sense of smell than most bird species. Roger Tory Peterson's book about birds in the *Life Nature Library* series contains a photo-graph of a Brazilian gaucho straddling a rhea who is pinned to the ground. The gaucho is tearing out feathers from near the tail to be used for making feather dusters. The rhea escaped with its life, but with a bare butt. Such treatment seems highly inappropriate for a bird named after a great nature goddess in Greek mythology who was called the "Mother of the Gods" and was the mother of Zeus, Hera, Poseidon, and Demeter.

29. FAIRY-WREN
Birds with Intense Colors

Have you ever seen a color so intense that it makes you want to shout? A tiny bird in Australia called a Splendid Fairy-wren has twice done this to me. The species is only five to six inches, about half of which is the tail. The plumage of the male has shades of blue that appear electric. Trinidad and Tobago naturalist David Rooks, who died in 2012, used to talk about brilliant blue butterflies in the Morpho family who "shoot blue laser lights at you." The Splendid Fairy-wren does similar blue laser surgery on your eyes.

Fairy-wrens are not related to American wrens. They are called wrens because they are small and energetic and frequently cock their tail like the little brown wren found in England. The Australian species have names such as Lovely Fairy-wren and Superb Fairy-wren, which are well deserved. The bright colors displayed by some of the males include turquoise, crimson, and purple. Female fairy-wrens are not as intensely colored, but still handsome.

Some fairy-wren species are common garden birds. When I stayed at the home of Graham and Sue Pizzey in 1996, I grated cheese to put on a windowsill for the Superb Fairy-wrens. The cheese had to be grated finely, because fairy-wren bills are tiny. The Pizzeys had problems with a male fairy-wren who repeatedly flew against windows to attack the reflection of what he perceived to be a rival male. Graham tried to stop the problem by rubbing a white substance on the windows to eliminate the reflection. Many bird species attack their own reflection in mirrors and windows.

A visually stunning moment on a 2003 trip to the Australian desert involved seeing two male Variegated Fairy-wrens in the same bush with a male White-winged Fairy-wren. The Variegated Fairy-wren, who looks like the Superb Fairy-wren, has a cap and sideburns that are electric blue. The White-winged Fairy-wren is a deep rich blue accented with white wings. Seeing one male fairy-wren can be stunning, but seeing three at once takes one's breath away.

One of the people who went on the desert trip was my artist friend Diana. Shortly after I returned to the United States, she sent me a painting she had done with a male and female Splendid Fairy-wren. She had based the painting on a photo in a book by Australian naturalist Steve Parish. The photo caption was as follows: "A 'furgling' male Splendid or Superb Fairy-wren may fly into a neighbouring territory intent on mating with a resident female. If he carries a flower petal in his beak, the resident males do not chase him away. DNA tests of chicks' parenthood prove that female fairy-wrens often succumb to 'furgling' strangers bearing gifts." I was not familiar with the word "furgling," so I looked it up online. The definition that I found was "to copulate rudely with a member of the opposite sex," and a possible source of the word was listed as Joseph Heller's novel *Catch-22*. In addition to not being sure what it means to copulate rudely, the definition did not seem to fit a scene involving two tiny birds.

The answer was not all that different from the definition that had puzzled me. According to an article that Diana found in a birding newsletter covering the far south coast of Australia, fairy-wrens are extremely promiscuous. Unless a male zealously guards a female mate during the breeding season, she will happily mate with other males who are in the vicinity, and the majority of the young born will not be the offspring of the male in the pair bond. The article calls this practice "kleptogamy," which means marriage by theft (even though only humans get married). But the practice is more rudely called furgling, which is a combination of fucking and burgling. Some fairy-wren species form groups of three males and many more females, usually with one male being dominant. The males might fertilize females in other groups, which diversifies the gene pool. Sometimes numerous females cooperate in raising the young.

Fairy-Wren

Male fairy-wrens can be quite devious in attracting mates. According to a study published in the journal *Behavioral Ecology*, male Splendid Fairy-wrens have a type of song they sing when in the presence of a much larger predator species called the Grey Butcherbird. When female fairy-wrens hear a male singing this song, they become more attentive because of the presence of a threat. But a male sometimes sings this song when there are no butcherbirds around merely to get her attention before making his moves. The journal article compared this to a human male taking a woman to a horror movie in the hope that she will move closer to him during the scary parts.

In addition to being devious, Splendid Fairy-wren males are extremely sexually potent. According to Olivia Judson's book *Dr. Tatiana's Sex Advice to All Creation*, each ejaculation of a Splendid Fairy-wren contains eight billion sperm, compared to 180 million from the average human ejaculation—more than forty-four fairy-wren sperm for each human sperm.

30. FALCON
Birds as Corporate Symbols

Humans often try to assume the qualities of animals they admire, such as desiring the bravery of a lion or the speed of a gazelle. In some instances, the associations go beyond metaphor, with people trying to assume the qualities by wearing part of a revered animal's body, consuming part of the animal, or even having cosmetic surgery to make themselves look more like the animal. Rhinoceroses continue to be critically endangered because of poaching to provide ground rhinoceros horn (which is powdered hair) to men who dream of enhancing their sexual potency. In the United States, symbolic associations with animals are widespread, particularly as school mascots or the nicknames for amateur and professional athletic teams.

Corporations liberally borrow from the animal kingdom for images to sell products. In the 1960s, the Ford Motor Company sold vehicles called Falcons. They were originally designed as a compact car, but Ford later used the name for a broad range of vehicles, including trucks. Ornithologists use the term "falconoid" to describe something that is like a falcon. The qualities of the Ford Falcon were not especially falconoid. Ford Falcons began as clunky little cars without much pickup. Before their demise in 1970, they became somewhat faster cars, but they never lost the clunky body.

Avian falcons are fast and powerful, with strong bodies and pointed wings. When perched, many falcon species appear short-necked and chesty. Their claws are falcate, or hooked like a sickle, which is the basis for their name. They live by killing and eating other creatures, and they have keen eyesight. Many falcons have a vertical black stripe running through each eye. These stripes serve a similar purpose to the blacking some athletes (such as football players on the Atlanta Falcons) put beneath their eyes to reduce glare from the sun.

For thousands of years, people have trained falcons to hunt and bring back prey. Such sport is known as falconry, even though it sometimes involves hawks rather than falcons. Although falcons have many similarities to hawks, they are in different families. The term "to bat an eye" comes from falconry, with the movement of the eye resembling the fluttering (beating/batting) of a bird's wings when perched on a falconer's hand. Bats (the flying mammals) are so named because they flutter in a similar way. Falcons were venerated in Ancient Egypt, and Horus, who was one of the most significant Egyptian deities, was usually depicted as having the head of a falcon. The name "Horus" comes from an Egyptian word that means "falcon" or "one who is above." Falconers in the Middle East and other areas have especially prized the Gyrfalcon, the largest of the falcon species. It is a bird of cold northerly climates, and it is the official bird of the Northwest Territories in Canada. In 2011, researchers Kurt Burnham and Ian Newton reported that after putting radio transmitters on Gyrfalcons in Greenland, they discovered that some of the birds were spending a lot of time at sea on pack ice, hunting seabirds.

There are more than sixty species in the world in the falcon family. Not all of them are big birds. The Pygmy Falcon in Africa measures less than eight inches—a little shorter than a European Starling. The smallest of the half-dozen North American falcon species is the American Kestrel, at about ten inches. The male is lovely, with blue-and-chestnut plumage. Kestrels are commonly seen in rural areas on utility lines or hovering low over fields. I also have seen them in flight over busy intersections in downtown Washington. Worldwide, there are about a dozen falcon species called kestrels, including a rare one on the island of Mauritius where Dodos used to live. In Africa, there is a species sometimes called the Neglected Kestrel, which is why I feel obliged to mention it. The one in Australia is called the Nankeen Kestrel. It was a favorite species of the late Australian naturalist Graham Pizzey, and an image of one was on the personal stationery he used for the letters he wrote to me. The bird's light-brown plumage resembles the color of unbleached cotton fabric that was imported from Nankeen, China. "The Windhover" is a poem that the nineteenth-century poet Gerard Manley Hopkins wrote about the species of kestrel he saw in England; he dedicated the poem "to Christ our Lord."

If the American Kestrel is the compact falcon model, the Merlin is the midsized. Merlins are small, dark, belligerent falcons whose name comes from an old word for a hawk; the "merlioun" was mentioned in Chaucer's poem "Parlement of Foules."[7] The name for the bird called the Merlin has no connection to the magician with the same name in the time of King Arthur. The names for the Merlin, Gyrfalcon, and many of the other falcon species come from Norman French, because the French introduced falconry to England after the Norman Conquest

---

7. "Parlement of Foules" contains the first recorded association of Saint Valentine with romantic love, which became the basis for Valentine's Day celebrations.

in 1066. Merlins combine speed, power, and maneuverability better than any bird-of-prey species I have seen. Rather than flying high above prey and attacking in a stoop (a swift, direct descent), Merlins fly low over potential victims. Their primary prey is other birds, but they also eat rodents, insects, and lizards. Along the Delaware coast, I saw a Merlin fly after a flock of shorebirds, and it seemed to shift into a higher gear as it approached them. Many species who form flocks fly in formation when attacked by a predator such as a falcon. A predator has much more trouble zeroing in on a bird in a group than on a solitary bird.

Moving up to the full-sized model, the Peregrine Falcon is almost twice the length of an American Kestrel. Peregrine Falcons are among the fastest-flying birds in the world, but most of their speed comes from gravity. If you put a Peregrine on a perch next to a Rock Pigeon, the pigeon can fly faster off the perch. But if the Peregrine gets above the pigeon and is able to dive, the pigeon has little chance to escape. Peregrines can make a fist with their toes, and the impact on another flying bird usually results in instant death, after which the Peregrine grabs the corpse out of the air and takes it to a place where it can be plucked and eaten. I once saw a young Peregrine flying among a group of gulls near the United States Capitol. The gulls glided and turned much faster than the Peregrine, who never came close to catching any of them. At no time did the Peregrine get above the gulls and go into a stoop.

Peregrines are found on every continent except Antarctica. They have wandered over a wide range, and their name means "wandering." During the twentieth century, they were nearly eliminated in the United States because of DDT and other pesticides. DDT prevented the production of adequate calcium for eggshells that could withstand the weight of the female during incubation. By 1970, there were fewer than forty nesting pairs in the lower forty-eight states, and the species was totally eliminated from the eastern United States. Through a captive breeding effort by Thomas Cade of Cornell University and many other committed people, a viable population of Peregrines was reintroduced into North America. As with Bald Eagles, Peregrine Falcon numbers have rebounded, and the birds are once again seen fairly regularly. There have been many instances of Peregrines being seen on tall urban buildings, which approximate the cliff ledges where they roost.

Regarding falcons and automobiles, Toyota sold a subcompact car called a Tercel during the 1980s and 1990s. In falconry, a tercel is a male falcon or hawk. The term for the small Toyota actually might be an accurate representation of the product rather than an exaggeration by marketers. The word "tercel" is derived from the Latin word *tertius*, which means third. One explanation of the origin is that male falcons are about a third smaller than females. Such a name would be appropriate for a car model that was about a third smaller than some of the larger vehicles Toyota was marketing.

31. FINCH
Birds as Measuring Devices

Environmental writers overwork a metaphor about small yellow finches called canaries. These birds were named after the Canary Islands in the Atlantic off the northwest coast of Africa, which in turn got their name from the Latin word for dog (the same root as canine). A cage with a canary used to be taken into coal mines as a way to detect harmful levels of odorless gas. The bird has a lower tolerance than humans for the gas, so if the miners saw a canary keel over, they would know to evacuate the mine. Environmental writers now refer to any species decline that indicates a broader decline in environmental quality as a "canary in the coal mine." These same writers rarely comment that putting a canary or other finch into a cage can cause serious environmental problems, even if no harmful gas is present. When I was in Trinidad in 1992, some of the native finches were rare in the wild because of trapping for the cage-bird trade. For every successfully trapped bird, many more die during the trapping process.

You do not have to go to Trinidad to find examples of environmental problems caused by caging wild finches. If you walk in downtown Washington during the spring, you might hear the loud, complex song of a House Finch. This species was not in Roger Tory Peterson's guide to eastern birds that I used as a youth. Shortly before World War II, an activist named Richard Pough, who later co-founded the Nature Conservancy, discovered that merchants in New York City were selling House Finches as "California Linnets." Macy's sold them for eighty-nine cents apiece. The birds were trapped in the western United States, where they are native, and taken east, where they are not. Trapping and selling the birds was illegal, so Pough notified federal authorities. The merchants, fearing prosecution, released the birds into the wild. House Finches now have established large populations all over the eastern United States, driving out native species.

The "California Linnet" name was based on a European finch called the Linnet, who like the House Finch is a sparrow-sized bird with a splash of red on the head and breast. Its name comes from the same root as "linen," because linen is made from flax, which Linnets eat. Linnets have been well represented over the centuries in British poetry. A Linnet was the torchbearer at the funeral after Cock Robin was killed in a famous old anonymous poem. Linnet was used as a generic term for various types of finches. Often, the references to Linnets mention the sweetness of their song, which many people associate with the joys of spring. William Wordsworth wrote a poem called "The Green Linnet," about a Greenfinch, which includes the verse:

> Oh have I marked, the happiest guest
> In all this covert of the blest:
> Hail to thee, far above the rest
> In joy of voice and pinion![8]

> Thou, linnet! in thy green array,
> Presiding spirit here today,
> Dost lead the revels of the May;
> And this is thy dominion.

Finches are a large, diverse group, and many small seed-eating birds with "finch" in their name are not necessarily in the same family or closely related to one another. They are popular as pets, because many are good singers and have pretty plumage. Being seedeaters, they also are easy to feed. The most familiar species of pet canary has bright yellow plumage and sings well.[9] In crime circles, informers are called

---

8. A pinion is a wing.

9. In Europe during the 1700s and after, musical instruments called serinettes were sometimes used to teach songs to canaries. The serinettes got their name from serins, who are finches in the genus *Serinus*, which includes the canaries. These instruments were small barrel organs about the size and shape of a shoe box.

canaries, because another word for informing is singing. Oddly, the pejorative word "fink," which also describes an informer, is derived from the German word for finch, perhaps to ridicule Germans who did not participate in certain social organizations (such as student fraternities and labor unions) and moved around like free birds. There is a thuggish-sounding African species sometimes called the Bully Canary, although the more common name is Brimstone Canary, which is not much better.

Finches are popular visitors to backyard feeders. The American Goldfinch is one of North America's most beloved feeder birds. Many people put out goldfinch feeders with niger seed, so named because it is black. The male goldfinch in breeding plumage has a bright-yellow body with black wings and a black skullcap. The female is duller, as is the male during the winter. A different species of goldfinch is popular in Europe, but its only gold is on its wings. The European Goldfinch is one of more than a dozen alien bird species with an established population in Australia. It primarily eats seeds from thistles and other

introduced plants that native birds do not eat. The spread of the exotic plants on which the goldfinches thrive has taken a greater toll on native Australian bird populations than has direct competition from the goldfinches.

The Zebra Finch, a native Australian species, is popular worldwide as a cage bird. It also is a popular subject for scientific experiments. One study determined that Zebra Finches sing in their sleep. Another discovered that male Zebra Finches sing much more loudly when other males are present. An unpleasant study involved injecting Botox into the vocal cords of Zebra Finches to determine how neurons might regenerate. The Zebra Finch is the most common finch in central Australia, where one often hears its tinny little song. These four-inch birds are among the songbirds who frequently build nests among the sticks at the bottom of the huge nests of Wedge-tailed Eagles.

The diversity of finches played a role in the formulation of Charles Darwin's evolution theories. When Darwin traveled to the Galapagos, he collected thirteen specimens of finches from the islands. Darwin had not noticed the differences among the bills and other physical characteristics of the finches while he was in the Galapagos. The differences were pointed out by the naturalist John Gould, who examined the specimens after Darwin returned to England. The idea of birds with similar bodies developing different-shaped bills to take advantage of local food sources helped Darwin realize that creatures are capable of changing over generations and that nature favors those who are best able to adapt to their habitat. While none of the Galapagos finches is named after Gould, a breathtakingly colorful bird in Australia called the Gouldian Finch is named in honor of Gould's wife Elizabeth.

One of the finches on the Galapagos is the Sharp-beaked Ground Finch, who uses its sharp beak to peck at the bodies of seabirds such as boobies and drink the blood from the wound. This species is sometimes called the "vampire finch." The bills of many other finches are extremely powerful, capable of crushing or opening seeds with thick coverings.

One of the most unusual bill adaptations belongs to a group of finches called crossbills. The tips of their upper and lower mandible do not meet in the front, but cross instead, which allows the birds to extract seeds from pine cones. I posted a video on YouTube of some who visited the National Arboretum in Washington in 2013. They typically travel in flocks, landing in an area, feeding awhile, and flying off to another feeding area. Crossbills usually are found far to the north of where I live, so I see them very infrequently. Nonetheless, I have a special place in my heart for them after reading a delightful 1917 book of poems called *How to Tell the Birds from the Flowers*, by Robert Williams Wood. Among Wood's comparisons are the crow and the crocus, the plover and the clover, and the lark and the larkspur. Because of my name, my favorite is his comparison of the crossbill with a flower called the Sweet William.

32. FLICKER
Birds and Space Travel

Few birds make national news headlines, but a pair of flickers at the Kennedy Space Center did so in 1995. They damaged the Discovery Space Shuttle by pecking at the foam insulation of its external tank, causing a mission to be delayed. NASA's security procedures for keeping human intruders from the rockets were not effective against birds. When the flickers damaged the Space Shuttle, NASA sprang into action and appointed a Bird Investigation Review and Deterrent (BIRD) Team. After consultations with leading ornithologists, the BIRD Team concluded that: ". . . the migratory Northern Flicker Woodpeckers were attempting to excavate a cavity in the external tank because they may have lost a nest or roost cavity to starlings. If a nest is overtaken before the female can lay her eggs, the pair becomes desperate for a nest. . . . This may explain the unusually aggressive pair that damaged the tank. In an effort to keep this problem from recurring and to reduce NASA's exposure to risk of flight hardware damage, the BIRD Team has recommended a three-phased long-term plan. Phase 1 involves establishing an aggressive habitat management program to make the pads more unattractive to flickers and to disperse the resident population of flickers. Phase 2 includes implementation of scare and deterrent tactics at the pads. Phase 3 is the formal implementation of bird sighting response procedures."

NASA's bird deterrent tactics included plastic owl decoys, Mylar strips, air horns, and water hoses. NASA also acquired tapes of bird predators to play near the launch pads. To NASA's credit, it did not take the easy way out by quietly killing the birds. Indeed, the response was anything but quiet. An airport in England discovered that playing Tina Turner records loudly works better than recordings of avian distress calls for repelling birds.

Flickers are atypical woodpeckers in that they often feed on the ground in addition to pecking for food on trees. They are plump brown birds who are about a foot long and show a white rump in flight. There are six species of flickers, and two are found in the United States. The Northern Flicker is a combination of what used to be two species—the Yellow-shafted Flicker, an eastern race who shows flashes of yellow in flight, and the Red-shafted Flicker, a western race who shows flashes of red. Unless you see a flicker in the hand or in a close-up photo, you are unlikely to understand the meaning of the term "yellow-shafted." The feathers have bright yellow shafts. Once when bird banding, a friend

and I caught a flicker. Our scale for weighing birds went up to 100 grams (about three and a half ounces) and was able to accommodate most songbirds. The flicker, who is not a songbird, weighs about 150 grams, or more than five ounces. I was especially interested in the fact that the flicker in the hand appeared larger than I expected. Most of the birds we banded appeared to be smaller in the hand than they looked when flitting in the trees. There also is an optical illusion that occurs when a bird in the hand is let go. For some reason, a bird appears to almost double in size the moment it leaves your hand. I have noticed this phenomenon with the release of both small songbirds and much larger birds such as hawks.

The Northern Flicker is the state bird of Alabama. I have read numerous conflicting origins of the name "flicker." One possibility is that the name comes from its call, which is a long, loud series of notes that sound like *flick-a-flick-a-flick-a*. Another is that it comes from the way it flicks its wings or bill, or from the flicker of yellow when it opens its wings. The flicker is sometimes called the yellowhammer because of the similarity of the eastern birds to a lovely European bunting of that name who also flashes yellow on its wings when it flies.

Very few bird species eat ants, because ants contain a high level of formic acid. Formic acid is pretty nasty stuff, and it is found in the venom from bee stings and ant bites. Even Neotropical species called antbirds do not eat ants—the name comes from these birds following swarms of army ants and eating the insects and other prey that the ants stir up. But ants are a favorite food of flickers. Once when I was at the National Zoo in Washington for a Sunday afternoon lecture, I saw a flicker on a paved pedestrian path. A large mass of small black ants was on the edge of the path eating a clump of ice cream someone had dropped. The flicker ignored the passing pedestrians and stood by the ants, zapping them like an anteater. He did not zap the ants straight on, but zapped them with his tongue curved to the side as he watched them with one eye. I was so fascinated by what he was doing that I missed the beginning of the lecture.

33. FLYCATCHER
Uncertainty in Identifying Birds

On a 1978 British comedy album called *Sir Henry at Rawlinson End* by Vivian Stanshall, there is an incident involving Sir Henry's brother Hubert, whom Stanshall describes as having the "assurance of a sleepwalker." Toward the end of the record, Hubert tries to entertain visitors by doing a bird impression. It consists of hopping on one leg, repeatedly saying "chirrup," and shoving a handful of worms into his mouth.

I am less interested in the worm-eating than in the metaphor of having the assurance of a sleepwalker. Occasionally, birders have experiences in the field that call into question how sure they should be about their bird identifications. A skilled birder friend who was leading a trip saw in the distance what appeared to be a perched adult Bald Eagle, with a dark body and white head and tail. Everyone in the tour group trained their binoculars on the distant shape and was pleased about seeing the eagle. After they returned to the bus, my friend decided to take one last look at the bird through a high-powered telescope. He saw a flimsy white grocery bag, a dark trash bag, and a piece of newspaper, all wedged into an eagle shape in the distant tree. What he had seen as a Bald Eagle was not even a bird. Had he relied only on his binoculars, he and the rest of the group would have been equally sure they had seen an eagle. A birder on a different trip was distressed when she saw a field that seemed to be littered with white plastic bags. Upon closer examination, she discovered that the white bags were actually Snowy Owls.

A more disquieting example involved two birds I saw in the hand. Some species of flycatchers are virtually impossible to tell apart in the field except by voice. If the birds are silent, you don't have much chance to identify them. There are field marks you might be able to examine if you have a bird in the hand. The size and color of the feet, which can be almost impossible to see on a bird perched in a tree, might be a basis for correctly identifying a hand-held bird. While bird banding, a friend and I caught a flycatcher in the genus *Empidonax*, whom we weighed and measured before attempting to identify it. About ten minutes later, we caught another *Empidonax* flycatcher who in the hand clearly showed longer legs and lighter-colored feet. This bird more closely resembled the description in the banding manual for the species by which we had identified the first flycatcher, so we had to change our identification of the first bird. If you can make such a mistake with birds in the hand, how can you feel confident about identifying these flycatcher species seen in a tree, unless you have the assurance of a sleepwalker?

The tyrant flycatchers are the largest family of birds found only in the Western Hemisphere, comprising roughly four percent of all bird species in the world. In some bird field guides for Central and South America, where hundreds of tyrant flycatcher species live, there are entire pages filled with different flycatchers who look similar. Some eat food other than insects, including fruit and even small fish. Because many species in various parts of the world catch insects, there are other birds called flycatchers who are not in the same family as the tyrant flycatchers. The word "tyrant" in Greek originally meant lord and only later developed the negative connotation of despot. As such, the tyrant flycatchers are the "lords of the flies." Among the tyrants in the bird world are the Pearly-vented Tody-Tyrant, the Agile Tit-Tyrant, and the Little Ground-Tyrant. I have seen both the Northern and Southern Beardless-Tyrannulets. Most flycatchers have stiff feathers called rictal bristles near their bill. These "beardless" tyrannulets do not have rictal bristles.

Some flycatcher species are smaller than many species of hummingbirds. In Panama, I saw a species called the Black-capped Pygmy-Tyrant, which is a long name for a bird measuring only 2.5 inches. I also saw a tiny (albeit friendly), drab bird with the oxymoronic name of Paltry Tyrannulet. Another name for this species is the Mistletoe Flycatcher, because it eats the berries from parasitic mistletoe plants.

Flycatcher

Mistletoe Flycatchers defecate or regurgitate the seeds, which are still covered with the viscous material from inside the berries, thereby allowing the seeds to stick to the surfaces of trees and germinate. Bird species in other parts of the world perform a similar function in spreading mistletoe seeds, including the Mistletoebird in Australia, who is not a flycatcher.

The scientific name of the Eastern Kingbird is *Tyrannus tyrannus*, which makes it the tyrant of tyrants. This very feisty bird, who is about the size of a cardinal, attacks much larger birds (including hawks) who enter its breeding territory. A tropical American species called the Piratic Flycatcher engages in behavior that is even more antisocial than the kingbird's.[10] This species does not build its own nest. Instead, it stays in the vicinity of another species who is building a nest. After the other species pair mates and lays its eggs, the pair of Piratic Flycatchers attacks it and commandeers the nest, dropping any eggs of the other species to the ground. The female Piratic then lays her eggs in the nest and proceeds with incubation.

Some tyrant flycatchers are attractive and eye catching. The Vermilion Flycatcher, a common species in parts of the southwestern United States, is a beautiful deep red. The Scissor-tailed Flycatcher, the state bird of Oklahoma, has a forked tail that is as long as its body. Other flycatchers have very long tails, including a South American species called the Strange-tailed Tyrant. The male Royal Flycatcher in Central and South America has a red, rounded crown (which is rarely seen raised in the field) that is bigger than his head. However, many tyrant flycatchers are quite plain, having names such as Greyish Mourner, Unadorned Flycatcher, and Drab Water Tyrant.

One of the most common flycatchers where I live is the Eastern Phoebe. This friendly little bird frequently pumps its tail while perched.

---

10. A species called the Social Flycatcher has a range that overlaps that of the antisocial Piratic Flycatcher.

One year, phoebes built a nest under the eaves of a nature center I often visit. Many build their nests under foot bridges. Their name is spelled the same as the Titan from Greek mythology who was the daughter of the Earth goddess Gaia, but it actually is merely a classical spelling of a representation of their song. To add to the confusing nature of tyrant flycatchers, some are named for vocalizations that they themselves do not make but that are made by a closely related species. The Eastern Wood-Pewee, a migrant who nests in eastern North America, says *pee-a-wee*. But the Greater Pewee, a Central American relative whose breeding range reaches as far north as Arizona, is sometimes called "Jose Maria," because his song is a slowly whistled *ho-say, ho-say, ho-say ma-RI-a.*

The genus that includes the pewees has fourteen species, and only one does not have "pewee" in its name. This species, the Olive-sided Flycatcher, is seen in the United States and has one of the most convivial vocalizations in the bird world: *QUICK, THREE BEERS!*

34. FROGMOUTH
Invisible Birds

Have you ever dreamt of being invisible and going about your life without anyone noticing? If you lack a magic potion to make yourself transparent, the next best thing would be to blend in closely with your surroundings. This latter strategy is used by a group of birds called frogmouths, who are some of the best camouflage artists in the animal kingdom.

Frogmouths are night birds who look like owls with big mouths, even though they are not in the same family as owls. Despite their stocky appearance, frogmouths are not especially strong. Were they not well camouflaged, they would be in much greater danger of being killed by large hawks and other predators. Birds of the night need effective camouflage so they can avoid detection while sleeping or roosting during daylight hours. Many owls have plumage that looks like the bark of trees. Birds called nightjars have plumage that resembles leaf litter. Frogmouths take the camouflage a step further. In addition to having feathers that look like the bark of a tree, they also can elongate their bodies to resemble a tree branch. This tactic is used by female frogmouths incubating eggs. I was with a birding group who discovered a female Tawny Frogmouth on a nest (a small cup) on the bare branch of a tree. Her feathers looked like tree bark, and from behind, her tail looked like leaves. She probably detected the presence of our group, monitoring us by sound rather than sight. She kept her eyes closed but moved her head back and forth. A moving head could resemble a branch swaying in the wind, but the appearance of large eyes might blow her cover.

Frogmouths are found only in Asia and Australia, and there are more than a dozen species. A similar ecological niche is occupied in the Americas by a family called the potoos. The three frogmouth species found in Australia are in a separate family from the rest of the frogmouths. The first ones I saw were a pair of Papuan Frogmouths at a daytime roost in a residential neighborhood in Cairns. They sat silently with their eyes closed and did not move. They had a peculiar facial expression, as if they were dreaming about something that made them smirk. They have a bush of bristles above their mouth, which helps with camouflage. I later heard the most common vocalizations of the Tawny and Papuan Frogmouths, both of whom sound like chanting Buddhists. The Papuan utters a deep *oom-oom-oom-oom-oom-oom*. The chant of the Tawny is a somewhat faster and higher-pitched version of the same mantra. The Buddhist chanting seems appropriate for birds who spend so much time in a seemingly meditative posture.

The vocalizations of the Marbled Frogmouth, the third of the Australian frogmouths, are my favorite of any bird species in the world, and they are anything but meditative. One vocalization sounds like Curly of the Three Stooges—a high-pitched *woo-woo-woo-woo-woo-woo-woo*. Another sounds as if the bird is shaking a large piece of wobbly sheet metal. There is a vocalization that sounds like a repetition of the phrase *koo-loo* and another that sounds like a series of two-part grunts, with the first grunt longer than the second. Many of the vocalizations end with a loud clap of the bill that sounds like someone hitting two blocks of wood together. The Curly vocalization actually sounds more like *woo-woo-woo-woo-woo-woo-woo-WHACK*, which is appropriate considering what happened to Curly in many Three Stooges films.

When camping in northeastern Australia, I sometimes heard these strange Marbled Frogmouth vocalizations coming from a distance in the middle of the night. Sounds emanating from the darkness can activate imaginations as people speculate about what they might be hearing. Many night sounds, coming from insects and frogs, create a wall of background noise you no longer consciously hear after awhile. But the sounds of some night birds stand out prominently from the background. In one of the areas where the Marbled Frogmouth can be found, there is another night bird called a Sooty Owl whose vocalization sounds like a falling bomb. I wonder what the Aboriginal people of Australia thought when they first heard these scary and mysterious sounds coming out of the darkness of the forest in the middle of the night.

35. GANNET
The Symmetry of Birds

The natural world contains wonderful examples of symmetry. If you draw a vertical line down the middle of most mammals and birds, the two sides resemble each other fairly closely. Biologists call this "bilateral symmetry." Sometimes, the symmetry goes further. The Duck-billed Platypus is one of the world's three monotremes, or egg-laying mammals. A platypus often swims flat on the surface of the water, with rounded shapes sticking out of four ends: its front (the bill), back (tail), and two sides (paws). Seabirds called gannets also have a four-sided symmetry: their bill, tail, and wings all are pointed.

A friend from Dublin sent me a handsome ceramic piece portraying five gannets. Their name comes from an old German word for goose, even though gannets are in the same family as boobies and not related to geese. There are about ten species worldwide in this family, and the three called gannets all look pretty much alike. When flying over water in search of fish, gannets can compress their body and wings and plunge quickly toward the surface, hitting headfirst with considerable force. The dives, sometimes from a considerable height, usually do not carry them far down into the water, but gannets have been known to dive more than seventy feet below the surface. As with woodpeckers, their skulls are adapted for absorbing impact, especially for deep dives.

Gannets nest in large colonies, and fishermen used to go into these colonies to kill the gannets and use them for bait. While this is no longer done, the Northern Gannets found off the coast of Britain are one of the species who has been victimized by a phenomenon called ghost fishing, in which birds and other sea creatures become tangled in nets abandoned by fishing vessels. Gannets are also victimized by oil spills. Ironically, in the North Sea off the coast of Aberdeen, Scotland, Royal Dutch Shell runs a massive operation called the Gannet Oil and Gas

Field Project. In 2011, there was a major leak at the project platform known as Gannet Alpha that resulted in a great many seabirds being coated in oil.

A sketch on *Monty Python's Contractual Obligation Album* features an impossibly annoying customer in a bookshop asking for the "expurgated" version of *Olsen's Standard Book of British Birds*. He says that the expurgated version does not contain the gannet; the customer does not like gannets "because they wet their nests." New Zealand is more tolerant than the Monty Python customer, having established a reserve for nesting Australasian Gannets. The reserve is on Cape Kidnappers, named by Captain James Cook after an unpleasant experience with the Maoris. This gannet species, which the Maoris call the Takapu, usually can live up to forty years. Gannet pairs produce only one chick at a time, and they use their big webbed feet to provide some of the heat for incubating the egg. Gannet chicks are born naked and helpless.

Boobies are basically gannets who inhabit more tropical habitats. A couple of booby species are best known for their foot color. The Blue-footed Booby appears to be wearing bright-blue webbed galoshes, while the Red-footed Booby appears to wear bright-red webbed galoshes. (If you enjoy tongue twisters, try saying "bright-red webbed galoshes" quickly ten times.) When these birds walk, they waddle and sequentially throw each foot out to the side rather than striding forward in a purposeful manner. The walking style calls additional attention to their colorful feet during mating displays, which can be quite elaborate. Kurt Vonnegut weaves a description of the courtship display of the Blue-footed Booby into the narrative of his 1985 novel *Galapagos*. Some booby species will lay two eggs that might hatch a few days apart. Both chicks will be fed if there is enough food; if there is not, the older chick will be fed and the younger one will die. The older chick can be very hostile and violent toward the younger one. Boobies are not graceful when alighting on the ground, and many descents end with a crash landing. They got their name because people thought boobies look and act dumb. Ornithologists have yet to ascertain the opinion of boobies about how humans look and act.

Boobies are being used as a symbol for a line of merchandise sold on Zazzle.com. One can buy a wide range of Booby Bird items, including T-shirts, mugs, pet clothing, tote bags, hats, mousepads, calendars, shoes, aprons, diapers, and lots of other things. You can buy these items in Booby Bird Blue, Green, Orange, Pink, Purple, and Yellow. The Booby Emblem insists that he is "100% fractal" and was created quite accidentally. He is content to live in a computer, which is probably just as well.

36. GNATCATCHER
Bird Nests

Birds lay eggs in nests, and some species roost in nests, but birds do not live in nests the way humans live in houses. In fact, many birds and their young wish to remain in their nest for as short a period as possible, because the nest is a stationary location that can attract predation. Not all species build nests before laying eggs; some deposit eggs on a rocky ledge or in a scrape in the ground. Nonetheless, many species are accomplished builders, even though they lack hands for manipulating their building materials—imagine humans trying to build similarly complex structures using only their mouth and bare feet. Birds such as eagles and ospreys make nests out of large sticks. Some smaller species make nests that creatively use twigs, sticks, mud, reeds, grass, leaves, moss, lichens, spider webs, string, human litter, and anything else that might be available. The Golden-headed Cisticola, an Australian species, is nicknamed the "tailor bird" because it punches holes in reeds and stitches its nest to them with thread from cocoons or spider webs. There are other bird species in the world who use a similar stitching technique when building nests. For most bird species, females do most of the building. In Europe, the female Red-legged Partridge sometimes builds two nests and lays eggs in both so that she and her mate can incubate at the same time, thereby increasing the number of offspring.

To avoid attacks from predators, some bird species conceal their nests on tree branches, while others conceal them in holes. Some build their nests near wasp nests or in swamps filled with alligators, while others build nests in trees with sharp thorns. Some prefer isolated nests, while others prefer to breed in large colonies. Species of sparrow-like birds called weavers build intricate colonies of nests and use numerous protective strategies to thwart nest robbers. For most songbirds, concealment is the most important defense.

Bird-finding strategies can be divided into two general groups, which I call "fishing" and "hunting." The fishing strategy involves staying in one place, like people trying to catch fish, and waiting for the birds to come. The hunting strategy is based on the idea that the more ground one covers, the more birds one is likely to see. Most birders I know seem to prefer the hunting strategy, but the strategy I choose depends on the location and what I am looking for. The fishing strategy is popular with many bird photographers, who set up a camera in one spot and wait. Fishing is also the preferred method when looking for bird nests. The best chance to find songbird nests during the breeding season is usually to follow the advice, "Don't just do something, stand there!" Staying in one place increases the chance you will notice an individual bird hanging around in an area or repeatedly flying to the same spot. Knowing birdsong can help if you recognize a particular species singing every day around the same place. One of the best ways to track down a nest is to look for birds carrying nesting material. Birds have little reason to carry a reed or other item unless they intend to use it for a nest.

The Blue-gray Gnatcatcher, the most common of the three gnatcatcher species regularly seen in the United States, is one of the first migratory songbirds to arrive in the Washington area each spring and begin nesting. It is a tiny bird with a long tail. Minus the tail, its body is not much larger than a Ruby-throated Hummingbird's body. Once when banding, we captured a Blue-gray Gnatcatcher, and after we had processed the bird, we decided that it was not ready to be let go. So we gave it some sugar water and I put the tiny bird into my breast pocket to warm up for awhile until it was ready to fly.[11]

---

11. When releasing a banded bird, you should never throw or flip it into the air to help it become airborne. Sometimes, the bird is still stunned from the banding process, and it might drop like a stone if thrown. The correct procedure is to put the bird on your flattened palm and let the bird fly when it is ready.

Gnatcatchers are active and fussy birds, uttering a complaining, nasal call. Because they arrive in April before the trees are fully leafed out, you have a good chance of finding where they are building a nest. They start by laying down a foundation on a branch that becomes the base for a solid cup held together with spider webs and other binding agents. The outside is decorated with lichens, and the finished product appears to be as sturdy as it is lovely.

Sturdy construction is not enough to ensure that a nest will survive the breeding season. In 2005, a pair of gnatcatchers built a nest in a tree next to an observation platform in a marsh I visit frequently. I saw the nest numerous times, and a photographer friend who went to the marsh every morning in the spring monitored and photographed the nest construction and subsequent incubation activities. Then one morning, the nest was gone. There was no trace of damage, because there was no trace that the nest had ever been there. Probably a raccoon climbed the tree and ripped the nest off the branch, chowing down on any eggs or nestlings.

The loss of eggs and nestlings is common for songbirds. The chances are low that any fertilized egg will eventually become an adult bird who successfully produces offspring. Migratory birds have a high survival rate in the winter, but they first must survive the migration. Small birds weighing less than an ounce often perish from exhaustion, weather factors, and other variables on journeys that can be thousands of miles. They sometimes arrive at their wintering ground to discover that it has been destroyed between the time they migrated north and flew south again.

Birds who arrive safely to their wintering grounds lead a much more relaxed existence than in the spring and summer. The expenditure of energy on wintering grounds is significantly lower than on nesting grounds, even for species with both parents sharing nesting duties. Birds no longer have to work hard to catch protein-rich insects that are needed so that the young will grow quickly and so that they themselves will be able to keep up with the demand to provide food. They can switch in the winter to a diet that features more fruit, which does not require as much effort to locate. Their only major concern is gradually putting on enough fat for their next migration journey. After two long migrations and the raising of young, birds such as Blue-gray Gnatcatchers are entitled to a leisurely winter vacation in a warm Central American or Caribbean climate.

37. GOOSE
Migratory Birds

In the twenty-first century, ornithologists still have many unanswered questions about bird migration. Little is known about how birds know where to go. If scientists are having problems in an era of rapid transportation and satellite communication, imagine the puzzlement of people five hundred years ago. Most of these people traveled little, because they did not have the means or interest to go far. They spent their lives in the same area, day after day, season after season, year after year, which allowed them to notice patterns of change in bird life. In the spring, songbirds appeared after being gone for the winter. And in the autumn, large flocks of waterfowl appeared after being gone for the summer.

The puzzle about waterfowl was how so many birds could materialize without a trace of nests or eggs. Some people believed that geese hatched from barnacles at the shore. For this reason, a European species is called the Barnacle Goose. A closely related species called the Brant has the scientific name *Branta bernicla*, with the species name meaning barnacle. "Brant" comes from a word meaning burnt, because its black head and neck look charred. To see Brant nests, you'll need to travel to the far northern tundra. No barnacles are in the nests.

An unusual Australian species called the Magpie Goose might explain another avian mystery. It might be an evolutionary link between the family of South American birds called screamers and the family that includes the ducks, swans, and the other birds we commonly call geese. Magpie Geese are black and white (the reason for the magpie name), but their feet are semipalmate, which means the webbing goes only halfway. Magpie Geese both swim and perch in trees. Their mating behavior is unusual, because a male typically will mate with two different females during each breeding season. The two females lay eggs in the same nest and share in incubating and raising the young. Males usually choose one older female and one younger female.

Geese were a major inspiration for my initial interest in birds. When I was only knee-high to an egret, my next-door neighbor Mr. Richman took me in November to Bombay Hook National Wildlife Refuge in Delaware, where we saw hundreds of thousands of Canada Geese and Snow Geese. At times, the sky would be dark with the Canadas or white with the Snows. The Canadas honked as they flew over, while the Snows uttered a high-pitched bark. These sights and sounds on a sunny autumn day captivated me, and I was hooked on birds. In those days, geese usually arrived in the autumn and left in the spring to nest in Canada or somewhere north. The long Vs of flying geese were an inspiring feature of autumn. The allure of migrating geese was captured in the 1996 movie *Fly Away Home*, in which young Anna Paquin pilots an ultralight plane to lead a flock of geese from Canada to North Carolina.

The birds who inspired me and Anna Paquin have since created considerable controversy. Were a young girl to lead a flock of geese to North Carolina today, angry North Carolina suburbanites might try to

blast both her and the geese out of the sky. Canada Geese have found ample food in suburban areas to raise their young and subsist through the year. Many of the geese who do not migrate are descendants of birds who were reintroduced into areas where goose populations had declined sharply during the middle of the twentieth century. A naturalist at one of the parks in Northern Virginia told me that his three biggest challenges in managing natural areas are beavers, deer, and Canada Geese. There continue to be migratory Canada Goose populations, but these birds are faring much worse than the nonmigratory ones; in addition to the inherent dangers of long-distance flight, migratory geese can be targets for hunters.

Part of the suburban anger has to do with goose physiology. Geese are basically defecation machines. They eat prodigious amounts of plant material that has little nutritional value, digest the sparse nutrients, and quickly eliminate the rest. The "rest" part can build up quickly in communities with large goose populations. Suburbanites have tried to control goose populations in a variety of ways. In some places, permits have been issued to allow the shooting of geese. Some states have tried to deflect public criticism of suburban goose hunts by feeding the dead geese to the poor, either as whole birds or as ground gooseburgers. Even if I were really hungry, I would have serious qualms about eating an animal who had been feeding mostly on chemically laden suburban lawns or golf courses. Some areas are attempting goose birth control. This does not involve little goose diaphragms, but rather involves coating eggs with oil to prevent hatching, or replacing real eggs with fake ones. Stealing the eggs does not work, because the geese lay new ones. Some areas have enlisted Border Collies to chase any geese who try to land. The problem with this strategy is that while the geese might disappear from the areas with the collies, they settle someplace nearby that does not have collies. Trying to frighten the geese away with loud noises, phony swans, and balloons has had little success. Some park officials have tried to humanely address the problem with the "send them back where they came from" approach. In Rockland County, New York, park officials once rounded up dozens of Canada Geese, put bands on their legs, and drove them in a truck a few days north into Canada. The geese beat the truck home.

Meanwhile in the tundra, increasing Snow Goose populations have eaten so much vegetation that the habitat is being destroyed. The population has increased because of conservation efforts in the United States, where the birds winter. This conservation success is causing severe damage to the tundra ecosystem in the summer. However, the proliferation has been a boon to Polar Bears. Instead of trying to survive on the ice that is breaking up because of global warming, the bears are coming onto land and eating large numbers of Snow Goose eggs.

Even before the problems in the suburbs and the tundra, geese had an image problem. One dictionary definition for goose is a simpleton or dolt, based on comparisons to the behavior of the bird. Nazis marched in goose step, a style resembling how a goose walks. Goose bumps, sometimes called goose flesh, are little bumps that rise on your skin in reaction to cold or stress, making your skin resemble that of a plucked goose. The technical term for goose flesh is "horripilation."

Airline pilots, both military and civilian, are not fond of geese. Geese often fly in groups and sometimes at very high altitudes—Bar-headed Geese have been seen higher than 29,000 feet flying over Mount Everest. The 2009 US Airways flight that Captain Chesley Sullenberger landed safely in the Hudson River had been downed by a collision with a flock of Canada Geese, some of whom had been sucked into the engines. This flight took off from New York's LaGuardia Airport. Nearby John F. Kennedy International Airport had a contract with a firm called Falcon Environmental Services to use falcons to try to keep geese and gulls away from airplanes. The contract was terminated in 2011 because of budget cuts, with the job going to the US Department of Agriculture, which uses guns rather than falcons to discourage unwanted birds. The US Air Force and other organizations have used a compressed air cannon capable of firing chickens at airplanes to simulate what would happen if a bird collided with the windshield or other part of a plane traveling at high speed. In fairness to the geese and other birds, they were using the skies for countless millennia before humans figured out how to become airborne, so they never had any reason to develop survival strategies for avoiding the Johnny-come-lately human flying contrivances.

Geese were part of a famous nineteenth-century German fairy tale by the Brothers Grimm. A princess is sent to a distant land by her mother (the queen) to marry a prince. A nasty maid accompanies the docile princess, and along the way manages to bully her into changing places in what was a very early instance of identity theft. When the two arrive, the king at their new home puts the princess to work as a goose girl (herding geese), while the maid tries to get cozy with the prince. The king eventually finds out about the switching of identities, but he does not tell the nasty maid. When he asks the maid posing as a princess what she hypothetically thinks should be done to a servant guilty of such a deed, she says that the person should be dropped nude into a barrel with protruding nails and then dragged through the streets by horses until dead. That is what was done to the real maid in this grim fairy tale, and the prince and the real princess lived happily ever after. In 2003, Shannon Hale won a literary award for youth fiction for a novel called *The Goose Girl* based on the Grimm fairy tale. The goose girl is also the subject of a popular painting in the National Gallery of Ireland, and the gallery has used the painting in its promotional efforts.

The most famous literary goose is Mother Goose. She was the narrator of French fairy tales originally published in 1697. Mother Goose nursery rhymes were first published in England in 1760. Before then, the rhymes were part of the British oral tradition. Also part of this tradition was the well-known violent goose verse:

Goosey, goosey, gander,
Where shall I wander?
Upstairs, downstairs,
And in my lady's chamber.

There I met an old man
Who would not say his prayers;
I took him by the left leg
And threw him down the stairs.

Sometimes, violence involving geese spills over into real life. In 1998, an Australian woman was awarded $125,000 in an out-of-court settlement after she fell into a flower bed at the National Rhododendron Gardens in Melbourne while being attacked by a flock of geese. The woman claimed to have suffered a potentially fatal blood clot in her leg when the geese knocked her over and chased her into a public restroom. Geese can be fierce and aggressive, and some people use them instead of watch dogs.

A well-publicized 1979 story in suburban Washington involved a doctor who killed a goose with his putter while playing golf at Congressional Country Club, site of the 2011 United States Open. The doctor claimed he accidentally hit the goose with his approach shot (which is not the birdie he was trying to shoot) and finished the goose off with his putter to put it out of its misery. However, another version was that the goose honked just as the doctor was striking his putt, inciting him to dispatch the bird in a fit of rage. Killing the goose for any reason would be a violation of the 1918 Migratory Bird Treaty Act, punishable with a jail sentence of up to a year or a fine of $10,000. The doctor ended up paying a $500 fine.

38. GRACKLE
Gangs of Birds

The word "flock" describes a benign group, such as sheep or church-goers. The word "gang" has a more sinister meaning, suggesting a rowdy or lawless group. One never hears about juvenile street flocks, or prisoners working on a chain flock, or a group of people flocking up on a victim. Large groups of birds typically are called flocks, but in the case of a few types of birds, gang might be more appropriate. An example is grackles, who are sleek, dark birds with a long keel-shaped tail. For some species of birds, individuals in a group appear to move in unison, but individuals in a group of grackles appear to act independently. Sometimes, a birder will be trying to look at small songbirds in the trees when a group of grackles shows up and takes over. Grackles utter a hoarse chatter that drowns out nearby birdsong. Unless the birder wants to view and hear a gang of grackles, the only option is to seek birds somewhere else.

Grackles continue their gang activities during the breeding season, often nesting in large colonies. Male Boat-tailed Grackles create harems, in which a male will select a territory to protect and then service the gang of females who join him. The females then are responsible for nest building, incubation, and the other tasks involved in raising young.

Grackles are in the same family as the American blackbirds, and many have beautiful iridescent plumage. Depending on where you live, male Common Grackles can be either a glossy purple or glossy bronze. The females are duller but have the same sleek profile. When separated from the gang, individual grackles can be endearing. In the Florida Everglades, I once heard a Boat-tailed Grackle perform a wonderful repertoire of chatters and whistles. The ornithologist Arthur Cleveland Bent tells of a wary, intelligent grackle who found a hardened crust of bread in a city park. The bread was too hard to eat,

so the grackle carried it to a bird bath. A pigeon was using the bird bath, so the grackle positioned himself so he was between the crust and the pigeon. He dropped the crust into the water, let it soften a few moments, and then took it to the grass to eat. Grackles also will dip living food into water. I have shot video footage of a Common Grackle in a stream dipping wriggling worms into the water. He then flew off with the wet worms, presumably to give them to his nestlings. Grackles sometimes steal worms from robins, and I have seen robins fly aggressively at grackles.

Grackles are scavengers and will eat almost anything. During the spring in a park near where I live, one can see many Common Grackles on a hillside, tossing dead leaves while looking for insects and other invertebrates. Watching them do this can be amusing. I uploaded a video to YouTube called "Gleaning with Grackles," which features video footage of their many different behaviors. Grackles are considered pests by farmers—one nickname for them is "maize thief." The poet Ogden Nash was not fond of them, writing, "I cannot help but deem the grackle an ornithological debacle." He referred to their harsh voice and hoodlum ways. I once saw a Common Grackle attack, kill, and eat a House Sparrow, dispatching his prey as a Sharp-shinned Hawk would.

There are about a dozen species of grackles, and three are found in the United States. The size of the gangs of Common Grackles I see in the Washington area is small compared to the gangs of Great-tailed Grackles in some southwestern cities. If you walk down Congress Avenue in Austin toward the Texas State Capitol around dusk, you might pass by and under hundreds of Great-tailed Grackles chattering in trees. Often, the sidewalks under the trees become quite messy with droppings. In 2007, dozens of dead grackles were found on Congress Avenue, which precipitated a closing of the area and a response from a crew in HAZMAT suits as well as other federal, state, and local responders. Some people were concerned about a link between the grackle deaths and a potential avian flu outbreak. After a lot of finger pointing by grackle lovers and grackle haters, the most likely cause of death was thought to be a combination of parasites and cold temperatures.

Someone named Michael Berry made a bizarre short film in 2005 called *The Day of the Grackle*, which can be viewed online. The promotional material describes the grackle as a large territorial bird who invades a man's life and turns his docile existence upside down. The bird calling in the film is alternately a crow and a raven, both of whom are much larger than a grackle. The film has no dialogue, but the scoldings by the man's shrewish wife sound like scoldings by the bird. The "chemical warfare" bombs that the bird drops on both the man and his car are incredibly prodigious. After several schemes to kill the bird go awry, the man finally manages to shoot it. A crow-like bird lands on the windshield of the car being driven by his wife, causing her to crash into a tree. The film is yet another attempt by someone to try to capitalize on human fears of both birds and dark-colored creatures.

39. GREBE
Bird Reproduction

The comedian Robin Williams once said his favorite word is "cloaca," which in Latin means sewer. More than 2,600 years ago, the ancient Romans built a large sewer system called the Cloaca Maxima. In ornithology, a cloaca is the hole underneath the back part of a bird through which reproductive and excretory functions occur. For males, it is where sperm come out. For females, it is where sperm goes in and eggs come out.

Because of the subject matter of this book, I will dispense with descriptions of bee reproduction and stick entirely to birds. Suppose you have a mommy bird and a daddy bird, and neither is a stork. For a male to pass his sperm to an as-yet-shell-less egg of a female, the two birds must press their little sewers together in what is called a cloacal kiss. While a few types of birds have a penis, the males of most species have only a cloacal protuberance, which is a bulge that helps them put the sperm where it needs to go. The only way you are likely to see a cloacal protuberance on a live bird is if you have him in your hand and blow on his underside. Bird banders use this technique to determine the sex of birds. The female then stores the sperm for a period as short as a week or as long as more than three months, depending on the species. The sperm then is used to fertilize the eggs as they come out of the female's ovaries. The shell develops around a fertilized egg, and the female lays it so that she will not be weighed down by developing young, which is very important for birds who fly.

The mechanics of bird mating are neither easy nor comfortable. Birds cannot lie on their backs, which means that two birds whose reproductive holes point downward must twist them around until they meet. This usually is accomplished with the male standing on the female's back. Because of the difficulty and awkwardness of the process, bird copulation typically does not last long. This is also why human sex manuals do not include the "bird position." According to Andrew Berger's book *Bird Study*, Song Sparrows copulate for only one second, while Great Blue Herons copulate up to fifteen seconds. With some species, a male repeatedly mounts a female, compensating for brevity with frequency. You sometimes can tell if songbirds are ready to copulate if you see them fluttering their wings as if tingling with excitement—a similar behavior to young birds begging for food.

Monogamy is more likely to occur when both parents have to work hard to find food for themselves and their young. When food is readily available, a male of a species can devote more of his energy to showing off, and the female can still survive and raise young without his help. Multiyear monogamy is not the norm for most bird species. Some birds engage in seasonal monogamy, pairing up for a breeding season. During the mating season, many species of birds engage in "extrapair copulations" (they get a little on the side), and some have been known to mount members of the same sex. There also have been instances of birds forming same-sex couples, such as when female-female albatross pairs raise young at a nest after being fertilized by males; they do everything that male-female albatross couples do in maintaining a pair bond except copulate. However, there are no "gay" birds, because homosexuality is a human concept that has no meaning in the avian world.

You might wonder what all this sex talk has to do with water birds called grebes, who are more similar to loons than to ducks. For most bird species who form pair bonds, copulation is much less important than foreplay and courtship rituals. Some of the rituals are elaborate and involve a lot of effort, so the "wham, bam, thank you, ma'am" ending should be viewed in the broader context of courtship. Some grebe species have elaborate courtship rituals. A rather spectacular one shown on many television nature programs is performed by the Western Grebe, found in western North America. The amorous couple do a running ballet together across the surface of the water.

These grebes have a long neck and a long, pointed bill, and the male and female stretch their necks and point their bills upward during the splashy run. After such a spectacular performance, copulation is an anticlimax.

There are more than twenty species of grebes in the world, and a South American species called the Hooded Grebe remained undiscovered until 1974. Grebes spend most of their lives in fresh water and have trouble walking on land. They build floating nests anchored to submerged vegetation. The young ride on the backs of their parents for a week or so until they are ready to fend for themselves. Seven grebe species are found in North America. The Western Grebe is one of the largest of all grebe species, at twenty-five inches. In Texas, you can see the Least Grebe, who is less than ten inches. Adult Horned Grebes have bright-red eyes and a narrow strip of pink skin running between their eyes and their bill, which can sometimes create the appearance that their eyes are bleeding.

Grebes are active swimmers who dive to seek food and sometimes to avoid predators. A small species called the Pied-billed Grebe, found throughout the United States, is nicknamed "hell-diver" for its frequent animated dives. Pied-billed Grebes sometimes stay underwater a surprisingly long time and resurface far from where the dive started. They arch their bodies to get momentum for the dive, swim rapidly to try to grab a fish or other critter, and pop up to the surface ready to dive again. The Pied-billed Grebe, along with other grebe species, eats its own feathers, and sometimes the feathers can occupy half of its stomach. The adults also feed feathers to their chicks. One function of the eaten feathers might be to assist in the formation of pellets containing sharp fish bones and other indigestible material, which the grebes cast out from their throats.

A midsized species is the Red-necked Grebe. They are uncommon in Washington; in some years, hardly any will be seen, while in other years, many will show up. The first one I saw was early on a wintry

Grebe

Sunday morning in 1982 in a channel of the Potomac River. It was across from the National Defense University, which teaches military people. Almost immediately after a friend and I took out a telescope to look at the bird, a military policeman materialized, seemingly out of nowhere. He asked what we were looking at, and I responded, "A Red-necked Grebe." The policeman glared at me for a moment and said we needed to move on.

40. GULL
Birds and Balls

A French tennis player named Julien Boutter gave a final blessing to a deceased bird during a semifinal doubles match at the 2002 Australian Open in Melbourne. Boutter and his partner Arnaud Clement were playing Fabrice Santoro and Michael Llodra. In the summer, swallows are common in Melbourne, flying through the air to hawk insects. During the tennis match, Llodra hit a shot that nailed a swallow flying low over the court. When Boutter saw the bird drop on his side of the net, he put his hand over his mouth, walked up to the bird, knelt, and made a sign of the cross. The chair umpire ordered the point to be replayed.

Bird kills at sporting events are not common, but incidents have occurred in golf, cricket, and baseball when a fast-moving ball unintentionally has hit a flying bird with the force of a Peregrine Falcon's feet. During a 2001 preseason game, Arizona Diamondbacks pitcher Randy Johnson threw a 97-mile-per-hour fastball that caused an unsuspecting dove to explode on contact. In 2006, a minor league game in Buffalo between the Durham Bulls and the Buffalo Bisons was interrupted when a pitch unintentionally hit a gull who swooped in front of home plate. The bird was stunned but later flew away. Many stadiums have large numbers of pigeons and/or gulls flying around. In West Coast cities such as San Francisco, Oakland, and Seattle, large flocks of gulls often show up around the seventh inning of baseball games, preparing to chow down on food scraps left in the stands as soon as the crowd leaves. In 2012, during an eighteen-inning night game in Seattle between the Mariners and the Baltimore Orioles, the gulls were confused about why people remained in the stadium much longer than normal. When Orioles pitcher Tommy Hunter entered the game in the sixteenth inning, he was not aware that some droppings from one of the impatient gulls had been deposited just above the oriole logo on his cap. In some cultures, being hit by bird droppings is considered good luck—which was the case for the Orioles, who later won the game.

A question of intent arose in an incident involving a gull killed by New York Yankees star Dave Winfield. In 1983, he was arrested for killing the bird during a game in Toronto against the Blue Jays (one of the three Major League teams with a bird nickname). Between innings, Winfield, an outfielder, threw a ball that hit the gull, causing its lifeless body to plummet to the field. Winfield claimed the death was an accident, but a Toronto police constable thought otherwise. After Winfield had done in the Blue Jays by driving in the game-winning run, he was taken to a local police station to respond to charges of cruelty to animals. In what must have been a surreal scene, the dead gull was displayed on a table in the room where Winfield was questioned. Winfield was freed on $500 bond, and charges were later dropped.

Gulls often are called "seagulls," which is a misnomer, because not all of them are seabirds. In many cities, gulls are as common as pigeons during some parts of the year. Washington in the winter is filled with Ring-billed Gulls, London is loaded with Black-headed Gulls, and Melbourne is filled with Silver Gulls. In 1981 when I was birding with a friend in an area of Washington called Hains Point, we were surprised to find a terribly out-of-place Silver Gull mixed in with a bunch of other gulls on a golf course—it had escaped from the National Zoo. Gulls are scavengers and often hang

around in garbage dumps. If you are inviting gulls to your home for dinner, try serving fish offal (innards), which is one of their favorite foods. Gulls who eat shellfish and mollusks will sometimes try to open them by taking them high into the air and then dropping them onto a hard surface. They also might try to do the same with balls they pick up from the fairways of golf courses they hang around. Many types of birds use this dropping technique, which clearly involves some intelligence, for trying to get into food contained in a shell or protective covering. A story about the ancient Greek playwright Aeschylus, probably apocryphal, claims that he died when an eagle dropped a tortoise on his head.

There are more than fifty species of gulls in the world, only five of which occur commonly in the Middle Atlantic states where I live. Many gull species are difficult to tell apart, having only subtle differences in size, shape, and plumage. The largest is the Great Black-backed Gull, who is fairly common along the East Coast. One of my favorites is the Heerman's Gull, found along the West Coast; this handsome gull is gray rather than white, and it has a red bill. In 1999, I went to Conowingo Dam in Maryland and saw three gull species I had never seen before. To find them, other birders and I had to look at thousands of gulls who were standing near the dam. The scene was a bit like a *Where's Waldo* drawing, except the three gulls were not as differently attired as Waldo usually is. Utah is the only state to have selected a gull as its state bird, and it is also the only state to select a bird named after a different state. California Gulls are revered in Utah for eating the huge swarms of "Mormon Crickets" (actually flightless cannibalistic katydids rather than crickets) infesting the crops of Mormon settlers, and there is a commemorative monument in the middle of Salt Lake City featuring two gulls.

Gulls have been the subject of numerous behavior experiments. The Dutch naturalist Niko Tinbergen performed a famous experiment involving the begging behavior of Herring Gull chicks. Herring Gulls and many other gull species have a red spot (called a gonydeal spot) on the lower part of their bill. When a chick is hungry, it pecks at the red spot, which causes the parent to regurgitate food. Tinbergen discovered that by substituting dummy gull heads of all shapes, sizes, and colors, the chick's food-begging response was elicited as long as the dummy had a red spot. A head painted black or shaped like an oval would elicit a response if it had the spot. The chicks did not respond to a perfect likeness of a Herring Gull head minus the red spot.

Another famous Tinbergen experiment involved the use of eggs of odd shapes and sizes. An enormous version of a Herring Gull egg was placed next to a real egg in a nest. The gull preferred to try to incubate the enormous egg, even though it was too large to sit on. Scientists refer to this phenomenon as responding to a supernormal stimulus. Before you criticize gulls for being stupid, remember that humans sometimes behave in a similar manner. Advertisements for pornographic movies often feature women with grotesquely large silicone-filled breasts. The purveyors of these movies believe that a certain type of male will be attracted to a supernormal stimulus; that is, the bigger the breasts, the more likely the male will want to see or buy the movie.

Even without Tinbergen's experiments, gulls have a reputation for being stupid. One definition of gull is a dupe or a person easily cheated. The verb form of gull means to cheat or deceive. To be gullible is to be easily deceived or misled, such as with the old joke of asking someone, "Did you know that the word 'gullible' is not in the dictionary?"[12]

---

12. All joking aside, nobody is sure of the origin of the word "bird." If you don't believe me, try looking it up.

41. HAWK
Changing Attitudes toward Bird Conservation

The National Geographic Society publishes one of the most popular field guides of North American birds. The introduction to a recent edition describes declines in the populations of birds of prey during the twentieth century, and it praises conservation efforts. In the twenty-first century, one could hardly imagine an organization such as the National Geographic Society suggesting that native hawk species be killed.

Yet in the 1920s, such statements were deemed acceptable. *The Book of Birds*, published by the National Geographic Society in 1921, contains color reproductions of 250 paintings by the noted wildlife artist Louis Agassiz Fuertes accompanied by species descriptions. It also has an article entitled "Common Birds of Town and Country," which includes a section with the subheading "Birds Should Everywhere Be Protected." Two subheads later is a section called "Most Hawks and Owls Beneficial," which contains the following: "A few hawks are injurious, and the bulk of the depredations on birds and chickens chargeable against hawks is committed by three species—the Cooper's hawk, the sharp-shinned hawk, and the goshawk. The farmer's boy should learn to know these daring robbers by sight, so as to kill them whenever possible. From the foregoing it will appear that the practice of offering bounties indiscriminately for the heads of hawks and owls, as has been done by some States, is a serious mistake, the result being not only a waste of public funds, but the destruction of valuable servants which can be replaced, if at all, only after the lapse of years."

According to this 1921 book, there are good hawks and bad hawks, and exterminating bad ones is acceptable. In those days, a lot of people did not make such distinctions. Into the 1930s, hunters went to the Kittatinny Ridge in the eastern Appalachian Mountains in Pennsylvania to shoot all kinds of hawks for sport during the autumn migration. Large concentrations of hawks funnel through this narrow passage along the ridge to take advantage of the rising air currents on their flight south. In 1934, conservationist Rosalie Edge successfully turned the area into a sanctuary called Hawk Mountain. The story of both the slaughter of the hawks and the creation of the sanctuary is recounted in *Hawks Aloft* by Maurice Broun, Hawk Mountain's first curator.

Around the time progress was being made in stopping the shooting of hawks, another threat appeared. Birds who eat high on the food chain sometimes absorb high concentrations of any poison that is in their prey. When pollutants such as DDT and other pesticides get into an ecosystem, hawks are especially vulnerable. Rachel Carson described the effects of DDT on birds in her 1962 book *Silent Spring*. DDT can cause eggshells to thin, preventing successful incubation. Carson cited a survey of Bald Eagle nests showing that between 1952 and 1957, 80 percent failed to produce young. Some nests had no eggs, while others had eggs that failed to hatch. She also cited migration data collected over the previous twenty years at Hawk Mountain to document that populations of many hawk species were seriously declining.

The U.S. Environmental Protection Agency effectively banned DDT in 1972, but DDT and other dangerous pesticides continue to be used in other parts of the world. Many of the hawks seen in North America spend part of the year in countries where environmental protections are weaker. In 1995–96, an estimated twenty thousand Swainson's Hawks, a spring and summer resident of the western United States, died in Argentina because of exposure to the pesticide monocrotophos. Pesticide use, including in the United States, is one of numerous factors contributing to hawk mortality in the twenty-first century. Many hawks are electrocuted or otherwise killed by power lines. And habitat loss, the biggest threat to hawks and other types of birds, continues unabated.

The family that includes hawks, eagles, harriers, and kites is both revered and maligned. These birds are included in a larger group called raptors, which includes the falcons, owls, and a few other predatory

bird families. The word "raptor" has the same root as rape and rapacious. Raptors live by killing and eating animals, and their killing ways have made them a symbol for warlike people and anyone who advocates aggressive or violent actions. Many humans consider raptors who kill mammals and other birds to be far more violent than predatory songbirds who kill invertebrates such as insects, even though both groups of birds live by killing living creatures.

Raptors show considerable variation in color and size. Some are as small as an American Robin, while others are more than a yard long. Female hawks usually are larger than males, sometimes significantly. For the chicken-killing Cooper's Hawk mentioned in the 1921 National Geographic book, the small male is in the size range of the birds hunted by the larger female. (Talk about love and death!) Hawks eat mammals, reptiles, amphibians, fish, insects, and other birds. Some hawk species concentrate on specific types of prey, while others have a more general diet. Not all raptors hunt from the skies or trees. In Africa, the Secretary Bird, a long-legged ground-dwelling raptor who is in its own family, specializes in killing snakes, which is why its scientific species name is *serpentarius*.

Hawk

Some birders who specialize in hawk watching are so skilled that they can identify a species by seeing only a minuscule dot in the distant sky. The autumn hawk migration can be an amazing spectacle if you visit an area on a flight path when the winds are favorable. In addition to Hawk Mountain, another outstanding hawk-watching venue in North America is Cape May, New Jersey. In Panama in the fall of 2012, I watched in amazement as more than ten thousand Broad-winged Hawks flew relatively low over my head during a fifteen-minute period—and this was not considered an especially large flight. In Veracruz, Mexico, more than five million hawks might pass through during a single autumn, and a birder might see more than a million hawks there in one day.

Some hawks are trying to adjust to habitat loss by living in highly urbanized areas. In 2011, a female Cooper's Hawk made the national news when she got into the main reading room at the Library of Congress in Washington. During the 1990s, a pair of Red-tailed Hawks received a lot of publicity when Marie Winn published *Red-Tails in Love*, which is about a pair who nested on a building on Manhattan's Fifth Avenue where both Woody Allen and Mary Tyler Moore owned units. Red-tails now can be found in many large cities. In the winter of 2010–11, numerous videos were posted on YouTube featuring hawks in Center City Philadelphia. One video shows a young Red-tail dismembering a pigeon while on top of a car, surrounded by people who are talking and snapping photos on their cell phones. There were feathers all over the roof of the car, but the video ended before the car's owner returned to find the mess.

42. HERON
The Liberating Quality of Bird Romance

Can romance help to liberate those who are locked behind bars? In the bird world, this question became relevant at the National Zoo in Washington. In the early 1900s, a small colony of wild Black-crowned Night-Herons lived on the zoo grounds. Over time, these birds began to build nests on top of the zoo's flight cage that held captive night-herons. The free-flying colony grew very large and spilled over into trees near the cage. Eventually, hundreds of wild night-herons flew free around the zoo and none were in the cage. There was no need for the zoo to care for captive night-herons when there were so many wild ones all over the grounds. Instead, the zoo has posted interpretative signs about the colony of wild night-herons and now during the breeding season does a public daily feeding in which fish and mice are thrown to the birds. If you visit the zoo at dusk during some times of the year, you will hear the calls of flying night-herons, who sound like barking dogs.

There are more than sixty species in the family that includes herons, egrets, and bitterns. Many are beautiful and sinuous. Some species who appear to be short and squat, such as bitterns and night-herons, look much sleeker when observed at close range. They are found almost everywhere in the world except some deserts and islands. Their primary need is a nearby wetland or body of water. While many heron species breed in colonies, some build isolated nests. In 2011, I was able to see an isolated active nest with Yellow-crowned Night-Herons high up in a tree next to a stream near where I live.

In the legal community, GBH stands for "grievous bodily harm," which involves doing serious physical damage to somebody. To birders, the letters stand for Great Blue Heron, the most common heron species in North America. It has long legs, a long neck, and a long, pointed bill that does GBH to fish and frogs. The top of the legs of

a Great Blue Heron resemble cooked turkey drumsticks. It you look closely at its body, you might see some of the bird's delicate plumes.

Herons typically hunt by stalking slowly and quietly through shallow water and striking with lightning quickness. The Green Heron, whose small body is a lovely combination of maroon and green, appears to be doing tai chi when it stealthily stalks a meal. Some have even been known to drop a feather or food into the water to lure fish, which is an example of intelligence and tool use. But not all Green Herons are smart. I have seen one who was so engrossed in pursuing prey from a log that it failed to pay attention to turtles who were sunning themselves on the log. The heron stepped on the back of one turtle, knocking it into the water and destroying any hope for a stealth attack.

Herons lack the ability to tear apart prey, so they swallow everything whole. Herons and some other types of birds have an esophagus that they are able to distend to accommodate large prey. The cartoonist Bernard Kliban, who is best known for his cat cartoons, released a book in 1976 entitled *Never Eat Anything Bigger Than Your Head & Other Drawings*. I once saw a Yellow-crowned Night-Heron ignore this advice when trying to eat a large fish. After about twenty minutes of flipping and turning the fish, the night-heron swallowed it. Other herons are not so fortunate and sometimes die from trying to swallow something that is too large.

The beauty of herons does not extend to their voices. Most herons utter harsh squawks, while some have vocalizations that are odd and entertaining. The diversity of nature allows the heron family, with its many stately species, to also include a species such as the American Bittern, whose nicknames include "thunder pumper" and "water belcher."

43. HONEYCREEPER
Birds with Multipurpose Bills

A tiny bird called the Akiapola'au on the island of Hawaii has the equivalent of a Swiss Army knife for a bill. The lower mandible is short and straight and is used for banging at bark like a woodpecker. The upper mandible is long and curved for digging out insect larvae. The two mandibles can work independently but also can work like a pair of tweezers for grabbing food. The Akiapola'au can use its long tongue to drink nectar. This species is only about five inches, with a yellow body and olive wings. I saw one in 1995 at the top of a tree on a foggy day, so the body color was not as visible as the silhouette of its remarkable bill.

The Akiapola'au is one of a group of native Hawaiian birds called honeycreepers. The name refers to the fact that some of the species creep in flowering foliage and drink nectar. (Honey is a term for nectar.) An unrelated group of birds called honeycreepers lives in Central and South America and on islands in the Caribbean. These honeycreepers are in the same family as the tanagers, and some of them are stunningly colorful.

The populations of the majority of Hawaiian honeycreepers are not doing well. According to the American Bird Conservancy (ABC), seventy-one bird species have gone extinct from the Hawaiian Islands since human settlement, with at least thirty-five of these being honeycreepers. ABC says that of the remaining twenty-four honeycreepers, seventeen are listed as endangered, and seven of these might already be extinct. Without a substantial conservation effort, the Akiapola'au and other honeycreepers could become extinct within a couple of decades. Two species of sickle-billed honeycreepers called 'Akialoas are already thought to be extinct. And on November 28, 2004, the last known Hawaiian honeycreeper called the Po'ouli died in captivity and now is believed to be extinct. The species had been discovered in 1973, so it was known to humans for only a few decades before possibly disappearing forever.

All of the known Hawaiian honeycreepers are thought to have evolved from a single species. While the Akiapola'au was developing its complicated bill, others evolved with bills suited primarily for eating seeds, eating insects, drinking nectar, or a combination of these. In some ways, the radiation of the Hawaiian honeycreeper species is similar to that which occurred with Darwin's finches on the Galapagos. On the island of Hawaii, you might see an I'iwi, a six-inch scarlet honeycreeper with black wings and a long, curved bill. You might also see honeycreepers called Amakihis, 'Apapanes, and Akepas. A variety of honeycreepers often feed in mixed flocks in flowering trees, and there is a pecking order among the species.

Islands throughout the world have suffered greater environmental devastation than any other ecosystems. They generally are isolated closed systems, so if new factors such as disease, invasive species, climate change, or extensive habitat loss are introduced, the resident life forms might not be able to adapt and survive. All of these factors have in one way or another affected Hawaiian honeycreepers. As bird populations decline within closed island ecosystems, the gene pool of an individual species can be reduced, which further compromises the ability of the species to survive. This "island" problem is not restricted to land masses surrounded by water. As humans continue to destroy habitat and relegate animals to nature reserves, the reserves become islands surrounded by development, and the dwindling populations of animals in the reserves might experience the same problems as on islands surrounded by water.

The feathers of honeycreepers were used to make feathered helmets (known in the Hawaiian language as *mahiole*) and feathered cloaks (known as *'ahu'ula*). The helmets and cloaks were worn by Hawaiian chiefs during battles and at special ceremonies. Captain Cook managed to bring back some of these feathered treasures from one of his voyages, so the British Museum in London now has a collection of them. The chiefs liked to use the feathers from the I'iwi and the 'Apapane, because both birds are red. Still, I wonder how imposing a chief could make himself look with his head and body enveloped in the feathers of small songbirds.

44. HONEYEATER
Birds Who Don't Sound Like Birds

People who do not have a good ear for music can have trouble remembering birdsong. One method for remembering is to associate the song with a familiar nonbird sound. The Black-and-white Warbler sounds like a squeaky wheel. The Field Sparrow's song is like a ping-pong ball bouncing on a table. The Pine Siskin makes a sound resembling a phonograph needle dragged across a record. The late Australian ornithologist Graham Pizzey likened the song of the Pheasant Coucal to water glugging from a bottle, and the song of the White-tailed Nightjar to an axe repeatedly striking a hollow log.

One afternoon when I was walking around in Melbourne for a few hours before catching a train to go to Graham Pizzey's house, I visited the Queen Victoria Gardens. As soon as I arrived, I heard what sounded like tinkling bells in the trees. The sounds were made by a species of honeyeater called the Bell Miner. The Field Sparrow's vocalization is compared to a bouncing ping-pong ball because of the similarity of the rhythm. The Bell Miner's call sounds so much like a bell that you might have trouble believing that a bird is producing it. There are unrelated species called bellbirds in the Neotropics, and the ones I heard in Trinidad are larger than the Bell Miner and sound like larger bells.

Honeyeaters are a large, diverse group of about 180 species in Australia and islands in the Pacific. They eat nectar in flowering trees and bushes, and some species pollinate plants. They occupy a similar ecological niche to the hummingbirds in the New World, and like hummingbirds, they also eat insects. Honeyeater species can be colorful, such as the Scarlet Honeyeater, or very plain, such as the Drab Myzomela. A skulking species in New Guinea is called the Obscure Honeyeater.

At Cassowary House in Australia, I watched honeyeaters drink from sugar-water feeders near the veranda. The feeders were generally pretty busy, and there was a pitcher of sugar-water on the veranda for refills. Once when the feeders were empty, a honeyeater called the Helmeted Friarbird, who is about a foot long, perched precariously on the edge of the pitcher and tried to drink without falling in. The MacLeay's Honeyeater was the most common species visiting the feeders, and its call is the memorable A FREE TV.

Birders who look in an Australian field guide will see the honeyeaters in a place similar to where warblers are in North American guides. While warblers show little variation in size, honeyeaters show enormous variation, ranging from four to eighteen inches. The biggest is the Yellow Wattlebird, found in Tasmania. It has two yellow pieces of skin hanging from the sides of its head like a pair of dangly earrings. Some large honeyeaters called friarbirds have bald vulturine heads.

Like hummingbirds, honeyeaters are feisty, but in a less endearing way. With hummers, there often is an appearance of the little guy defending against bigger foes, even though they sometimes are aggressive against each other. Honeyeaters seem more like bullies. One often sees them driving off smaller species. Bell Miners are especially aggressive. In his book *The Australian Bird Garden*, Graham Pizzey explains how a flock of Bell Miners will form a colony and exclude all other bird species. If you see a flock of Bell Miners, chances are you will not see much species diversity in that area. Among the birds excluded are many of the insect eaters, which means that the trees near a Bell Miner colony often suffer insect damage. Graham said that researchers removed a colony of Bell Miners from a patch of land, which resulted in a marked improvement in the appearance and health of the trees.

Noisy Miners, who are closely related to Bell Miners, likewise gather in flocks and become very vocal when alarmed. Rather than sounding like bells, they make noises resembling a loud smoke detector that relentlessly beeps after you accidentally burn something on your stove. The name of this species is one of the better puns in the bird world, being an apt description for screaming children.

45. HORNBILL
The Sound of Bird Wings

Some birds make sounds that do not emanate from their throat. Mourning Doves make a whistling sound with their wings. A displaying male Ruffed Grouse (the state bird of Pennsylvania) makes a drumming sound by beating his wings rapidly; the accelerating thumping noises result from air being compressed against his body. Some birds allow a close enough approach so you can hear them pecking at something or stepping on leaves.

One of the most memorable nonvocal bird sounds I have ever heard was in Thailand when two Wreathed Hornbills flew over. These forty-inch birds have big heavy bodies, so flying requires considerable effort. As they were overhead, their wings made a noise that sounded like *WHOOOOSH-WHOOOOSH, WHOOOOSH-WHOOOOSH*. Each *WHOOOOSH* was long, loud, and slow. The birds have a prehistoric look and appeared to have escaped from the movie set for *Jurassic Park*.

The Wreathed Hornbill is not the largest hornbill species in Thailand. I saw a pair of Great Hornbills eating figs in a tree. Great Hornbills measure more than four feet long and have a big horn on their bill. When they fly, they show a black, white, and yellow striped wing pattern. Some have been known to live close to fifty years. The male has red eyes and the female white eyes. As I watched the pair in the fig tree, the male fed the female. Feminists who applaud male cassowaries and emus for assuming the responsibility for incubating eggs would not approve of the behavior of male hornbills. After a nest is prepared in a hole in a tree, the female climbs onto it and uses her own feces to cement shut the hole, except for a small space through which the male can pass food to her. She remains cemented in for months until the young are ready to come out.

Hornbill

There are about sixty species of hornbills. They can be seen in Africa and Asia, but none are in the Americas. They are forest birds, and their numbers have declined because of hunting and deforestation. Not all of them are as huge as the two species described above, with the smallest species being only about a foot long. Hornbills are in the family Bucerotidae, which comes from the Greek words meaning "cow horn," because that is what people thought the bills looked like. The large bills usually have a horny casque on the top, which is the basis for their common name. The casque can be large and colorful. The Rhinoceros Hornbill, who is about the size of a Great Hornbill, has what looks like a large red-and-yellow rhino horn stuck onto its forehead above its bill. The Helmeted Hornbill, who is even larger than the Great Hornbill, appears to be wearing a small red fireman's helmet, and its casque can comprise close to ten percent of its body weight. The need to support the weight of the bill and casque is the reason that hornbills have their first two neck vertebrae fused—an anatomical feature found in no other family of birds. The casque is made out of keratin, the same protein that is in the beaks, claws, and feathers of birds as well as in human skin, hair, and fingernails.

Hornbills may play an important role in preserving the health of rain forests. A 1998 study by biologists at San Francisco State University and the University of California at Davis found that hornbills disperse seeds from almost a quarter of the rain forest tree species. Hornbills are omnivorous, eating fruit, small animals, and insects. To find the fruit in their diet, they sometimes range more than one hundred miles, which covers a much wider area than some of the mammals (such as elephants and primates) who also disperse seeds. As the mammal populations dwindle, the role of the hornbills in seed dispersal becomes even more important.

Some hornbills have long eyelashes that resemble the false eyelashes worn by human females. Birds in numerous families have conspicuous eyelashes. Bird eyelashes are not made out of hair as human eyelashes are (or polyester, in the case of false ones). They are feathers called rictal bristles, like the ones that many insect-eating birds have near their bill.

Much has been written about how birds might be a living link to dinosaurs. I have not spent much time studying such theories, because I am more interested in living creatures than fossils. Hornbills are much further along the evolutionary ladder than ostriches and many other bird species, but few bird families look as prehistoric.

46. HUMMINGBIRD
Jewel-like Birds

No family of birds features more entertaining names than humming-birds. In what other group can you find a Bearded Mountaineer, Shining Sunbeam, Mexican Woodnymph, White-necked Jacobin, Royal Sunangel, Empress Brilliant, Coppery Metaltail, Green Mango, Black-thighed Puffleg, and Purple-crowned Fairy? There are Festive Coquettes, Frilled Coquettes, and Spangled Coquettes. Some hummingbirds have the names of jewels, including the Blue-chinned Sapphire, Ruby-topaz Hummingbird, Purple-throated Mountain-gem, Golden-crowned Emerald, Amethyst Woodstar, and Garnet-throated Hummingbird. The scientific names of some hummingbirds are similarly imaginative, with the Red-tailed Comet being *Sappho sparganura* and the Black-tailed Trainbearer being *Lesbia victoriae*.

The British naturalist John Gould helped to popularize humming-birds by producing a 360-plate monograph about them in the mid-1800s. In 1851, he displayed his collection of 1,500 hummingbird specimens at the London Zoo, and about seventy-five thousand people paid to see it. Among the attendees were Queen Victoria and Prince Albert. Around the beginning of the twentieth century, the popularity of these jewel-like birds on both sides of the Atlantic resulted in large numbers being killed to bejewel women's hats.

All of the more than 330 species of hummingbirds are found exclusively in the New World. The closer you get to the equator, the more hummingbird species you can see; the United States has about twenty, but Ecuador, which in land area is about the size of Colorado, has around a hundred and thirty. The Arawak Indian name for Trinidad is *Iere*, which means "land of the hummingbird," and the coat of arms of Trinidad and Tobago features two hovering hummers. My friend Bill Murphy, who wrote *A Birder's Guide to Trinidad and Tobago*, has a gorgeous photo of a Tufted Coquette on the cover. The photo is larger than life-size, because this species is only 2.75 inches from the tip of its bill to the end of its tail. The male looks as if he has been decorated with items pasted on by a collage artist. On his head is a red tuft that is wavy on top like Bart Simpson's head. Red tufts with black spots stick out from both sides of his throat. At the Asa Wright Nature Center in Trinidad, the tiny Tufted Coquettes do not visit the sugar-water feeders near the veranda, and instead hover around small flowers below the veranda.

The Bee Hummingbird of Cuba is not only the smallest bird in the world, but also one of the smallest homeothermic creatures (along with a tiny species of bat). "Homeothermic" means maintaining a constant body temperature and is a more accurate term than the more commonly used "warm-blooded." The male is less than 2.2 inches—a little shorter than a toothpick—and weighs less than a sixteenth of an ounce. The Bee Hummingbird's tiny nest is an inch across. The female

lays two eggs, each of which is roughly the size of the nail on my pinkie and weighs only about a hundredth of an ounce. At the other size extreme for hummers is the Giant Hummingbird, who lives in the Andes and measures eight inches. The Sword-billed Hummingbird in South America has a bill that is four inches. A Caribbean species called the Western Streamertail has tail streamers that can be longer than seven inches.

Hummingbirds get their name from the hum of their rapid wingbeats. They are the only birds who can fly backwards. They also can hover and maneuver in all directions. Hummers are aggressive and will challenge much larger birds. I have seen them dive-bomb crows and Pileated Woodpeckers. What they lack in size, they more than make up for in speed and spunkiness. When I was in Panama in areas with feeders sometimes visited by more than ten species of hummingbirds, there was a definite pecking order that was not based on size—some of the smaller hummers were driving away the larger ones. Because many hummers are relatively fearless, you sometimes can walk close to them when they visit feeders. I have been close enough to see the long tongues of the hummingbirds lapping up sugar-water. A friend in Costa Rica patiently kept one of her fingers near the feeders, and hummingbirds eventually perched on it to drink.

Hummingbirds have the fastest metabolism of any animal. Their diets consist mainly of insects and flower nectar. In gathering nectar, some hummingbirds perform the important ecological function of pollination. The length and shape of the bill for any hummingbird species is an adaptation for drinking nectar from its flowers of choice. A group of about thirty hummingbird species called hermits get their name because they usually wander alone in the forest and do trapline feeding. Instead of picking a particular patch of flowers and defending it, as is done by some species of hummers, hermits visit flowers along a line that typically stretches anywhere from a quarter to a half mile.

A 2004 report about fossil discoveries indicates that there might have been birds similar to hummingbirds in Asia and Africa. A niche for nectar-eating birds in these areas now is occupied by a group called sunbirds. They are not related to hummingbirds, but many have glittering iridescent plumage.

The best place to see hummingbirds in the United States is southeastern Arizona, where there are many species, including large ones such as the Blue-throated Hummingbird and Magnificent Hummingbird. These two hummers measure about five inches. In the east, the Ruby-throated Hummingbird is the only species you are likely to see. The male's throat is not actually red but reflects red light; if the throat is turned away from the light, it looks black. Ruby-throated Hummingbirds arrive in North America in the spring and stay until autumn when they journey back across the Gulf of Mexico to their winter homes from Mexico to Costa Rica. This long and perilous journey by such a tiny creature amazes me almost as much as the migration of Monarch butterflies over roughly the same course. During the spring, I typically discover at least one Ruby-throated Hummingbird nest, which is a tiny lichen-covered cup attached to a branch. The female's body minus the bill is only about three inches, and she appears to sink her belly into the middle of the nest while her head and tail spill over the sides. The nest typically holds two white, elliptical eggs that are about half an inch long.

One fall on a visit to Rock Creek Park in Washington, some friends and I found a dead Ruby-throated Hummingbird unable to escape from burdocks to which it had been stuck throughout the previous evening. Burdocks inspired the invention of Velcro, and the unfortunate tiny hummer was Velcroed to death. I broke off the stalk with the dead bird, took it to the park's nature center, and asked the rangers to please cut down the burdock plants, which are a non-native species. A photo of the dead hummingbird stuck to the burdocks was published in a National Park Service publication, and I subsequently saw someone from the Nature Conservancy use the image in a slide presentation about the problems caused by invasive plants. The hummingbird died because it was unable to regulate its body temperature during the cool of the evening. In *The Life of the Hummingbird*, Alexander Skutch used the term "noctivate," which he coined to describe how hummingbirds conserve energy by allowing their body temperature to drop to that of the air around them, thereby slowing some of their vital body functions. This is equivalent to hibernating for an evening or becoming temporarily cold-blooded like a lizard. The process will not work if the hummer is stuck in the cold against its will, as happened to the Rock Creek Park bird. Many birds in cold climates, especially small songbirds, can maintain their proper body temperature by shivering. Some mammals do this as well, including humans.

I once heard the late ornithologist Rick Blom suggest that identifying hummingbirds is like trying to identify gnats. Someone gave me a three-hour video about how to identify all the hummingbird species in North America. It includes explanations such as how the third tail feather on one species might have slightly more indentation than the third tail feather on another. In reality, you might not be able to make an identification. Living in an area with only one regularly occurring hummingbird species saves me the trouble of having to deal with the complex identification challenges that some hummingbirds pose. In the spring of 2005, I saw a male hummingbird do a display flight to attract females. He rapidly flew in numerous large parabolas, back and forth. I assumed he was a Ruby-throated even though I never saw his field marks, because he was moving much too quickly.

Some hummingbirds use sounds made with their wing and tail feathers in courtship displays. Christopher Clark of Yale University studied fourteen species of hummingbirds by putting their tail feathers into a wind tunnel to see how the feathers would respond both individually and with adjacent feathers to produce sounds at different wind velocities. The stronger winds, which approximated what happens when a hummingbird is doing a courtship flight, caused the feathers to vibrate and make sounds.

Occasionally, hummingbird species other than the Ruby-throated show up in the eastern United States. In November 2002, my friend Haji, who loves hummingbirds, sent me an excited e-mail saying that an unusual hummingbird was visiting the feeders at her home in Northern Virginia. In order for this to happen, many unlikely events had to occur. The bird—a Rufous Hummingbird, whose typical range does not extend east of Texas—might have traveled from as far away as Alaska. Somehow, its migration compass went awry, and instead of migrating south, it went east. After this tiny creature, who weighed about a ninth of an ounce, ended up a couple thousand miles from where it was supposed to be, it managed to locate within an enormous metropolitan area one house that had full hummingbird feeders, even though there are no regularly occurring hummingbirds in the area in November. The Washington winter of 2002–03 was very harsh, with snow and ice storms starting in November. Haji spent a couple hundred dollars for halogen lamps, umbrellas, and special plants to accommodate her tiny friend, who hung around for a month before departing in mid-December.

An even stranger incident occurred the following year. In November 2003, two species of out-of-place hummingbirds showed up in gardens outside one of the Smithsonian buildings in Washington. One was a Black-chinned Hummingbird, a western species similar to the Ruby-throated, and the other was a Rufous Hummingbird.[13] The birds initially fed in flowers in the gardens, and the Smithsonian staff later put up hummingbird feeders. The Rufous is the more aggressive species and eventually chased the Black-chinned from the area. Before

13. The Rufous Hummingbird in nonbreeding plumage is so similar to another western species called the Allen's Hummingbird that the only way to make a definite identification is to have the bird in the hand. The hummingbird expert who banded Haji's hummer initially misidentified it in her hand as an Allen's before determining that it was a Rufous.

this happened, a hummingbird expert trapped both birds to band and identify them. Because there are office buildings and tourist attractions nearby, birders and other interested people visited the gardens every day to look at the hummingbirds. In January 2004, the nature writer and bird bander Scott Wiedensaul sent an e-mail saying that the Rufous Hummingbird who had been banded in the Smithsonian gardens was discovered dead after hitting the window of a school in Pennsylvania, about 125 miles north of Washington. The response of some people to the news was disbelief—not because they could not accept the death of the bird, but because they were continuing to see a Rufous Hummingbird in the Smithsonian gardens. In fact, they were seeing a different Rufous Hummingbird than the one who had been banded.

In 2003, Haji moved from Virginia to southeastern Arizona so she could live somewhere that has more hummingbirds. I can understand why she went.

47. IBIS
Sacred Birds

In *How to Tell the Birds from the Flowers*, Robert Williams Wood juxtaposes the ibis with the 'ibiscus and writes, "The sacred Ibis, one might say, was classified a Bird-of-Pray." The pun is a reference to how the ancient Egyptians regarded the ibis as sacred. They used the head of an ibis to represent Thoth, the god of wisdom and magic. Thoth, a learned old bird, was the measurer of time, inventor of numbers, and scribe of the gods. Originally he was the moon god. Later, he recorded the weights of people's hearts in the judgment hall of Osiris, who was the Egyptian god of the underworld. The Tour Egypt website states a common belief that rather than being born, Thoth created himself through the power of language. This is a strange concept, because it presupposes that Thoth would have had the power of language before he could create himself. The extent to which the ibis was revered by the ancient Egyptians is reflected in the fact that in addition to mummifying pharaohs and other prominent people, they also mummified many ibises. At the beginning of Herman Melville's novel *Moby-Dick*, the narrator Ishmael, when talking about the job of cook on a ship, says, "It is out of idolatrous dotings of the old Egyptians upon broiled ibis and roasted river horse, that you see the mummies of those creatures in their huge baked houses the pyramids."

Ibises look like herons with long, hooked bills, but they are not in the same family as herons. They are in a family called the Threskiornithidae, which means "sacred birds." There are about twenty-five species of them in the world, including one called the Sacred Ibis. This species, which is common in parts of Sub-Saharan Africa, has not bred in Egypt for more than a century, but it has become an invasive species in parts of Europe. The British Ornithologists' Union calls its quarterly journal *The Ibis*. One often sees ibises in groups walking slowly in marshes, feeding on small fish and shrimp. Some feed in rural areas,

and there has been a campaign to educate Australian farmers about how the large numbers of ibises in agricultural fields are beneficial, eating only insects and other animals, but no grain.

There are three ibis species in the United States. One is the White Ibis, who is common in Florida. When driving through the state, one often sees them flying around or feeding near the side of the road. Another is the Glossy Ibis, who is also found on other continents, including Australia. The third is the White-faced Ibis, who looks like a Glossy Ibis but has a thin line of white around the base of its bill.

The Scarlet Ibis, found in the Caribbean islands and northern South America, gets its feather color from its diet, which includes crustaceans, small fish, insects, and other items. This diet is rich in carotenoids, the same compounds that make tomatoes red and carrots orange. Without the proper diet, the birds will fade from bright scarlet to a washed-out pink. The Scarlet Ibis is the national bird of Trinidad and is on the Trinidad and Tobago coat of arms. When I took a boat ride through Trinidad's Caroni Swamp before sunset, I saw an area where the Scarlet Ibises came in to roost. Roosting in the same trees were Snowy Egrets and Little Blue Herons. Because the birds tend to stick with their own kind, I saw rows of red, white, and blue, which was an appropriate display to show a visitor from the United States.

48. JAY
A Bird in the Hand

Having a bird in the hand occasionally allows you to notice a behavior you never would have known about otherwise. On a bird-banding trip, a friend and I caught a Blue Jay. When my friend held the bird, it put its head back and pointed its bill straight upward. We later caught another jay who did the same thing. No other species we caught exhibited similar behavior when held the same way. Bitterns, stocky-looking herons who live in marshes, point their bill into the air and stay still when trying to escape detection. Their posture and plumage provide effective camouflage when they stand among reeds, but they try the same trick when standing in an open area. Perhaps the jay behavior is an instinctive posture to try to become less conspicuous when confronted with danger.

During migration and the nesting season, birds often do things by instinct that seem inappropriate. One spring, I saw a female American Robin on a path, and she was crouching down as if simulating the brooding of eggs. She would walk a bit and then crouch down again. In the same park during spring migration, I saw a Prothonotary Warbler gathering nesting material. This species does not breed in the park, and no potential mates were there. Migratory birds often exhibit territorial behavior such as singing from a perch or chasing others of the same species, even though they have not yet reached the area where they intend to establish a territory and breed.

The jay is the only bird whose name is a letter of the alphabet. There are about fifty jay species in the world. They are related to crows and ravens but are generally smaller, sleeker, and more colorful. Magpies are in the same family, and they look a lot more like jays than crows and ravens do. The word "jay" comes from an Old French word *gai*, and the Italian word for magpie is the similar *gaza*. A diminutive form of *gaza* is *gazette*, and it is thought that the publications called gazettes

Jay

(such as my university's alumni magazine) got their name from cheap publications in Venice during the Renaissance that were intended for people who chattered like magpies. The connection with the dissemination of news is maintained in the noun of assemblage for these birds, which is a tidings of magpies.

Jays are raucous, aggressive birds, and some species are known to dive-bomb cats for the same reason small songbirds dive-bomb jays. Jays view cats as bird killers, just as many songbirds view jays as bird killers (in both cases, with good reason). Jays are omnivorous and eat almost anything, including the young and eggs of other bird species. Blue Jays are accomplished mimics and are adept at imitating hawks. If you think you hear a hawk, you might need to see the bird to confirm that you are not hearing a jay. The jays might do this for the same reason that crows engage in hawk or owl mobbing behavior when none is present: to cause small birds to investigate the threat, possibly revealing the location of eggs and nestlings. Some jay species are known to store food for the future by burying acorns a distance away from where they are found, and Eurasian Jays are thought to be responsible for the germination of a great many of the wild oak trees in Britain.

The Blue Jay is a popular backyard bird in the eastern half of the United States. It is large, handsome, and easy to see. Its feathers do not contain blue pigment but look blue because of the way light interacts with their internal structure. A Blue Jay feather appears blue if you turn it toward the light and gray if you turn it away. In the western United States, a similar species called the Steller's Jay has plumage that is black in a lot of the places where a Blue Jay is white. Easterners tend to think Steller's Jays are more attractive, while people from the West tend to think that Blue Jays are prettier. It might have something to do with the beauty of something you see all the time losing its impact.

The Green Jay is more colorful than either the Blue Jay or Steller's Jay. It has a blue cap and face. It has a black bib, some of which extends to the facial area. Its body and breast are various shades of light green, and it flashes yellow around the tail when it flies. I was in a park in Texas where Green Jays were being banded, and they look even gaudier in the hand. Southern Texas is the northern edge of the range of this species that is found through Central America and parts of South America. Other jays from Central and South America can be quite large. While the Blue, Steller's, and Green Jays all are roughly a foot long, some birds called magpie-jays measure more than two feet.

The Gray Jay, a North American species found in northern habitats and high-elevation areas, has a personality more colorful than its plumage. It is a mostly gray bird who lives in coniferous forests. Its nickname is the "camp robber," because it often loiters around campsites and tries to steal food. Gray Jays are brazen enough to steal bacon or hot dogs frying in a pan.[14]

In *The Minds of Birds*, Alexander Skutch tells of an adult hand-reared Blue Jay who tore a long piece of newspaper from the bottom of its cage and pushed the paper between the wires of an adjoining cage to rake pellets of food within reach. The jay's keepers then gave the bird other objects, including a paper clip, a straw, and a tie for a plastic bag, all of which it used successfully to rake in food. Since Jane Goodall's discovery in 1960 of tool use by chimps, many creatures have been

---

14. In Australia, I heard about a kookaburra (a kingfisher) trying to steal bacon while it was frying in a pan.

discovered to be able to use tools, including numerous species of birds. While jays are very smart birds, the term "jay" when applied to a person suggests someone stupid or inexperienced, which might be where the term "jaywalking" comes from.

When I was helping to band birds during the breeding season, most Blue Jays seemed smart enough to avoid our nets, so we could not draw many conclusions about population trends from our banding data. There are other surveys that yield better results. In many parts of the country, people do a survey of the breeding birds in their area. Volunteers are sent out during the breeding season to record the species they hear and see, along with any evidence of nesting activity. I have participated in a couple of these surveys in Washington, DC, and the area I helped to survey included Theodore Roosevelt Island in the Potomac River. To hear birds on their territories, it is best to be in the field right before first light when the birds are singing their dawn chorus. A problem I encountered was that the main access to Roosevelt Island is over a footbridge that has a locked gate during the evening. The rangers from the National Park Service sometimes would not come to unlock it until after first light. I could get onto the island regardless, because on the south end was a hole in the chain link fence which had been made by homeless people who slept on the island. I was not crazy about the idea of crawling through an illegal hole in the fence in the dark, so I asked one of the rangers if there were some way I could get a key so that I could get onto the island before sunrise to do the survey. The ranger said that he would contact headquarters and get back to me.

A few days later, I received a letter from the ranger. He said that the Park Police open the gate on the pedestrian bridge at an early hour, but should it still be locked when I arrive, there is an alternate way onto the island. He said there was a hole in the fence on the south end of the island, and he attached a map showing me where to find it.

49. KINGFISHER
Birds and Mythology

The name of a genus of kingfishers—*Halcyon*—comes from ancient mythology. Alcyone was the daughter of Aeolus, king of the winds. She was married to Ceyx, the son of Lucifer, the light bearer. Ceyx went off to sea, and his ship got blown onto the rocks—Aeolus played a role in this. Alcyone waited patiently for Ceyx to return and did not know he had drowned. Then one night, Morpheus, whose father was the god of sleep, came as a messenger while Alcyone was sleeping and let her know in a dream that Ceyx was dead. Both Morpheus and Alcyone have given their names to sleep-inducing drugs: morphine and Halcion.

This story of Ceyx and drugs and rocks and roles has a happy ending. The next morning when Alcyone awoke, she ran to the beach, and by an amazing quirk of fate, the body of Ceyx was floating toward the shore. As she ran to the water where Ceyx's body was, she was transformed into a kingfisher, as was Ceyx. The two lived happily ever after as seabirds, which kingfishers are not. According to the myth, there are seven days every year when the wind and seas are calm so Alcyone can lay her eggs on a floating nest. As soon as the eggs hatch, her father becomes windy again. This period of calm has lived on in the phrase "halcyon days," which describes a period of tranquility and peace.

The association of kingfishers with wind led to the odd practice in bygone days of hanging the dried body of a kingfisher by a thread for use as a weathervane to tell which way the wind was blowing. Kent, a character in Shakespeare's *King Lear*, refers to this practice. Metal cocks have been used as weathervanes since the early days of Christianity because the cock is an emblem of Saint Peter, but to my knowledge, real dried cocks were not used.

There are more than ninety species of kingfishers in the world. Most North American birders see only the Belted Kingfisher, who looks

Kingfisher

like a big chunky Blue Jay and has a crest resembling the ruffled hair of a German composer. The two other kingfisher species seen in the United States are found only in southern Texas and southern Arizona. Australia has ten kingfisher species, and I have seen all but the smallest, appropriately called the Little Kingfisher. This bird is only 4.5 inches, and a good bit of that is its bill. An even smaller kingfisher is found in African rain forests. The largest is another African species called the Giant Kingfisher, who is eighteen inches. Most kingfisher species excavate a nest rather than build one. In Australia, some dig a nest in a termite mound, while others dig a tunnel into a stream bank.

In 1999, I met David Hollands, who had recently written a book entitled *Kingfishers and Kookaburras: Jewels of the Australian Bush.* He is not guilty of overstatement in the title. Some of his photographs of these stunning species look more like art photography than nature photography. The Buff-breasted Paradise-Kingfisher is one of Australia's most beautiful birds. It has blue wings and a mustard breast. Its white tail is as long as the rest of its body, trailing like a long, stiff train. Another beautiful Australian species is the Yellow-billed Kingfisher, who has a lovely deep-golden head and a gold-tinged breast. It has the odd scientific species name of *torotoro.*

One of the most popular birds in Australia is the Laughing Kookaburra, the largest kingfisher on the continent. (The "kook" part is pronounced the way Americans say "cook.") It is one of the five kookaburra species in the world, and all are restricted to Australia, New Guinea, and Indonesia. Laughing Kookaburras have a lot of personality and are not especially wary of humans. In a famous song, the kookaburra sits in an old gum tree (a common name for a eucalyptus). The Laughing Kookaburra's call is a loud, long, raucous laugh. The call is used as an African jungle sound in some Hollywood movies, even though Laughing Kookaburras are not found in Africa and do not live in jungles. A group of noisy kookaburras can sound like a laugh riot. Most other kingfisher species are solitary and are seldom seen in groups. Kookaburras are in the genus *Dacelo*, which has an unusual origin. There is a large group of kingfishers in the genus *Alcedo*, and *Dacelo* is an anagram of *Alcedo*. The Banded Kingfisher of Southeast Asia is in the genus *Lacedo*, which is likewise an anagram of *Alcedo*. There is also a kingfisher genus named after our drowned friend Ceyx.

David Hollands says that the characteristics common to kingfishers are an oversized bill, top-heavy bearing, tubby body, short tail, and in many species, some iridescent blue feathers. Kingfishers spend a lot of time perched, waiting for some source of food to come into sight. A lot of kingfishers have collars of white or some other color, primarily for camouflage. A break in the color between the head and the body makes the bird's profile more difficult for a predator to discern. From a distance, the head and body look like two separate shapes rather than one bird-like shape.

The kingfisher name is somewhat of a misnomer. The most common European kingfisher species, who is the basis for the name, hunts for fish, but the majority of kingfisher species in the rest of the world seek other food, including insects, worms, lizards, frogs, and snakes. Most kingfisher species are not adept fishers, which is another example of why you should not make assumptions about a bird based on its name.

50. KITE
Birds and Snake Venom

The Letter-winged Kite of Australia is the only nocturnal hawk in the world. I was with a group who looked for this species in 2003 during a trip to the Australian desert, but a colony where many had bred in the recent past had been wiped out by feral cats. Before the trip, I had read some of the research done about Letter-winged Kites by Jack Pettigrew, a professor at the University of Queensland. His information about the kites helped me to understand why many Australian snakes have such astoundingly toxic venom—in some instances more than a hundred times what is necessary to kill a human.

Letter-winged Kites hunt Long-haired Rats (also called Plague Rats), who are large and nocturnal. Not counting the tail, these rats measure six to nine inches. While hunting at night, a Letter-winged Kite will hover over a rat and then drop feet-first from a considerable height, splatting the rat from the impact of the collision. The kite has strong legs and needs to kill the rat instantly, because a struggle with such a large animal could injure the bird. An injury to the kite could be fatal, because there are no hospitals in the wild where injured birds can recuperate until able to hunt again. Predatory birds who are too injured to hunt probably will starve to death, which is why they tend to initiate only conflicts they can end quickly. Letter-winged Kites live in the same habitat as the Desert Taipan, the deadliest snake in the world. This snake hunts and eats Long-haired Rats, and likewise needs to be able to kill the rats without getting into a struggle. Therefore, the snake needs to have venom powerful enough to immediately incapacitate a rat. After the snake strikes, it backs off for a moment while the rat quickly dies. The same venom that can quickly incapacitate a rat also works quickly on humans, even though taipans do not actively hunt people.[15]

Kites are a group of hawks who are generally medium-sized with narrow wings. There are about two dozen birds called kites in the world. Some kites hover, while others soar. The children's toy called a kite is named for the bird. In Florida and Costa Rica, I have seen Swallow-tailed Kites, who are lovely hawks with deeply forked tails. They gracefully chase insects in the air like giant black-and-white swallows. In Trinidad, I saw a Pearl Kite, who is mostly black and only nine inches (smaller than an American Robin). The Brahminy Kite in Australia is more than twice the size of a Pearl Kite; it has a rich chestnut body and a handsome white head and breast. The White-tailed Kite in the Americas, the Australian Kite in Australia, and the Black-shouldered Kite in Asia and Africa are all similar; they are mostly-white hawks whose ghost-like image can be seen hovering over open fields.

In the Everglades and other areas near the Gulf Coast of the United States, one can see Snail Kites. These birds have strongly hooked beaks for eating apple snails, the main component of their diet. Snail Kites are rare and endangered in Florida but more common in other parts of the American tropics. I once went to a section of the Everglades called Shark Valley because I had heard that Snail Kites could sometimes be seen from the tram tour. When I arrived, I was told that I had just missed a couple of perched Snail Kites near the visitors center. The tram ride was worthwhile, but I did not see any kites. I drove back to the Tamiami Trail, and about a mile after I got onto the road, I saw six Snail Kites in bare trees next to the other side of the road. There was not much traffic, so I did a U-turn and pulled off the road right next to them. My car was like a blind, so I had really long looks at them at close

---

15. When I was typing my field notes from the 2003 trip, my spell-checker rejected "Desert Taipan" and suggested that I make it "Desert Tampon."

range. Their scientific species name is *sociabilis*, which means sociable and reflects their habit of gathering in groups.

Australia has no vultures, but the species that most closely fills that niche is a scavenger called the Black (or Fork-tailed) Kite. A similar species in England is the Red Kite, who centuries ago was a common scavenger of dead bodies in London. In the twentieth century, the British population of Red Kites plummeted, but they are making a comeback.

The associations with scavenging and dead bodies might be a reason the word "kite" developed some negative meanings. Kite is a derogatory term for a person who is rapacious and behaves like a rogue or rascal. This meaning is connected to the practice of kiting checks, which involves writing checks based on funds that are not in your account but that you hope to obtain and deposit between the time you write the check and the time it clears. In an age of computers and electronic fund transfers, such a practice might become extinct.

51. LOON
Heavy Birds

Loons are one of the few groups of flying birds with solid bones. The heavy bones aid their efforts to dive and stay underwater for long periods in search of food or to avoid predators. Europeans refer to loons as "divers." Loons have longer bodies than ducks, and they have heavy, pointed bills. In flight, loons hump their back and appear to be flying upside down. Their flight is fast and direct.

There are five species of loons in the world; all can be found in North America, and four can be found in Europe. They breed in northern latitudes, but they winter in areas farther south where the water does not freeze. The loon species most likely to be seen in the United States is the Common Loon, the state bird of Minnesota. The loons used to be the first species featured in North American field guides, meaning that they were thought to have evolved to their present state before all other North American birds, but they have recently been placed further down on the list.

Loons sometimes dive for small stones at the bottom of a body of water and swallow them. Loons and other birds do not have teeth, so these stones, called gastroliths, help the loons to grind the bones and shells of some of the fish, crustaceans, and amphibians that they eat. The stones stay in the loon's gizzard, which is a specialized digestive chamber of a bird's stomach. The word "gizzard" comes from a Latin word meaning giblets, a term familiar to people who prepare and/or eat poultry. While loons prey on fish, some large fish, such as sharks, sometimes prey on loons. Humans sometimes cause significant problems for loons. The popularity of boating on many lakes inhibits the nesting of the loons. And the burning of fossil fuels produces acid rain, which affects the lakes by killing the prey that loons seek.

Common Loons can weigh fifteen pounds, and they need to run along the surface of the water to achieve adequate lift to become airborne. If you are next to a body of water and suddenly hear a lot of splashing, that might indicate a loon is running along the surface, trying to take off. Common loons cannot take off from dry land. Sometimes in ice storms, loons become confused and land on icy ground rather than water. The only way they can fly again is to be taken to a body of water where they can run and achieve lift; the same problem exists for some species of seabirds. If you find a loon accidentally grounded on land, you cannot make it airborne by throwing it into the air, just as you cannot make a small airplane airborne by throwing it into the air. The Red-throated Loon, who can be seen in coastal areas in the eastern United States, can take off without running along the water.

In 1998, a western species called the Pacific Loon showed up in a Potomac River channel in Washington. At times, this loon was so close to a walkway near the shore that I could see it swimming underwater. The legs and webbed feet are much farther back on the body than on most aquatic bird species and are used for propulsion in much the same way as a frogman's legs are used. The positioning of the legs is effective for swimming but not for walking. That is why loons build their nests either by the edge of a lake or on a clump of grass in a lake so

they can enter and exit without having to walk. The young (often two per nest) sometimes ride on the back of a swimming parent.

Loons are known for their laughing, yodeling, and maniacal cries. These vocalizations were heard in the film *On Golden Pond,* for which Katharine Hepburn and Henry Fonda won Oscars in 1981. According to Ernest Choate's *The Dictionary of American Bird Names,* the name "loon" comes from a Scandinavian word meaning lame, based on the bird's inability to walk on land. But Edward Gruson suggests in *Words for Birds* that the name comes from the same Indo-European root as lament, which refers to its call. The term "loon" sometimes is used to describe a crazy person, but this might be a pun on the word "lunatic." Lunatic is derived from the same root as lunar, because such people were thought to howl at the moon—making sounds like the cry of a loon.

52. LYREBIRD
Birds Who Mimic and Mock

Lyrebirds are big, they are beautiful, they can sing, they can dance, and they can do impersonations. They have the whole entertainment package. The lyrebird is an important part of Australian culture and is featured on the country's ten-cent coins.

There are two species of lyrebirds, and they are found only in Australia. The Superb Lyrebird, the more common of the two, is found in southeastern Australia. The Albert's Lyrebird, named after Queen Victoria's husband, is limited to a small range of subtropical rain forest around the border between Queensland and New South Wales.

Lyrebirds are the largest songbirds in the world. Their brown bodies have the size and shape of a pheasant. The male is about a yard long, but about half of that is his magnificent tail. When raised, the two outer tail feathers look like the frame of a lyre, which is the basis for the bird's name. In between the lyre feathers are about a dozen lacy plumes. When shaken during a sexual display, the male's tail plumes create a stunning visual effect. The display is usually performed from a perch or the top of a mound. The female also has more than a dozen tail feathers, but they are not as ornate.

Lyrebirds are among the great mimics in the bird world. David Attenborough's *The Life of Birds* series includes footage of a lyrebird mimicking the sounds of a camera motor and a chain saw. I have a tape of lyrebird songs recorded by Paul White, who says that lyrebirds have been known to imitate trains, whistles, car horns, and barking dogs. He tells the story of a clan of lyrebirds in New South Wales who fifty years earlier had an ancestor who was kept as a household pet before being released into the wild. One of the household members played the flute, including the tune "The Mosquito Parade." The lyrebird learned this song, and the birds in the clan used it as their territorial song for the next four generations.

You are more likely to hear lyrebirds than see them. They often stay in heavy foliage on the forest floor. The first one I saw was a rain-soaked bird walking near a picnic table. Lyrebirds have large feet that they use to scratch in the dirt for worms and insects. A way to find lyrebirds is to look for their scratchings. One day when I was with a group looking for an Albert's Lyrebird, I saw not only scratchings but also droppings, which were white with little green flecks.

My best look at an Albert's Lyrebird came in the botanical gardens at O'Reilly's, a lodge in the Lamington National Forest in southern Queensland. While birding at 5:40 one morning, I heard a lyrebird singing loudly. I walked toward the singing and saw a male perched on a rock and then on a branch, giving me a clear look at the tail plumes. He then disappeared into the nearby forest outside the gardens. I went back to the same spot early on the next few mornings but never saw him again, even though I heard him singing. A few years earlier, I had heard a male lyrebird singing in about the same patch of forest behind the botanical gardens. I looked for him and eventually saw only his tail as he moved through the understory. As I retraced my steps to leave the forest, I discovered a twelve-foot Carpet Python (a nonvenomous snake) stretched across the only path out. I gingerly made my way around it.

Another great mimic in the Lamington National Forest is the Rufous Scrub-bird, a small songbird who might be related to the lyrebird. The Rufous Scrub-bird is extremely shy and skulks on the rain forest floor like a mouse. One particular scrub-bird was responsible for the most memorable experience I have ever had as a birder. At O'Reilly's in 1996, I was with a group led by the naturalist and filmmaker Glen Trelfo. He is the first person to shoot video footage of a Rufous Scrub-bird, and he also shot and produced a twenty-minute video that includes amazing footage of a displaying Albert's Lyrebird. While I was with Glen and the group, I had about a five-second glimpse of a Rufous Scrub-bird, which is a longer look than most people ever get of this elusive bird.

Lyrebird

Our group was listening to a scrub-bird who was within ten feet of us but concealed in the dense understory of the rain forest. This bird, whom Glen nicknamed "Whistling Rufus," was singing a broad repertoire of songs of other bird species found in the forest.

As we were listening, we heard a pair of Eastern Whipbirds singing a short distance away. The male whipbird's song is a long whistle, followed by a sound resembling a loud whipcrack. The female often answers with a two-note *choo-choo* immediately after the male's whipcrack. The remarkable incident was that once, during the male whipbird's long introductory whistle, the scrub-bird supplied the whipcrack before the whipbird did. Another time, during the male whipbird's introductory whistle, the scrub-bird supplied the female whipbird's two-note response before the male whipbird sang the whipcrack. Birds sometimes mimic other species, but I had never witnessed or read about one bird mocking another by mimicking a portion of the other bird's song while the other bird was singing it.

When I returned to the United States, I wrote a letter about this episode to the ornithologist Alexander Skutch in Costa Rica. I thought he would be interested, because he had written a book about the minds of birds. Along with the letter, I sent a tape with scrub-bird song on one side and lyrebird song on the other. I received a reply from Dr. Skutch, thanking me for the letter and tape. He wrote: "I was especially glad to hear the lyrebird, which is so highly praised. Lyrebirds are certainly one of the world's most extraordinary birds, not only the male, with his unique tail and versatile voice, but likewise the female, who builds a covered nest that may weigh up to thirty pounds, incubates in midwinter, and takes nearly a year to raise her single young from laying to independence."

Knowing that an ornithologist whose writing has greatly influenced my life was sitting on the porch of his home in the forests of Costa Rica and enjoying the song of this remarkable bird who lives on the other side of the Earth makes the lyrebird seem all the more special to me.

53. MANAKIN
Improbable Birds

I have a gorgeous eleven-by-fourteen-inch photograph of a Golden-headed Manakin that I obtained in 1992 from a photographer in Trinidad named Roger Neckles. The photo is an extreme close-up of a captive male bird whose head, shoulders, and neck fill the entire frame. The species measures only 3.5 inches—by comparison, a Ruby-throated Hummingbird is 3.75 inches. The male's head is an intense gold, while the body is jet black, except for two crimson garters at the top of his legs. The intensity of the colors is impossible to capture in a photo, but Roger came pretty close. In the field, the bird appears to have a large white eye-ring, but the photo reveals that the white actually is the iris rather than skin or feathering around the eye.

Manakins are manic little Neotropical birds. Some of them are black and white, while others are in dazzling Technicolor. They should not be confused with finches called mannikins; both types of birds, as well as the mannequins that stores use to display clothing, probably come from the same Dutch root, meaning a little man. Manakins are fruit eaters, and the fifty or so manakin species all live in Central or South America, except for a few who live on Caribbean islands. One Trinidad species is the White-bearded Manakin, a small bird (4.5 inches) who is white underneath and whose cap, back, wings, and tail are black or gray. Manakins have a short bill and a chunky body. If you are familiar with the inflated images in the paintings of the Colombian artist Fernando Botero, a White-bearded Manakin resembles a Botero image of a chickadee minus the black bib.

At Trinidad's Asa Wright Nature Center, I visited a lek of White-bearded Manakins. A lek is an area filled with horny males who show off in the hope of catching the attention of a horny female. If you are a female who wants to have your eggs fertilized, you visit the lek, pick the show-off whose act impresses you most, get fertilized, and leave to raise your young. The father does not help with building a nest, providing food, or protecting eggs and nestlings. Males hang out at the lek for most of the year, and there is little overt conflict among them, despite the intense competition for females. The use of a lek by displaying males is not unique to manakins. The same strategy is used by some species of grouse, birds of paradise, hummingbirds, and shorebirds.

The males of different manakin species have different ways of trying to impress females. Male White-bearded Manakins show off at their lek by darting from branch to branch at a speed too fast for the human eye to follow. While they are doing this, they make noises with their wings that sound like the snapping of twigs. It is the type of sound that will cause you to wonder how the bird could possibly be making it. Some manakin species display high in a tree. Others display on a log. The male Wire-tailed Manakin brushes the wiry feathers of his tail against the face of a female to try to turn her on. With some manakin species, two or more cooperating males display to a lone female, performing a special dance so one of them can mate with her.

Research is revealing what incredibly improbable creatures manakins are. Ornithologists Richard Prum and Kimberly Bostwick discovered that the male of a South American species called the Club-winged Manakin can produce a violin-like sound by rubbing one of his feathers against the ridges of another. Bostwick made an even more amazing discovery about the male Red-capped Manakin, a species I saw in Panama. The males are jet black with a bright red cap. One sometimes can see what look like little yellow garters when they are perched. Bostwick used a special camera that can record images at five hundred frames per second (similar to the cameras that were used at tennis matches to show whether a shot was in) and discovered that some male manakins do a moonwalk-type slide during their display, resembling Michael Jackson in his *Thriller* days. During the dance, the yellow garters become long yellow leggings that extend down a major portion of the bird's legs. Videos of Bostwick's moonwalking manakins are available on YouTube and have been shown on countless nature programs and other television shows.

While Michael Jackson was a fairly improbable character as humans go, he was not nearly as improbable as some of the male manakins. And I find the manakins to be much more thrilling.

54. MERGANSER
Birds and Hunters

My favorite North American duck is the Hooded Merganser. On a 2005 trip to Penticton, British Columbia, I was surprised to see that a casino in the town had a restaurant called "The Hooded Merganser." When I told the hostess that the Hooded Merganser is one of my favorite birds, she said I was the first person she encountered in the restaurant who knew what a Hooded Merganser was.

Mergansers are diving ducks, so they swim underwater to find food. Their name comes from the two Latin words *mergere*, meaning plunge (the same root as submerge), and *anser*, meaning goose. Hence, a merganser is a goose who plunges below the surface of the water. The name has nothing to do with the French word *mer*, which means sea. There are seven species of mergansers in the world, of which three are seen regularly in the United States. They are sometimes called sawbills, because they have a long, thin, serrated bill to grab and hold fish, frogs, and other slippery meals. The Common Merganser and Red-breasted Merganser are found in both Britain and North America, except the British call the Common Merganser a Goosander. Both of these species are long and sleek; the females have a ruffled crest, as does the male Red-breasted Merganser.

The Hooded Merganser is smaller than the Common and Red-breasted. The handsome male is mostly black and white, with russet flanks. His black head has a large white ear patch that he can open and partially close. The patch is not an ear, but the male has the look of a creature willing to listen. The female has a New Wave frizz in the back of her head. Her body is mostly brown on top and white underneath. I once observed a female in the Lincoln Memorial reflecting pool with three Mallards. The Mallards are longer and chunkier, and they have a typical duck bill rather than the merganser's sawbill. While the dabbling Mallards were sticking their butts into the air to reach for submerged vegetation, the agile little merganser was diving for food at the bottom of the pool. At times, she was below the surface more than above. The glare from sunlight and the murkiness of the pool did not allow me to see her swimming underwa-

ter, but I could follow some of her bubbles while she was submerged. Seeing a Hooded Merganser at such close range is unusual, because the species tends to be skittish when humans approach. At one point, the female merganser stepped onto the pavement around the pool. I could see her white belly, which was completely hidden while she swam, and I also noticed that she looked a lot chunkier out of the water than in it.

As a nonviolent bird-loving type, I have to strain to show toleration around hunters, who for recreation enjoy killing many creatures I love. I once was talking to someone from the Midwest who hunted ducks. I mentioned how much I like Hooded Mergansers, and he said that hunters refer to them as "lawn darts" because of the pointed bill and rounded body. Even worse was an incident at the 1998 Waterfowl Festival in Maryland. The festival has an area featuring federal and state duck stamps. I saw a beautiful framed print of a Hooded Merganser that had been used for the 1995 Rhode Island duck stamp. The artist was Robert Steiner, who won the 1998 federal duck stamp competition. While I was filling out the paperwork for the purchase, Steiner offered to inscribe the back of the print. He wrapped it in brown paper and I took it home. When I went to hang it in my bedroom, I noticed his inscription: "To Bill Young, a true patron of the arts and a great shot!" Fortunately, that side of the print faces the wall.

55. MOCKINGBIRD
Birds Who Sing All Night

The Northern Mockingbird is one of the few songbirds who sing all night. A lot of people love the song of the mockingbird until they hear it throughout a spring or summer evening next to their bedroom window. I know an ornithologist who has loved and studied birds for many decades, yet even he complained when, on a camping trip, a singing mockingbird kept him up all night.

Mockingbirds are mimic thrushes, related to the catbird and the thrashers but not to the thrushes. Their name comes from their skill at imitating the songs of other birds. A mockingbird might be able to sing up to a couple of hundred different songs. Once a new song is heard and learned, it stays in the repertoire, even if the original singer is no longer around. Some species of birds sing songs they know by instinct. Other species learn songs by listening to birds of their own kind. Northern Mockingbirds take this a step further by expanding the learning of new songs to birds of other species. A human has the anatomical equipment to learn to talk, but our vocal equipment can be used in different ways. Where people are born will determine what language they speak, which is the equivalent of birds learning by listening to their own kind. But some humans can go beyond simple speech and train their voices to sing opera or other types of music. Species such as mockingbirds might be doing something similar by expanding their repertoire to include songs of other species. On breeding territory, only the male mockingbird sings. After the breeding season when the male and female go to different wintering territories, both will sing.

There are about fifteen species of mockingbirds, all in the New World. Only the Northern Mockingbird is resident to the United States. It is a sleek gray, black, and white bird, measuring about ten inches. In flight, it shows patches of white on its wings. These patches assist the bird when hunting insects. Sometimes, a mockingbird on the ground will raise and lower its wings quickly. The sudden flash of white on the wings might startle an insect, causing it to jump and become easier for the mockingbird to see and catch. Four species of mockingbirds live in the Galapagos, and one of them likes to drink blood, sometimes from living creatures.

An unrelated species who resembles a Northern Mockingbird and has similar white wing patches to startle prey is the Loggerhead Shrike. The "loggerhead" in the name comes from the bird's heavy-headed appearance; it was at one time a very disparaging term, such as in Shakespeare's *Love's Labours Lost* when Biron says to Costard, "Ah you whoreson loggerhead! You were born to do me shame." Shrikes are songbirds who want to be hawks. Loggerhead Shrikes hunt insects, mice, small birds, reptiles, and almost any living creature they can catch. They take their prey to a perch and either pin it there with a spike or hang it on some type of natural hook.[16] Shrikes do not have strong feet like hawks, so they cannot grasp prey tightly enough to rip it and eat it. By pinning it up, shrikes anchor their prey sufficiently to be able to eat it. When driving through rural areas of Texas, I saw a lot of Loggerhead Shrikes perched on fences, sometimes near impaled prey. The impaling of prey is the reason shrikes are sometimes called "butcherbirds." The Northern Shrike, the other shrike species regularly seen in North America, can mimic the calls of other birds, but not as adeptly as the mockingbird.

Mockingbirds do not impale prey, but they can be very aggressive. The feistiness of mockingbirds is captured in a John James Audubon painting featuring four adult birds at a nest defending against a rattlesnake. They have been known to attack cats, dogs, and other animals. I once saw a mockingbird repeatedly fly after a squirrel, who looked terrified and eventually sought refuge under a parked automobile. A

---

16. On the soundtrack for the 2012 movie *This Is 40*, British singer Graham Parker teamed with a band called the Punch Brothers on a song about deteriorating love called "What Do You Like?" It contains the line: "You started out a lovebird, now you're a shrike." In the next line, Parker assumes his partner is ornithologically ignorant by singing: "Look it up in the dictionary, what do you like?"

mockingbird also might fly at humans who walk near its nest. An elderly couple in the city of Washington had to call the fire department to knock down the nest that a mockingbird had built at the base of their driveway because the protective bird would fly at their faces whenever they tried to come outside.

The Northern Mockingbird is an important part of American culture. In addition to being the state bird of Arkansas, Florida, Mississippi, Tennessee, and Texas, it is the subject of the popular song "Listen to the Mockingbird," which is the theme for Three Stooges films. The CIA started a secret program in the 1950s called Operation Mockingbird to infiltrate American and foreign media and influence the stories they produced.

Mockingbirds have been an inspiration to many creative people. The mockingbird's most famous poetic reference is in Walt Whitman's 1859 poem "Out of the Cradle Endlessly Rocking," which begins, "Out of the cradle endlessly rocking, Out of the mocking-bird's throat..." This poem of more than 180 lines uses the mockingbird's song as an extended metaphor for Whitman's voice. James Taylor and Carly Simon had a hit record in 1974, covering a song called "Mockingbird." The original version was recorded in 1963 by Inez and Charlie Foxx. *The Munsters*, a television sitcom from the mid-1960s, featured a family of monsters who lived at 1313 Mockingbird Lane in the town of Mockingbird Heights. Harper Lee won a 1961 Pulitzer Prize for her novel *To Kill a Mockingbird*. And Bennett Cerf once told a *What's My Line* audience about a Mexican stripper named Tequila Mockingbird.

Walt Whitman, Harper Lee, Bennett Cerf, the actors who played Herman and Lily Munster, and all the Stooges are deceased; James and Carly have split up; and nobody knows what became of Tequila. But mockingbirds continue to sing all night during the spring and summer.

56. NIGHTINGALE
Birds Who Inspire Human Emotions

The Common Nightingale is closely associated with the British poet John Keats, who died in 1821 at age twenty-five. In 1819, a nightingale built a nest near the house in which Keats was living, and he loved to listen to the bird sing. One spring morning, Keats sat under a plum tree for a few hours and dashed off his "Ode to a Nightingale" that begins, "My heart aches, and a drowsy numbness pains my sense, as though of hemlock I had drunk." His feelings are juxtaposed with the song of the nightingale:

> 'Tis not through envy of thy happy lot,
> But being too happy in thine happiness,
> That thou, light-winged Dryad of the trees,
> In some melodious plot
> Of beechen green, and shadows numberless,
> Singest of summer in full-throated ease.

In 1645, John Milton wrote a sonnet that begins:

> O Nightingale, that on yon bloomy Spray
> Warbl'st at eeve, when all the Woods are still,
> Thou with fresh hope the Lovers heart dost fill,
> While the jolly hours lead on propitious May.

Milton's sonnet refers to the bird singing "at eeve," because the nightingale can often be heard singing at dusk and in the early evening. The name "nightingale" describes a bird who sings at night. In England, they sing from mid-April into June. The song begins with a series of about ten individual notes and ends with a twittery bit, but it is impossible to capture the song's quality in words. When hearing the introductory notes, you are not quite sure when they will end, which makes you get a bit lost in the song—you do not know where it is taking you.

Visually, nightingales are not especially exciting, although seeing one can be a challenge because they tend to skulk in the bushes. They are about six or seven inches long, with a brown back, russet tail, and light underparts. They look like the Hermit Thrush in North America, without the breast spots. Nightingales are now thought to be in the same family with the Old World flycatchers rather than being grouped with the thrushes. They are found mainly in Europe and are closely related to the European Robin.

Nightingales are not known to sing in Berkeley Square (which is in the Mayfair section of London) as is suggested in the lyrics of a 1939 British popular song, but they have long served as the archetype for beautiful singing. Other bird species noted for their song have "nightingale" in their name, such as nightingale-wrens, the Nightingale Reed-Warbler, and a group of Neotropical species called nightingale-thrushes. The nineteenth-century opera singer Jenny Lind was known as the Swedish Nightingale. Mark Forsyth, in his 2012 book *The Horologicon*, refers to the entry "nightingale floor" in the *Oxford English Dictionary*. Such floors were constructed in medieval Japan to make a sound like a chorus of chirping birds should any miscreant try to sneak up on the shogun while he slept.

Not everyone has regarded the nightingale's song as happy and hopeful, as Keats[17] and Milton did. In an ancient Greek myth, a woman named Aëdon plots to kill the son of someone named Niobe but accidentally kills her own son instead. Zeus takes pity after hearing Aëdon's loud laments about her dead child and turns her into a nightingale, whose song was thought to be similarly melancholy. The scientific species name for the House Wren is *aedon* because of the bird's loud and persistent singing like the figure from mythology. In more recent times, Carole King had a hit single in 1974 with a downer of a song called

---

17. F. Scott Fitzgerald took the title for his novel *Tender Is the Night* from a line in Keats' "Ode to a Nightingale."

Nightingale

"Nightingale" about a lonely guy who has lost his hope and confidence. The song has lyrics such as "When his strength is slowly going, his pride is all but gone, she makes a foolish dreamer listen to one last song." On her enormously successful 2002 recording *Come Away With Me*, Norah Jones sings a song called "Nightingale" that includes the lyrics "Does it seem like I'm looking for an answer to a question I can't ask?"

Sometimes, famous authors have written things about nightingales that are not true. For instance, Portia says in Shakespeare's *The Merchant of Venice*: "The nightingale, if she should sing by day, when every goose is cackling, would be thought no better a musician than the wren." Shakespeare's line is triply erroneous, because nightingales often sing during the day, the males rather than the females are known for their song, and the only wren found in Europe is one of the most accomplished songsters in the bird world. That is why Shakespeare is studied in English class and not biology.

57. NIGHTJAR
Birds with Rude Names

How would you like to be called a goatsucker? That is the name of a group of more than 120 bird species around the world in the order Caprimulgiformes. The "capri" part is the Latin word for goat (as in the zodiac sign Capricorn), and the "mulgi" part means milker. Some goatsucker species fly around goats and other livestock in agricultural fields, and many people thought the birds sometimes sucked the milk of goats. In fact, the movement of the goats flushes insects from the grass, so flying low near the goats presents good feeding opportunities for the birds.

A less rude name for many of the goatsuckers is nightjar. Many night-jars are either nocturnal (active at night) or crepuscular (active at dusk or in low light). I saw the sixteen-inch Great Eared-Nightjar, the largest nightjar in the world, perched in a tree in Thailand, and it sometimes raised its ear tufts as it uttered its haunting *Come Heeeeere!* song. A closely related Indochinese species used to be called the Satanic Eared-Nightjar, but its name has been changed to the Diabolical Nightjar, which does little to improve the bird's image. A South American species called the Lyre-tailed Nightjar is about ten inches long, but the male's two tail streamers are up to twenty-seven inches long. The North American nightjar species range from eight to twelve inches, and none have ear tufts or tail streamers. The most commonly seen nightjars in the United States are Common Nighthawks, who are not related to hawks. They are active at night, including in cities, and you can hear their nasal one-note call coming from the sky during some times of the year. They have a big mouth for catching insects, and they especially like to fly among swarming insects in the lights at the tops of buildings. The white slashes near the tips of their long wings might startle fly-ing insects and make them easier to catch, much as the mockingbird's white wing patches make insects easier to catch on the ground.

Nightjar

Nightjars are some of the most cryptically colored birds in the world. When perched, they look exactly like leaf litter or tree trunks. The same is true for their chicks. In Australia, I saw a tiny Large-tailed Nightjar chick who still had its egg tooth and was only a day or so old. An egg tooth is a small, hard calcium protuberance on the end of the bill of almost all newly born birds that helps them break out of the shell; it usually falls off a few weeks after hatching. The nightjar chick looked exactly like a tiny cream-colored leaf. It was so well camouflaged that if I looked away for a moment, I had trouble relocating it, even though it was close enough for me to touch. Nightjars do not build nests. They lay their eggs on the ground, and the eggs are as well camouflaged as the birds.

Nine nightjar species can be seen or heard in the United States. I say "seen or heard," because some of the species call loudly and persistently but are difficult to see. The Poor-will, who is found in the western United States, is named for its call. It is the only bird in the world known to hibernate. Another name-saying species is the Common Pauraque. It can be seen in Central and South America, and the northern part of its range extends into southern Texas. If you drive slowly along certain roads just after dusk, you sometimes can see the eye-shine of a pauraque sitting on the pavement. The eye-shine is caused by a reflective layer of cells in the bird's eyes. A similar effect (the red-eye effect) is produced sometimes when humans are photographed by a camera with a flash.

The name-saying Whip-poor-will is the best known of the bunch. It was celebrated in the song "By a Waterfall," sung by Dick Powell and Ruby Keeler in the 1933 movie *Footlight Parade* during a huge production number choreographed by Busby Berkeley. According to one description, this elaborate production number "with dozens of swimming chorines" culminates in the image of a human fountain. "Chorine" is a slang term for a chorus girl, so the water in the film was highly chorinated. In the song, one-syllable words such as "you" are sung as *you-hoo-oo-oo*. It has sentimental verses such as:

There's a whippoorwill
That's calling you.
By a waterfall
He's dreaming too.

Whip-poor-wills are loud, persistent singers who sometimes repeat their song nonstop hundreds of times. Another nightjar with a three-syllable song is the Chuck-will's-widow. Some birding groups go on trips at dusk to look for Whips and Chucks, which sounds even kinkier than looking for goatsuckers.

58. NUTHATCH
Nonconformist Birds

Nuthatches are strange little nonconformist birds. Many of them forage on the trunks of trees for food. While most trunk foragers land on a tree and work their way up, many nuthatches go down head-first. Their different way of viewing the world might enable them to see insects and grubs that woodpeckers and other trunk foragers miss by moving upward. An analogous situation might involve people who have hiked along a path and then noticed that the same portion of the path looks different when they hike in the opposite direction back to the starting point.

Nuthatches are small, round birds, many of whom both look and sound like toys. The Brown-headed Nuthatch sounds like a small squeeze toy. The Red-breasted Nuthatch sounds like a toy trumpet. The jerky hopping movements of nuthatches on a tree trunk make them look like wind-up toys. When a Red-breasted Nuthatch comes to a bird feeder, it often quickly takes a seed and flies away with it rather than lingering. The White-breasted Nuthatch seems to be less wary, spending more time at feeders. I have gotten so close to a White-breasted Nuthatch foraging on a tree that I have heard its feet grasping the bark.

Brown-headed Nuthatches have been known to use tools. They sometimes look for insects by taking a piece of bark in their bill and using it to scrape away another bit of bark. This discovery was made in 1968, eight years after Jane Goodall's discovery that chimpanzees use tools by poking twigs into termite mounds. Over the years, there has been a strong prejudice within the scientific community that humans are the only creatures intelligent enough to use tools. Scientists who have believed in the uniqueness of humans as tool users did not bother to observe what was being done by creatures who lack opposable thumbs. There has been a similar prejudice among scientists that humans are the only creatures capable of learning and that other

species do everything by instinct. This too has proven to be false; for instance, many songbirds are born not knowing the song commonly sung by their species and learn it from listening to older birds.

Nuthatches are often found in mixed flocks of small birds such as chickadees, titmice, and woodpeckers. They get their name from their habit of hacking nuts open. There are about two dozen nuthatch species in the world and four in the United States. In Thailand, I saw a species called the Giant Nuthatch, whose name involves a bit of overstatement. The bird is eight inches, which is larger than the four to six inches for most nuthatches but hardly large enough to be called giant. In the same tree, I saw a lovely species called the Velvet-fronted Nuthatch, who has a violet back and a red bill. In Doi Inthanon National Park, which contains Thailand's highest mountain, I bought a pin featuring a Velvet-fronted Nuthatch. I sometimes wear the pin on my lapel—pointing head down.

59. ORIOLE
Confusing Bird Names

Bird names can be confusing. I took a photograph of a lovely Orchard Oriole in the hand on a bird-banding trip. I e-mailed the photo to an Australian friend, but had to explain, "Your orioles in Australia are not related to our orioles in America, who are blackbirds, who are not related to the blackbird in Australia, who is an introduced species from Europe closely related to the American Robin, who is not related to the Australian robins." When I sent the same photo to an American friend, I said, "Look at this beautiful Orchard Oriole!"

The name "oriole" comes from *aurum*, the Latin word for gold, because the adult male of the only oriole species seen in Europe is gold and black. European settlers thought the orioles in the New World look like this species. Orioles in the Americas are unrelated to the orioles native to Europe, Asia, Africa, and Australia. There are about thirty species of American orioles, and seven or eight breed in North America. The plumage for breeding males generally is a combination of black and some other color, ranging from bright yellow to deep chestnut.

A Major League Baseball team is named after the Baltimore Oriole. The avian Baltimore Orioles are seen in the eastern half of the United States during most of the baseball season—spring through autumn—and spend the rest of the year in the tropics. During my lifetime, the Baltimore Oriole has gone from being a distinct species to being lumped with a western species (and being called the Baltimore race of the Northern Oriole) to being re-reclassified as a distinct species. While all of this was happening, the baseball team never changed its name.

Orioles are among the most skilled nest builders of American birds. Some oriole species weave a long sock-like nest, while others make a cup-shaped nest. During the spring, you sometimes can watch an

oriole weaving one of the large sock nests. Depending on the stage of completion, you might not see much of the bird, because a lot of the weaving is done from inside. This type of dangling nest high in a tree helps to protect eggs and young from predators.

Orchard Orioles sometimes nest in small colonies, but even more unusual, they sometimes nest a second time after leaving their primary nesting area in the United States. An ornithologist named Sievert Rohwer from the University of Washington reported in 2009 that Orchard Orioles, Hooded Orioles, and three other non-oriole species were sneaking in a second nesting during a migratory stopover point in western Mexico before continuing to their final wintering ground.

The songs of American orioles are sweeter and more melodious than the songs of most of their blackbird relatives. The Baltimore Oriole sings a series of flute-like whistles that lack a consistent pattern. One spring morning, I listened to a male Baltimore Oriole sing for more than twenty minutes. He would whistle six notes and stop. He then would whistle another six notes and stop. He sounded as if he were trying to compose a song but could not get it right.

A species whose coloration is similar to some of the American orioles was the subject of a remarkable discovery that made international headlines in 1992. The ornithologist Jack Dumbacher was banding birds in New Guinea, and a species called the Hooded Pitohui often became caught in his nets. The bill and claws of pitohuis are sharp, and people removing the birds from nets sometimes were cut. Once after Dumbacher was cut, he put his finger into his mouth and suddenly felt his mouth tingle and freeze. He talked to native people who said they do not eat these birds. Dumbacher had the feathers and skin of the Hooded Pitohui tested and discovered they contain the same powerful neurotoxin found in poison dart frogs. He tested two other pitohui species in New Guinea and discovered the same toxin. Pitohuis are so toxic that even snakes and lice avoid them. Some bird species eat things that are poisonous to humans, thereby making themselves poisonous for humans to eat; for instance, quails in Europe eat nightshade berries that can poison humans. But such circumstances are different from a bird producing a neurotoxin as a defense mechanism.

A poisonous bird's name that is similar to the sound made when someone spits out something distasteful is probably based on more than a punny coincidence. Hence, this oriole look-alike might be the only bird species in the world named for the way it tastes.

60. OSPREY
Birds with a Worldwide Distribution

Hank Snow had a hit song in 1962 called "I've Been Everywhere," which was repopularized four decades later by Johnny Cash. Only about a dozen of the roughly ten thousand species of birds naturally occur in all the major nonpolar regions of the world. There are a few shorebirds, a couple of terns, and a couple of long-legged wading birds. Peregrine Falcons are found throughout the world, as are Barn Owls and Barn Swallows. When birding in a foreign country, seeing some old friends you are used to seeing at home can provide a respite from trying to identify species you have not seen before.

Another old friend who appears in all corners of the world is the Osprey, also known as the fish hawk. If you are near an area with water, you might be able to see an Osprey flying around. From below, Ospreys have a lot of white on their underwings, but each wrist (the part where the front of the wing bends) has a dark patch that gives the appearance of a bite taken out of the wing. When Ospreys are not actively fishing, they never seem to be in a hurry. Their whistle is shrill but not exceptionally loud.

As with the Peregrine Falcon, Osprey populations have plummeted in many areas but are making a comeback. In the United States, the primary problem was DDT and other pesticides, which thinned eggshells and prevented new birds from being born. In Great Britain, the principal problem was persecution by fishermen and others who did not like fish-eating hawks. The hobby of egg collecting further threatened their survival—the rarer the bird became in Britain, the more in demand its eggs were. Likewise, Osprey skins became a valuable trophy. By the beginning of the twentieth century, Ospreys were rare in most parts of Britain and entirely eliminated from Scotland. However, conservation efforts have yielded some positive results. In 2011, an Osprey in Scotland made headlines for being the oldest known member of her species in the world. The Osprey was called Lady and was thought to be twenty-six years old when she returned to a reserve near Dunkeld from her winter home three thousand miles away in the Gambia in Africa. She laid three eggs, bringing her total to sixty-one during her twenty-one breeding seasons. None of the 2011 eggs hatched, but she previously had raised forty-eight chicks. Typically, a female Osprey will live to be eight years old and produce about twenty eggs.

To assist breeding Ospreys in some areas, platforms on poles are erected to provide a suitable place for them to build their nest of large sticks. I have seen such structures with active nests at locations as varied as the Chesapeake Bay Bridge in Maryland, a condominium development on the Gulf Coast of Florida, and a sagebrush habitat in central British Columbia. A nest location will be suitable as long as it is near shallow water where the birds can find fish, the primary component of their diet. Some populations of Ospreys are migratory. Where I live, Ospreys generally can be seen from spring through autumn, after which they are likely to winter in South America. However, an

Osprey or two occasionally hangs around into December or through the winter.

A fishing Osprey is one of my favorite spectacles in the bird world. Ospreys are majestic, hovering over the water with purposeful wing-beats. When they dive toward the water, they must stop their momentum and keep flapping hard at the moment of contact with the fish to avoid plunging too far below the surface. They then must be able to quickly lift themselves with a heavy object in their talons. Their feet have special adaptations for grabbing and holding a fish, and the fish is always pointing forward when the Osprey yanks it from the water.

The name "Osprey" represents a case of mistaken identity. The "os" part means bone, as in ossify, and the other part suggests breaking, even though ospreys do not break bones. The name of another raptor species who does break bones was pinned on the Osprey. A colloquial name for the Osprey is seahawk, and this nickname was chosen for Seattle's professional football team. I am not aware of the football team choosing its name because of associations with bone breaking.

61. OWL
Mean Birds

Owls are not birds to trifle with. If you see an injured owl on the road, particularly one of the larger species, leave it alone and seek assistance from someone experienced in handling such wildlife. No matter how well they are treated, some injured owls kept in captivity never lose their dislike for people. The renowned British nature photographer Eric Hosking lost an eye after being attacked by a Tawny Owl near its nest. The title of Hosking's subsequent book of memoirs is the macabre pun *An Eye for a Bird*. I once saw a perched Rufous Owl, the second-largest owl in Australia, holding a large dead possum in one of its feet. It was the meanest-looking bird I have ever seen. Some people who have tried to photograph Rufous Owls will confirm their meanness.

Relatively few birders see owls often. The majority of owl species are nocturnal and have plumage with excellent camouflage. Among land-based predatory birds, hawks generally work the day shift and owls the night shift. Some owls are diurnal (active in daylight hours), but most roost inconspicuously between dawn and sunset, and their plumage often looks like the trunks of the trees in which they roost. I used to regularly observe a Great Horned Owl's winter roost on Theodore Roosevelt Island in Washington. The owl was so faithful to the site that I could sometimes point my telescope at the roost spot without looking for the bird, and the owl would be in view. Some passers-by who wanted to see the owl in the telescope had trouble finding it because of the camouflage, even when they were looking right at the bird. Species such as the Eastern Screech Owl have different color phases that assist with camouflage. The Tawny Owl does also, and a 2011 study by researchers at the University of Helsinki found that climate change might be affecting the survival value of the colors. Brown Tawny Owls stay better hidden when there is no snow on the ground, while gray

Tawny Owls prefer a snow cover. As the amount of snow in Finland has decreased, the brown phase is doing better compared to the gray phase.

The word "owl" is related to the word "howl" because of the sounds the birds make. Owl vocalizations vary greatly. Some owls hoot; two of the best-known hoot owls in the United States are the Great Horned Owl, who says *Who's awake? Me too!*, and the Barred Owl, who asks *Who cooks for you all?* The screech of the Eastern Screech-owl sounds like a descending whinny. Owls in the genus *Tyto*, including the Barn Owl, make a hissing noise—they are in a different family than the other owls. The naturalist and filmmaker John Young, who is known as the "Prince of Australian owl men," says *Tyto* owls call with their bill open, while hawk-owls (who are more closely related to most of the owl species in the United States, but not to hawks) call with their bill shut. To understand the difference in techniques, try producing a hooting sound with your lips closed. It will sound much richer than if you try to make the same sound with your mouth open. Opening your mouth softens the sound and makes it more dove-like. Similarly, you will have trouble making a loud hissing sound if you keep your lips shut. When I was in the field with John one evening listening to owls calling, he pointed out how the call of the female Southern Boobook (an Australian hawk-owl) is lower-pitched than the call of the smaller male boobook.

In the Bible, owls are mentioned in the book of Leviticus as one of the birds of abomination, which means they were not to be eaten. In ancient Greece, Athena, the daughter of Zeus and goddess of wisdom, took the owl as one of her symbols.[18] Her association with owls is why they are thought to be wise. The ancient Romans did not revere owls nearly as much. Shakespeare refers to owls as ill omens in *Julius*

---

18. There is an owl genus called *Athene*, named after the Greek deity. One member of this genus is the Little Owl, who was introduced to Britain in the mid-1800s and sometimes kept indoors as a pet to eat cockroaches and other indoor pests.

Owl

Caesar and *Macbeth*. Many cultures in Europe, India, and the Middle East regard owls as bad omens, which might be connected with the nocturnal character of owls and the fear that people have of the dark and the night. The predatory ways and creepy-sounding vocalizations of owls do nothing to soften their image.

Edward Lear's "The Owl and the Pussycat" is a much-loved children's poem. It tends not to be read much in American schools because of verses such as:

> The Owl looked up to the stars above,
> And sang to a small guitar,
> 'O lovely Pussy! O Pussy my love,
> What a beautiful Pussy you are,
> You are,
> You are!
> What a beautiful Pussy you are!'

Owls have enjoyed a resurgence in popularity with children because of Harry Potter's owl Hedwig, whom he received as a birthday gift. In India, people have been trying to make their children feel like Harry by giving them caged owls, even though J.K. Rowling, the author of the series, told people not to do this when she found out about it.

There are more than two hundred species of owls in the world if one includes the barn-owls. They come in a wide variety of shapes, sizes, and colors. Some are as big as eagles, while others are as small as sparrows. Some are dark colored and some are light. Some eat mammals, some eat fish, and some eat insects. Owls have evolved to kill with stealth and precision. Their camouflage allows them to remain inconspicuous until they attack, and their feathers are edged to muffle sound when they fly toward prey. The eyes of some owl species are almost as large as human eyes and far better adapted to see for distance and in low light. Their hearing also is acute. The ears of owls are positioned at slightly different points on either side of their face. Sound reaching

each ear at slightly different times allows owls to locate prey by triangulation. Some owls have ear tufts, but these are only feathers and have nothing to do with hearing.

Sometimes, young owls run into trouble. In the early 1980s, a Great Horned Owlet on Theodore Roosevelt Island was learning to hunt, and it unwisely went after some Mallards swimming in a large fountain. Baby owl had to be fished out of the water and was sent to a rehab center to dry out and recover. Around the same time, I was on a bird walk along the C&O Canal towpath in Maryland when our group saw a Barred Owlet who appeared to have its wing caught in a branch by the water's edge. My friend who was leading the trip anchored himself on the shore and tried to dislodge the branch with his foot. As soon as his foot went toward the owlet, mama owl seemed to materialize out of nowhere, exhibiting a threat posture to make herself look bigger. My friend decided that the owlet was probably okay, and he quickly withdrew his foot.

Owl

The Barn Owl, who is spectral and monkey-like when flying at night, has the widest range of any owl, being found on every continent except Antarctica. During the latter part of the nineteenth century, they used to nest in the tower of one of the Smithsonian Institution buildings in downtown Washington. During the early 1980s, I saw them roosting in a tree near one of the subway stops in the northeastern part of the city, but they have long since abandoned the area. John Young's video *Wings of Silence*, which contains remarkable footage of the nine Australian owl species, shows that male and female Barn Owls enter their nest hole differently. The nest in the film is in the hollow of a tree, well below the entry hole. The female eases down the inside walls of the tree, while the male drops like a rock. At this same nest, the video shows an owlet killing and eating its smaller and weaker sibling. Such gruesome events occur if there is not adequate food for all the nestlings. Barn Owl females lay their eggs a day or two apart and begin incubation as soon as each egg is laid, meaning that the eggs are likely to hatch at different times rather than all at once, and one nestling will be larger and stronger than others. A webcam site showing a Barn Owl nest box in Southern California was very popular in 2010, attracting tens of millions of hits. The pair of owls successfully raised four owlets in their first clutch. The second clutch also had four owlets, but two died, and the camera was turned off so that people would not see the dead owlets being eaten.

North America has about twenty owl species. Among the best places to see owls in the United States are northern Minnesota for the northern species and southeastern Arizona for the southern ones. If rodent populations or other food sources crash in the far north during a particular winter, many northern owls will come much farther south than usual. Such a circumstance is called an "irruption," which literally means a breaking into.

Not all owls roost in trees. The Burrowing Owl has long legs and is about the size of an American Robin. Burrowing Owls spend much of their time on the ground and are active during the day. They hang around golf courses, airports, graveyards, and other open areas. I once went to the airport in Homestead, Florida, and one of the workers drove me down the runway in a pickup truck to see some of the Burrowing Owls that hung around there. Other Burrowing Owls roosted in one of the hangars. An especially good place to see them is in prairie dog colonies. Short-eared Owls are found in open fields and marshes. They often sit on the ground, although they sometimes perch in trees. In some wetlands, hawks called harriers fly low over the grass looking for rodents during daylight hours. Around dusk, the harriers punch out for the day, and the Short-eared Owls take over and hunt the same prey in the same area. These owls have long wings and a moth-like flight. During the breeding season, a male might clap his wings over his head as part of his courtship display.

Some owls are not afraid of approach by humans. One February on the Upper Peninsula of Michigan, I walked up to a utility pole on which a Snowy Owl was perched, and it merely glared at me. In their habitat, Snowy Owls are at the top of their food chain and do not seem afraid of anyone. In Northern California, I saw a Great Gray Owl, North America's largest owl, and was able to walk up close to the tree where it was perched. On the same trip, I saw the endangered Spotted Owl at close range, and it did not seem bothered by my presence. This species has been at the center of a conservation battle about protecting habitat in the Pacific Northwest. Owls eat high on the food chain, so fluctuations in their population can be an indicator of changes in environmental quality. The decline of the Spotted Owl suggests a broad problem in its ecosystem.

The Elf Owl, who can be seen in Arizona, is one of the two smallest owl species in the world. These little birds, who are less than six inches, have a call that sounds like the laugh of a crazed elf. While they are about the same length as a sparrow, they are much heftier, as one would expect for a predator. The Northern Saw-whet Owl is the smallest owl in the eastern United States—about eight inches.[19] Its name comes from its call, which sounds like someone sharpening a saw on a whetstone. You can imitate it by whistling the same note about eight times in four seconds. One night in 2002, I visited a Saw-whet Owl banding station in Maryland. The banders set up mist nets near a speaker that boomed out the bird's call. Around midnight, a young female owl flew into a net. The age of a Saw-whet Owl can be determined by its eye color. The bander had a card with four paint swatches with different shades of yellow; the darker the eyes, the older the bird. This particular bird did not vocalize, but when something happened that she did not like, she clicked her bill. With a bird in the hand, I was able to observe the owl's feet, which have three toes pointing forward and one back. But unlike the feet of most other types of birds, one of the front toes can slide around and become a back toe to aid in grasping prey.

The ornithologist Paul Engman told a story about a Saw-whet Owl found in a bird-banding net one autumn morning in Cape May, New Jersey. Because Cape May also is a major flyway for hawks, the netted Saw-whet Owl could not be safely released during daylight hours. Instead, it was taken into a hawk blind and placed on a shelf next to the cans of bird bands until it could be released safely after nightfall. All day, the tiny owl watched a procession of large hawks being processed by the banders. The little bird probably had nightmares for the rest of its life.

---

19. Theodore Roosevelt, who along with Jimmy Carter was more knowledgeable about birds than any of the other US Presidents, kept a list of birds he saw on the White House grounds. He said that in June of 1905, a pair of Saw-whet Owls spent a few weeks by the south portico of the White House. He also reported that the Screech Owl was a steady resident on the White House grounds.

62. PARROT
Bird Names That Are Verbs

While many people's names have entered the dictionary as nouns—boycott, ohm, Mae West, etc.—names that have become verbs are much less common. An unfortunate example from the 1990s was to "bobbitt," which is derived from the act of Lorena Bobbitt, who was so angry at her husband that she performed a penectomy without anesthetic or surgical tools. Marine biologists have also used her name as an adjective for Bobbitt Worms (*Eunice aphroditois*), small deep-sea creatures whose female lops off her partner's sex organ after mating and feeds it to her young.

Ornithology has given the English language a few verbs based on the behavior of birds. To "goose" means to reach up between someone's legs and poke them from behind, derived from the habit of domestic geese doing this to people who are bent over doing farm chores. To "crane" one's neck is to make it long like the neck of a crane. One of the most common bird verbs is to "parrot," which means to repeat exactly what someone else has said without thinking about the meaning of the words.

Some bird species, including many parrot species, are able to repeat sounds they hear. If the sounds are words uttered by humans, the birds will create the illusion of talking, even though they usually have no idea what the words mean. However, an African Gray Parrot named Alex was taught to associate certain words with certain concepts, so the utterances resembled simple human speech rather than mere parroting. Irene Pepperberg, an animal psychologist, trained Alex to associate words with objects and colors. She then determined that Alex was capable of processing information to make requests or to combine colors with objects to identify a particular colored object. While similar experiments have been performed with chimpanzees and gorillas who have been taught sign language, birds capable of mimicry can say the actual words. The success in teaching Alex suggested that birds are capable of much more complex mental activity than previously thought.

Some of the best-known parrot species are the common pets called parakeets, even though many of these pets actually are an Australian species called the Budgerigar (which is why the British call them budgies). *Monty Python* fans might remember a skit in which Mrs. Premise and Mrs. Conclusion discuss the best way to put a budgie down. When told that a neighbor had flushed one down the toilet, Mrs. Conclusion says you should not do that, because "they breed in the sewers, and eventually you get evil-smelling flocks of huge soiled budgies flying out of people's lavatories infringing their personal freedom."

A more famous *Monty Python* sketch involves an irate John Cleese in a pet shop trying to return a dead parrot. The angry Cleese ends his tirade by shouting, "This is an ex-parrot." If you look at a list of about 370 known parrot species (including the cockatoos and the

New Zealand parrots who are in separate families but the same order), about ten of them now are ex-parrots, as in ex-tinct. About seventy-five others are classified as threatened, endangered, or critically endangered. The only parrot species native to the United States went extinct around the beginning of the twentieth century. The Carolina Parakeet was a victim of habitat destruction and the perception by some farmers that it was an agricultural pest. These lovely green-and-yellow parrots had a behavior that allowed farmers to kill large numbers of them. If one parakeet was shot, others in the flock would come to the fallen bird. Farmers waited nearby and then shot a lot more. Another theory about the cause of their extinction is that introduced honeybees took away the birds' nest sites. Some of the parakeets were collected as cage birds. By 1918, they were all gone. The only parrots now seen flying wild in the United States are escaped cage birds.

The principal parrot family (not including the cockatoos and New Zealand species) includes birds called parakeets, parrotlets, macaws, lories, lorikeets, rosellas, lovebirds, and other names. Parrots range in size from tiny, short-tailed birds of only a few inches to large, long-tailed birds who are more than a yard long. They are found in Central and South America, the Caribbean, Asia, Africa, Australia, New Zealand, and islands of the Pacific.

Parrots are gregarious. In the wild, one usually sees a pair, a small group, or a large flock of parrots; rarely does one see a solitary bird. Parrots are one of the few groups of birds with zygodactyl feet, which means they have two toes pointing forward and two pointing back. They are adept at using their feet to assist with climbing and eating. In Australia, I frequently saw wild parrots picking up fruit or other food with a foot and raising it to their beak. A 2011 study by Culum Brown of Macquarie University in Australia found that fifteen of the sixteen parrot species studied showed a preference for using the eye and foot on one side of their body—the equivalent of a human's being either right-handed or left-handed—and that young Sulphur-crested

Cockatoos all end up being left-footed. Parrots also can be remarkably long-lived. A two-foot-long endangered parrot in New Zealand called a Kakapo has an average life expectancy of more than ninety years and can live to be one hundred and twenty.

Many parrots have brightly colored plumage. Nonetheless, birds who appear colorful in a cage have the ability, when flying freely, to land in a tree and seem to disappear. The reason for the effectiveness of the camouflage is evident when looking at an Australian species called the Scaly-breasted Lorikeet. It has mostly bright-green plumage, yellow horizontal streaking on the breast, and a red bill, and it spends a lot of time in flowering trees, some of which have red flowers. The green plumage blends in with the leaves on the tree. The yellow streaks look like the spaces between the leaves, so at a distance the green on the lorikeet no longer has the shape of a bird's body. And the red bill looks like a red flower.

Parrots and other birds who consume the nectar of flowers in trees have been known to get drunk from doing so. Any food that contains sugar has the potential to ferment, and birds consuming the fermented nectar sometimes behave strangely. Large birds such as pheasants have been known to consume fermented berries and then fly into the windshields of moving cars, which can cause serious harm to the bird and driver. The intoxicants sometimes can be fatal to birds.

Macaws are the largest parrots in the American tropics. Their name comes from a Portuguese word for a type of fruit some of them eat. They are sleek and have a long, pointed tail. Of the eighteen macaw species, two are extinct, and the populations of four others are dangerously low. They often fly in flocks, and their wingbeat is distinct and deliberate. Scarlet Macaws are bright, colorful, and loud. According to the naturalist Dan Janzen, they rarely eat the fleshy part of fruit, but instead try to extract the seeds. Some species of South American macaws eat clay to obtain sodium and essential trace minerals. Because macaws are big and colorful, they are popular as cage birds and are used by some people as a fashion accessory. In a 2000 fashion spread in the *New York Times Magazine,* women models wore a line of Yves Saint Laurent clothing and added a decorative flourish by having various species of macaws perch on their arms and shoulders. Street vendors sometimes try to attract customers by having a macaw on their shoulder.

Parrots have suffered greatly from the cage-bird trade. In some areas of the tropics, macaws and other types of parrots have all but disappeared. Some parrot species can fetch enormous sums when sold on the black market. The problem feeds on itself, because the rarer a species becomes, the more each bird is worth. The trapper, middleman, exporter, and seller all take a cut of the money. For tropical birds intended for sale in other countries, the number eventually sold is substantially smaller than the number who die between capture and sale. Parrots who survive the trip often die shortly after being sold from the shock of trying to adjust to an alien captive environment.

Because parrots have the ability to mimic human speech, many people have thought it humorous to teach them to curse. In some instances, the motive is revenge rather than humor. In 2012, a complaint was filed against a Rhode Island woman who lived next door to a couple consisting of her ex-husband and his new lady friend. The lady friend complained that the parrot repeatedly called her a whore and sometimes would curse for up to fifteen minutes.

63. PEAFOWL
Birds and the Visual Arts

The Peacock Room, designed by James Whistler, is a major attraction in the Freer Gallery of Art in Washington. This room used to be in the home of a wealthy London ship owner named Frederick Leyland before it was purchased by Charles Lang Freer and taken to the United States. Whistler initially was asked for advice only about the paint colors to be used in the room, which had been designed by someone else. He soon began to make major, costly revisions without consulting Leyland, who balked at the price of the changes. Leyland eventually agreed to pay only about half of what Whistler asked. In retaliation, Whistler covered one of the walls with a large painting of two fighting peacocks. Near the feet of one of the birds are coins, which represent the dispute over the money for Whistler's efforts. The decorations contain other symbolic insults to Leyland.

There is no species called a peacock. There are three species called peafowl, with the males being peacocks and the females peahens. They are related to pheasants and the species from which domestic chickens were bred. The male Indian Peafowl has a blue body that is about three feet long. His absurdly long tail coverts (feathers that cover the tail) are another three or four feet long. During sexual displays, these feathers are spread and shaken to make a swishing noise to attract a peahen's attention. Some florists and other vendors sell the long peacock feathers, which are bluish green and have large eyespots. Peacocks do not have the largest feathers of all wild birds; the Crested Argus Pheasant, an Asian species, has tail feathers that are five feet long and six inches wide.

Peacocks and other male pheasants feature some of the most outrageous plumage of any birds. Peafowl sometimes are acquired by celebrities and other rich people to add an exotic and decadent air to the properties where they live. Bono, the lead singer for the rock band U2, has had peafowl at his home in Ireland which, because of their noise and messiness, have not endeared themselves to his neighbors. Just as with human rock stars, gaudy plumage on birds can be useful in luring mates. But elaborate plumage is not functional for other aspects of life—imagine if women had to dress every day in a bridal gown with a long train. The showiness of peacocks would be a liability around the nest because of the greater likelihood of attracting predators. The peahen, who is a large bird without excessively long trailing feathers, is responsible for hatching the eggs and raising the young.

In Thailand, I visited a facility that breeds various species of birds and mammals, including a species called the Green Peafowl. Wild Green Peafowl have come to the site, and they walk around near their caged brothers and sisters. When you see one in the wild, you have trouble believing such an improbably showy creature could be real. They look as if they are wearing a costume. Green Peacocks are more than seven feet long. They have a green head and tail coverts, blue wings, and a patterned face. Their call is a loud KEE YOW. The ones I saw were wary but not especially shy.[20]

In the 1950s, the National Broadcasting Company pioneered in showing television programs in color. Before each NBC color broadcast, a cartoon peacock spread his tail while the network made an announcement about the show being in "living color." When I was growing up, the televisions in my household were black and white, so the eleven colors in the peacock's tail appeared to be shades of gray. In the 1980s, when color television was the norm, the peacock remained as NBC's logo, even though the announcement about color no longer

---

20. Another peacock who was not shy was the Australian Liberal Party leader Andrew Peacock, whose party lost in the 1990 federal elections to the Labour Party led by Bob Hawke in a rare contest involving two candidates with bird surnames. Bird surnames can be found in languages other than English. The last name of baseball pitcher Matt Garza means "heron" in Spanish. The surname of Cuban boxing champion Kid Gavilán, who fought in the 1940s and 1950s, is the Spanish word for "hawk," which is why he was nicknamed "the Cuban hawk."

was necessary before each show. The bird's tail was reduced to six colors, with each color representing one of the six divisions of NBC.

Peacocks are prominent in literature and fable. Each Greek god had a favorite bird, and the peacock was the favorite of Hera, the wife of Zeus (who preferred the eagle). One of Aesop's fables involves a peacock asking Hera to make him be able to sing as sweetly as a nightingale rather than being stuck with a loud, ugly squawk. Hera told him to be satisfied with his beauty, because you can't have everything. The Roman name for Hera is Juno, and the Irish poet William Butler Yeats wrote a poem in 1922 called "Meditations in Time of Civil War" in which the third section ends with the words, "Juno's peacock screamed." Two years later, the Irish playwright Sean O'Casey wrote an acclaimed play called *Juno and the Paycock* about a poor Irish family who mistakenly believes it will be receiving a large inheritance. The play was made into a 1930 film directed by Alfred Hitchcock. Peacocks also have played an important role in the cultures of India, Tibet, China, Iran, and other countries, as well as in the Buddhist and Hindu religions.

The American writer Flannery O'Connor, who lived from 1925 to 1964, raised peafowl on her Georgia farm for many years. She wrote a long article about peacocks called "The King of the Birds," which appears in a collection of her prose called *Mystery and Manners*. Rarely do accomplished fiction authors write a life history of a bird species, and O'Connor's essay is as amusing as it is informative. She talks about the significant demands of caring for these imperious birds, saying she was at their "beck and squawk." She says that when first graders visited her farm each year to see the peafowl, they often commented on the male's "underwear," which is the stiff gray portion of the tail under the showy long tail coverts. O'Connor seemed to take comfort in the revealing of the underwear, just as when the high and the mighty in the human arena expose some behavior or characteristic that makes them seem more like the rest of us.

64. PELICAN
Birders with Bird Names

An aptronym is a person's name that is related to some characteristic or activity of the person. For instance, George McGovern was a senator involved in governing. The sprinter Usain Bolt bolted from the starting blocks during his Olympic races. The birding community has many aptronyms. John Flicker has served as president of the National Audubon Society, while the chair of the board in 2011 was B. Holt Thrasher. I belonged to a bird club whose president at one time was Byron Swift. The author of *The Bird Almanac: The Ultimate Guide to Essential Facts and Figures of the World's Birds* is David M. Bird. I do not know whether these names caused the people to become interested in birds or whether they would have developed the interest anyway. In some instances, the aptronym is a homophone: it is pronounced the same as the name of a bird but spelled differently. A former editor of an American Birding Association newsletter was Matthew Pelikan.

Pelicans have been responsible for other variations in spelling. There is a famous limerick, written in 1910 by a Nashville newspaper editor named Dixon Lanier Merritt, about the pelican having a bill that can hold "more than his belican." It ends with the statement, "But I don't know how the helican." Pelicans are much-loved birds, primarily for their wise appearance and large bills. The limerick is not entirely accurate. The part that can hold the substantial volume (more than its belly can) is a throat pouch with elastic skin attached to the lower mandible. If you go to a museum that has bird skeletons, you will see that a bird's lower mandible is an open frame, similar to the human jawbone (which also is called a mandible). Birds must find food that will fit into this frame and down their throat. Unlike humans and other mammals, birds cannot chew food to make it small enough to go down their throat, although some are capable of pecking or tearing small pieces from food sources that would be too large to swallow. The large frame and throat pouch of pelicans allows them to scoop up fish and water at the same time. The throat does not work like a sieve, but pelicans are able to let water spritz out the sides of their bill before swallowing.

All of the world's eight pelican species are found near water, but not necessarily in coastal areas. On a camping trip to central Australia, I frequently saw groups of Australia's only species of pelican swimming in the creeks near where we pitched our tents. The Australian Pelican holds the distinction of having the longest bill of any bird in the world. North America has two pelican species, including the White Pelican, who is the largest bird on the continent. Its wingspan is nine feet—the same as a California Condor, who has a much smaller body. The White Pelican's body is sixty-two inches—slightly longer than a Trumpeter Swan, whose wingspan is much shorter. The Brown Pelican is smaller than the White Pelican but still a large bird. On a trip to the Gulf Coast of Florida, I saw Brown Pelicans standing on a dock near men who were fishing. The fishermen gave small fish and the innards of cleaned fish to the pelicans, so the pelicans followed the men wherever they went on the dock.

Pelicans are gregarious, and they often fly and swim in groups. When not seeking handouts from fishermen, they show a lot of variety in their feeding methods. Some catch fish by plunging from high in the air and hitting the water with considerable force. Others participate in cooperative fishing, which can involve a group of pelicans swimming in a gradually closing circle to herd fish into a small area where they can be more easily caught. Another method involves a group of pelicans driving the fish into shallow water to facilitate capture.

Scientists who believe that the ultimate purpose of all animal behavior is to pass genes to future generations might have trouble explaining some cooperative behavior among pelicans. Proponents of selfishness theories could argue that each individual bird has a better chance of surviving by fishing in a group, thereby increasing the chances of passing on its genes. But they would have trouble explaining an example cited in *The Audubon Society Encyclopedia of North American Birds* in which a group of White Pelicans fed and kept alive a blind member of their colony. There would be little genetic advantage to the other individuals taking time away from their own feeding activities to feed another adult bird. If any biologist wants to suggest that such behavior is not based on altruism, I don't know how the helican.

65. PENGUIN
Birds and Paperback Books

During the 1930s, a bird became the symbol for a revolution in the publishing industry. An Englishman named Allen Lane began to publish inexpensive paperback books. His original goal was not to make a lot of money, but to encourage a greater number of British readers to buy books at bookshops rather than only borrowing books from libraries. People could buy each of these books for about the same price as a package of cigarettes. Within a year, Lane's company, which was called Penguin Books, had sold a few million paperbacks. The company is still in business and now has many competitors in the paperback market.

Penguins are associated with Antarctica, but they are found throughout the Southern Hemisphere, as far north as the Galapagos Islands near the equator. As such, the penguin family experiences as great a range of temperatures as any bird family. Their average body temperature is one of the lowest in the bird world and roughly equal to that of humans. None of the roughly twenty penguin species is found in the Northern Hemisphere.

Humans often consider penguins to be irresistibly cute. Penguins stand upright, resembling the erect posture of a human. They waddle when they walk, and their black-and-white plumage resembles a tuxedo. They spend much of their time at sea and are fast and mobile swimmers. They are incapable of flight, but they use their vestigial wings as flippers to "fly" through the water. Penguins are the only birds capable of porpoising—propelling themselves through the water by arcing their body above the surface, as porpoises do—which allows them to swim faster than any other type of bird. They also can dive deeper and hold their breath longer than any other type of bird.

The first penguin I saw in the wild was a dead one who had washed ashore on the southern coast of Australia. It was a species called the Little Penguin, the smallest penguin in the world at less than a foot and a half tall. I subsequently visited a colony of Little Penguins in Tasmania. Each of the penguins had a burrow. As night fell, the penguins swam to the shore and trudged across the beach, resembling a mass of workers leaving a factory at quitting time. They wait until dusk, because they are small birds and would be more vulnerable to attack by predators in broad daylight. Their feathers have a hairy appearance, which when wet resemble cloth. These penguins walk with their bodies tilted forward, a bit like the way Groucho Marx walked for comic effect in some of his movies. One of the penguins tried to slide across the beach on its stomach as far as it could. Little Penguins bray like donkeys, which adds to the comic effect; a species found on the coast of South Africa is called the Jackass Penguin for the same reason.

The Emperor Penguin, the largest penguin species in the world, is about three feet tall and roughly twice the height of a Little Penguin. Emperor Penguins star in the 2005 movie *March of the Penguins*, which examines the life cycle of the species. The birds leave the seas off Antarctica to march to their nesting area, where they pair off and mate. The female lays an egg and helps with incubation. She then marches all the way back to the ocean to feed, leaving the male to stand on the polar ice and incubate the egg for two long, dark winter months. He eats nothing while holding the egg on his feet. Around the time the egg hatches, the female returns with food, and the family eventually goes out to sea as the winter turns into spring.

Some political and religious groups have praised the movie for promoting strong monogamous family values. But in the bird world, one must be careful about making generalizations about behavior. Regarding penguins, the devoted parents often do not stay together for the next breeding season. For some penguin species, the "divorce rate" is higher than it is for humans. And penguins sometimes engage in behavior that would be less likely to be found in a book about family values than in a book such as *Lady Chatterley's Lover*, for which Penguin Books was prosecuted (and acquitted) under Britain's 1959

Obscene Publications Act. Adelie Penguins, who are smaller and more numerous than the Emperors, also nest in the Antarctic. Rather than balancing eggs on their feet, they make simple nests featuring an indentation in the ground ringed with stones. The stones are much sought after during the mating season, and Dr. Fiona Hunter of Cambridge University in England discovered that some female Adelies act like prostitutes, offering sex to males in exchange for stones. In a 1998 study, Hunter observed that some mated females would copulate with an unattached male who had gathered stones, take a stone or two, and return to her own mate's nest. The BBC website had fun with the story, showing a doctored photograph of a female human prostitute standing on a dreary street at night with a forlorn-looking penguin next to her.

A penguin species has a connection to a famous American song. The species has yellow feather tufts on its black head. Because of the "feathers in its cap," it is called the Macaroni Penguin, just as Yankee Doodle had a feather in his cap. While the basis for the "called it macaroni" line in "Yankee Doodle" is not entirely certain, it might be ridiculing both foppish Englishmen called macaronis as well as colonists who acted like the fops. Despite the negative lyrics, Americans adopted the song, mainly because they liked the tune.

66. PLOVER
Birds Who Deceive

Ethicists love to wrestle with issues such as whether a person is ever justified in lying to protect family members or friends. Some bird species engage in a similar type of dishonesty. I once saw a Killdeer, a species of plover, skittering away and pretending to have a broken wing. Adult Killdeers at the nest or with chicks are known to use such deceptions. Predators like to catch prey with as little effort as possible, and an injured bird presents an inviting target. When the predator has chased the supposedly injured adult Killdeer a sufficient distance, the Killdeer flies away, leaving the predator far away from the eggs or young. Bird species in many other families use similar distraction displays.

Plovers are mostly wading birds, but some prefer to forage in fields rather than wetlands. The name comes from the Latin word *pluvia*, which means rain, but it is not clear why plovers were considered rainbirds. There are more than sixty plover species in the world, including birds called lapwings, dotterels, and other names. Some plovers are among the bird species who have the longest annual migrations between their nesting area and their wintering ground.

About ten plover species are found regularly in the United States, and some have become endangered because of encroachment from humans. Piping Plovers nest on beaches and dunes, and people driving around in dune buggies and all-terrain vehicles have destroyed a lot of nests and young. Conservationists have waged campaigns to set aside areas for the nesting plovers. The nest of the Piping Plover is a scrape in the sand lined with small stones or pieces of shell. Some plovers do not bother to line the scrapes where they lay their eggs. The making of the scrape is an important component of the courtship ritual of many plover species.

The Egyptian Plover is found in Africa and was called the "crocodile bird" because the ancient Greeks believed that it would hop into

the open mouth of a crocodile and peck at food that was between the teeth. While the Egyptian Plover is not so rash as to seek food in such a dangerous place, it does have an unusual way of incubating its eggs. It covers them with sand and then uses its body and the sun to maintain the proper egg temperature.

The Killdeer is the most common plover in North America. It has a white breast with two black bands. The Killdeer gets its name from its distinctive call, which it makes loudly and often; its scientific species name is *vociferus*. Killdeers sometimes are found in urbanized areas. Once while walking around Las Vegas after dark, I located silhouettes of calling Killdeers on a vacant lot.

One of the strangest-looking plovers in the world is the Masked Lapwing, who is common in eastern Australia. It looks as if it were designed to be an adolescent's action figure, with a yellow flap of skin hanging from each side of its face and a nasty yellow spur sticking forward from the edge of each wing. Masked Lapwings are noisy and aggressive, and they frequently harass hawks and other birds.

There are roughly a couple dozen species called lapwings in the world. The Northern Lapwing, who is found in many parts of Eurasia, is one of the best known of the group, and it is probably the species from which the word "kibitz" is derived. The Yiddish word for lapwing is *Kiebitz*, and a busybody or someone who offers unasked-for criticism is thought to be kibitzing, or behaving like a loud and aggressive lapwing.

The Crab Plover is not in the same family as the birds described above. It is found along the coast of the Indian Ocean. In *What's in a Name*, Paul Dickson talks about a race horse with the seemingly innocuous name "Little Lass," which caused problems when said quickly during a race. The name Crab Plover would cause similar problems.

67. PUFFIN
Birds Near the Maelstrom

The word "maelstrom" comes from a whirlpool near the Lofoten Islands off the coast of Norway north of the Arctic Circle. To see it, you need to catch a ferry from the town of Bodo. The ferry will take you to an island called Moskenes. On the southern tip of Moskenes is a town called Hell, from which you can pay someone to take you on a boat to the Maelstrom. Norwegian is a Germanic language, and *hell* is the German word for light; for instance, the color "light green" in German is *hell grün*. The word "maelstrom" now is used metaphorically to describe a state of confusion. Another word for a state of confusion is pandemonium, which has links to Hell—the place in the underworld rather than Norway. In John Milton's *Paradise Lost*, Pandemonium is the principal city of Hell.

In the summer of 1989, I took a ferry from Bodo, but instead of going to Hell, I went to a small island called Røst on the south end of the Lofoten chain. I arrived on the island at about ten at night, and it was still very light. I went to the only bar in town, along with two Norwegian seminary students who had been on the ferry. When the bar closed at midnight, a guy we met in the bar offered to take us for a tour of the tiny island, and there was still enough light to see the various landmarks. I then went back to a guesthouse and was shown to a room that had on one of my windowsills an active nest of a gull called a kittiwake. All that was between me and the kittiwake was a thin piece of glass, and I was close enough to the bird to see the texture of the skin around her eye. She did not act at all disturbed by my presence.

The reason I went to Røst was to see the *lunde*, which is the Norwegian word for puffin. During the summer, many thousands of puffins nest there. The Atlantic Puffin is about half the size of a Mallard. Puffins look pudgy and ungraceful; the word "puffin" comes from their puffy appearance. A young puffin is called a puffling. The most

noticeable characteristic of a puffin is its huge triangular bill that is blue, red, and yellow. With this remarkable bill, they are able to catch fish and hold onto them while catching additional fish. The colorful portion falls off when they are not breeding. Puffins have big orange feet that stick out when they fly and help them to brake and steer when they land. When a puffin is about to land, it looks as if it is flying too fast and is going to crash.

There are three species of puffins. They are in the genus *Fratercula*, which means "little brother," in the sense of a small member of a religious order—the black-and-white plumage makes them look priestly. Puffins are in a family called the Alcidae (also known as the alcids), which includes auks, auklets, guillemots, murres, and murrelets. "Auk" has been used as a generic term for an alcid, but the only species left with auk in its common name is the Little Auk, whom Americans call the Dovekie. A tall, clumsy, flightless bird called the Great Auk became extinct by the middle of the 1800s due to mass slaughter by human hunters. A huge colony of Great Auks was wiped out on Funk Island, just east of Newfoundland. The island, named because massive accumulations of bird excrement gave it a funky smell, now is used by other alcid species and gannets for nesting. The Great Auk is the symbol of the American Ornithologists' Union.

In winter plumage, the Great Auk had a patch of white on its head between the bill and the eye. In the Welsh language, the two words for white and head are *pen* and *gwyn*, and some dictionaries regard this as a possible origin of the word "penguin." Alcids occupy the same ecological niche in the Northern Hemisphere that penguins occupy in the Southern Hemisphere, but the two families of birds are not closely related. Their visual similarities are due to convergent evolution, which involves organisms of different lineages developing similar characteristics. Most alcids and penguins are black on the back and white underneath, which provides camouflage from predators. Both groups spend most of their lives at sea. If a predator looks down from above, the surface of the ocean looks dark, and a black back will be difficult to see. If a predator looks up from underwater, the surface of the ocean looks light because of the reflection of the sky, and a white belly will be difficult to see. The white belly also will be more difficult for the birds' potential prey to see. The color configuration also helps the birds to regulate their body temperature. Birds who spend most of their life in frigid water need black feathers on their back to absorb as much heat as possible. During nesting season when summer heat might be intense, they can turn their white breast toward the sun to reflect heat. Black feathers contain a pigment called melanin that makes them more durable. Feathers of birds living in the middle of the sea, exposed to the elements, will suffer greater wear and tear than the feathers of birds in a more sheltered environment. Penguins cannot fly, but all of the remaining alcid species can. Among the major predators of penguins are seals and other sea mammals, from whom they can escape by means other than flying. Some of the predators of alcids are land based, so alcids need flight to escape. Both penguins and alcids are among the relatively small group of birds who have only three toes on each foot rather than four.

The alcids who most closely resemble the Great Auk are the murres. There are two species of murres and seven smaller species of murrelets. Murres nest by the ocean, while murrelets often nest in forests. Murre eggs are irregularly shaped, being fat on one end and thin on the other.

A likely reason for this is that murres lay their eggs directly onto bare, rocky ledges; an egg that is narrower at one end will roll in a circle rather than rolling off the ledge. "Murre" is pronounced like the myrrh that the three wise men brought in the nativity story. Myrrh is a resin mixture used in incense and perfumes and as a medical remedy. Mary and Joseph probably were glad that the wise men did not bring gold, frankincense, and seabirds.

As with many species of alcids, puffins have been affected by a lot of environmental problems. On their nesting grounds, rats, cats, and other predators have prevented successful reproduction. Being seabirds, puffins are vulnerable to oil spills and the effects of toxic residues. Their food supply is being depleted as the oceans are overfished. And around Britain, the rapid expansion of the population of a species called the Snake Pipefish, which was virtually unknown near Britain in the year 2000, is also causing problems for puffins and other seabirds. A 2008 report by British biologists said that puffin chicks were choking to death on the rigid bodies of the pipefish, and that adult puffins were eating the fish even though they have little nutritional value.

I have seen some alcids from coastal vantage points in the United States. But the only way to see most alcids, barring a storm that blows them toward the shore, is to either take a boat trip into the ocean or visit their nesting grounds. One of the most popular starting points for such boat trips in North America is Monterrey, California. On one of these trips in 1994, I saw an alcid called a Rhinoceros Auklet, whose name sounds like an oxymoron. Rhinoceros Auklets, who are about fifteen inches, are named for the small horn at the base of their bill. Because of the horn, a colloquial name for them is the Unicorn Puffin, and they are thought to be in the same genus with an extinct species called the Dubious Auklet (one of my favorite bird names). They do not in any other way resemble the huge mammal after whom they are named. On that same boat trip, I saw the hugest mammal of them all when a Blue Whale swam close to our boat. This incredible creature was more than eighty feet long, much longer than the boat I was on. I was glad that Blue Whales do not bow-surf the way dolphins do. Although I went on the trip to look for seabirds, my memories of the Blue Whale are more vivid than my memories of the fifteen-inch auklet.

68. QUETZAL
A Life Devoted to Birds

Before a 1997 trip to Costa Rica, I had hoped both to meet the ornithologist Alexander Skutch and to see a male Resplendent Quetzal in breeding plumage. The Resplendent Quetzal possesses a magic that transcends the bird world. The quetzal is the national emblem of Guatemala and the name for the Guatemalan unit of currency. An Aztec deity called Quetzalcoatl (which means quetzal serpent) is a god of peace. In some cultures, only royalty and nobles have been allowed to wear quetzal feathers.

The name "quetzal" comes from an Aztec word meaning precious or beautiful. And quetzals are beautiful! From the back, the male looks almost entirely Day-Glo green. The green head appears to have a shag haircut. The bill is yellow, the breast is green, and the belly is bright red. The bird is fourteen inches long, but some males have two bright-green plumes that extend another two feet beyond their tail. (As with the peacock, the showy plumes are actually feathers above the tail rather than tail feathers.) The female is smaller and plainer. Her green coloration is not as bright, her belly is gray, and she never has tail plumes. During the nesting season, quetzals live at high altitudes. After nesting, they migrate to lower altitudes where they feed in fruit trees—they are especially fond of wild avocados. Costa Rica has created reserves to protect quetzals, but poachers still try to trade in both feathers and live birds.

My first look at quetzals in Costa Rica was at a lodge near the cloud forests at Monteverde (which means green mountain). I saw five males, but none of them had long tail plumes. The owner of the lodge showed me a couple of tail plumes he had found on the ground. Resplendent Quetzals nest in holes, and the plumes fall off when a male helps with incubation. After leaving Monteverde, I saw a plumed male who might have been unsuccessful in mating that year. I viewed the bird through a high-quality telescope called a Questar, and I had such a good look that I could see the central shaft of tail plumes. Quetzals tend to perch quietly in trees without moving much. When taking off, they seem to fall off a branch and glide to the next one. In flight, the quetzal's plumes trail like long streamers wafting in the wind. This is a breathtaking bird!

The Resplendent Quetzal is in the trogon family. Trogons are found in warm climates around the world, including the New World, Asia, and Africa. The trogons are uniformly beautiful birds. Because they tend to sit still in trees, they can be difficult to find. Also, for large, brightly colored birds, they can blend in well with foliage. The only trogon species who nests regularly in the United States is the Elegant Trogon, found in southeastern Arizona. Of all the lovely birds in that part of the United States, the Elegant Trogon ranks near the top of the list of species visiting birders wish to see. The male has a green-and-red color scheme similar to the Resplendent Quetzal's, but the Elegant Trogon is smaller and lacks the tail plumes and shag haircut.

The best description I have read of the characteristics and behavior of the Resplendent Quetzal is in Alexander Skutch's 1983 book *Birds of Tropical America*. Skutch was one of the most important ornithologists of the twentieth century, but a lot of birders in the United States do not know much about him because he lived most of his life in Central America. Skutch was a naturalist and philosopher who, like Henry David Thoreau, built a house in a secluded woodland, but instead of remaining for thirty months, Skutch stayed for more than sixty years. In May 2004, he died at his home in Costa Rica about a week shy of his one hundredth birthday.

Skutch was born in Baltimore, and his family moved to a farm outside the city when he was three. On the farm, he developed a love for nature. Skutch entered Johns Hopkins University at seventeen and earned a doctorate in botany at twenty-four. His first experience with tropical habitats came on a trip to Jamaica in 1926 to study banana plants. After completing school, he went to Panama to study bananas and realized that he preferred the tropics to northern habitats. He worked in Honduras and Guatemala before going to Costa Rica in 1935 and living there almost continuously until his death. He discovered plants that were not previously known to science, including one that is named after him (*Kohleria skutchii*). In 1950, he married Pamela Lankester, the youngest daughter of one of Costa Rica's best-known naturalists. Mrs. Skutch died in 2001, not long after their fiftieth wedding anniversary.

During the late 1930s, Skutch worked in the botanical section of the national museum in Costa Rica, but he did not enjoy being indoors looking at lifeless specimens. He left the job and went to live in the woods. In 1941, he built a wilderness home about fifty miles south of the capital in San José. He named the home *Los Cusingos*, the Spanish name for the Fiery-billed Aracari (a toucan). Los Cusingos became a destination for many birders and naturalists visiting Costa Rica.

Skutch believed that there are two callings that few people can resist: the voice of religion and the voice of nature. An encounter with a Rufous-tailed Hummingbird opened his eyes to the possibilities of bird study and inspired him to fulfill his yearning to learn about the secret lives of free animals. When Skutch looked at existing bird research, he was deeply disappointed. He found a great many specimens that had been shot, measured, and catalogued, but little information about behavior or nesting habits. Skutch was not alone in his antipathy for museum ornithologists. In his 1989 book *The Appreciation of Birds*, the naturalist Louis Halle commented that because all species tend to vary more or less continuously and almost imperceptibly over their range, it is too easy to "discover" new subspecies. Halle quotes Jacques' Rule, which says that the number of subspecies in any given area is inverse to the distance from the nearest natural history museum.

Skutch did more than any Neotropical ornithologist to remedy this lack of information about the behavior and habits of birds. Over

Quetzal

the decades, he observed birds in the field and produced three volumes of *Life Histories of Central American Birds* (published in 1954, 1960, and 1969). Cumulatively, they include more than 150 species, with more than 1,600 pages of text. The magnitude of this achievement seems more astounding when one reads the case studies. A typical description of his time-consuming, meticulous research is found in the account of an incubating Sulphur-bellied Flycatcher: "In nearly seven hours of watching in the afternoon of June 14 and the following morning, she took 15 completed sessions which ranged from 5 to 32 minutes and averaged 17 minutes and 15 recesses which varied from 1 to 21 and averaged 8.5 minutes." Skutch later produced additional volumes of studies of tropical American birds as well as co-authoring a field guide to Costa Rican birds. He also produced numerous books about families of birds worldwide, including hummingbirds, woodpeckers, tanagers, pigeons, flycatchers, blackbirds, antbirds, and ovenbirds.

Some of his best work involves behavioral studies. *Parent Birds and Their Young* (1976) is a five-hundred-page study of all aspects of the mating and breeding behavior of the birds of the world. A related book is *Helpers at Birds' Nests*, which deals with birds giving assistance at the nest to others who are not their mate or their young; Skutch was the first to report this behavior when early in his career he observed Brown Jays doing it. *Birds Asleep* (1987) is a survey of an activity that even the most avid birders rarely observe, but Skutch compiled enough material to write a book about it.

The Minds of Birds (1996), one of his most controversial works, presents evidence that the mental capacities of birds are greatly underestimated. Skutch had trouble finding a publisher for the book, because the scientific community has a deep prejudice against suggestions that creatures other than humans are capable of certain types of mental processes. The views Skutch expressed in this book were vindicated shortly after his death when scientists discovered that the brains of birds are far more complex, flexible, and inventive than was previously thought by most ornithologists—especially ornithologists who spend most of their time looking at museum skins rather than observing the behavior of wild birds.

Skutch learned about nature by immersing himself in it and becoming part of it. Skutch's autobiographical works intersperse events from his life with field observations, because he did not perceive a strict demarcation between the two. In *Nature Through Tropical Windows* (1983), he describes sightings from the windows of his home. Skutch had no glass or screens on his windows (with one exception), which prevented many bird deaths from collision as well as removing barriers between himself and nature.

Skutch was well read in literature, philosophy, world religions, and history. He became a vegetarian after reading Shelley's poetry and essays. He did not like to feel that any of the humans or animals who assisted in the work on his property were acting under compulsion. He believed in the Indian concept of *ahimsa*, which is the bedrock of Jainism. It means "without harm," and it entails a compassionate concern for all life forms, from the largest animals to the tiniest organisms. He extended this tenderness for living things to plants, and he thought that there is a strong relationship between a society's agricultural practices and its spiritual level. Skutch believed that nobody with an adequate appreciation of our planet's uniqueness, beauty, and bounty would wage war, which he regarded as an example of our technical skills outrunning our moral competence. He thought we should consider the possibility that the Earth can support only a certain total of human beings throughout its entire existence, so that the greater the number of people who crowd it today and drain its resources, the fewer it will be able to support in future ages. He believed that conservation is where ecology and ethics meet. Two years after his death, his book *Moral Foundations* was published. It examines morality and ethics and their antecedents in the animal kingdom and the universe at large.

Quetzal

Skutch thought that the great tragedy of biology is the difficulty of acquiring certain kinds of information without harming living things. He was proud that during his seventy years of Neotropical bird study, he never intentionally harmed, for science or otherwise, any adult or young birds he studied. He admitted to killing a few raptors who preyed upon birds he was studying, and he killed numerous snakes for the same reason. To Skutch, refusing to come to the aid of a bird whose nest is menaced by a snake would be like failing to help a family member or friend being brutalized by a stranger.

Skutch said that much of his life was a revolt against the harsher aspects of nature, especially predation. He believed that the process of evolution deserves our approval only to the extent to which it makes existence more satisfying and desirable, and it does not deserve our approval when it is harsh and wasteful. He considered photosynthesis to be the highest achievement of evolution and the basic good in the living world, upon which all of the Earth's constructive processes, beauty, and joy depend. He thought predation and overpopulation are basic evils, causing most of the ills in nature. He took the naturalist Aldo Leopold to task for suggesting that the Grizzly Bear is nature's outstanding achievement in the wilderness. Skutch thought that many small, weak animals, especially songbirds, are far more outstanding and admirable evolutionary achievements by any criterion we choose, except weight and strength. He said that perfection is most often found in little things, noting that our planet, which he saw as the fairest in the solar system, is tiny as celestial bodies go.

My personal library includes more than thirty books written by Skutch. I met him during my Costa Rica trip. He was at a birding conference, during which he released a book of fictional stories called *Tales of a Naturalist*. On the morning when he was supposed to attend a book signing, I saw Mrs. Skutch on a telephone in our hotel lobby having some sort of trouble getting information. I asked if I could help, and she said she was trying to find the location of the signing. I knew it was scheduled for the convention center next to the hotel, and I offered to take her and Dr. Skutch over. At the time, Dr. Skutch was ninety-three and frail, so Mrs. Skutch asked me to take one of his hands while she took the other. As we walked slowly, I told him how much his work meant to me and how it has encouraged me to become much more interested in observing bird behavior than in merely trying to see a lot of birds to put on a checklist. Dr. Skutch said, "I'd rather know a few birds well."

At the time, Alexander Skutch knew a great number of bird species as well as anyone has ever known them. Including the Resplendent Quetzal.

69. RAIL
Trying to Catch a Wild Bird

Rails, like owls, are common birds whom birders seldom see. Owls are hard to find because of cryptic coloration and nocturnal habits. Rails are hard to find because they often hide in marshes that are difficult for birders to access. In Virginia, hunters are allowed to kill up to fifteen of some rail species and twenty-five of other rail species daily during a hunting season that lasts from September into November. By going into marshes in boats and flushing the birds, some hunters are able to kill more rails in a day than many birders have seen in a lifetime. From a distance, some rails look like dumpy little chickens, but up close, their bodies appear much thinner. Hunters use the term "skinny as a rail" to describe the bird's ability to squeeze through extremely narrow openings. Rails stalk when they walk, and they scoot away quickly in the face of danger.

I live near a wetlands area in Virginia called Huntley Meadows that used to be one of the best places to see breeding King Rails in the United States, but changes in the habitat and an influx of Canada Geese have caused most of the rails to leave. During breeding season, you could see King Rail chicks, who are little black fluffballs. Often, you hear rails without seeing them. One call of the King Rail sounds like someone dragging a stick along the slats of a wooden fence. The most difficult North American rail species to see is the Black Rail, a dark bird about the size of a sparrow and not much different in size and color than a King Rail chick. Black Rails spend most of their time silently walking through reeds, and during breeding season the male calls most actively in the middle of the night. Finding a tiny black bird at night in a marsh is virtually impossible without shining lights and playing tapes of the bird's call, which greatly disturbs the bird.

There are about 150 species of birds in the rail family, which includes coots, gallinules, crakes, flufftails, and birds with other names; not all of them are marsh birds. My favorite rail names are the Snoring Rail, Invisible Rail, and Inaccessible Island Rail (the smallest flightless bird in the world). Other rails are flightless, including a species on Guam who was nearly wiped out when Brown Tree Snakes were introduced to the island in the 1950s. By 1985, only twenty-five Guam Rails remained in the wild. The population has increased somewhat through a captive breeding program, but remains perilously low.

In 1998, a Virginia Rail, a species the size of an American Robin, visited downtown Washington in July. It stayed in gardens in front of the Castle, which is the main administration building of the Smithsonian Institution. These gardens were an odd place for a secretive marsh bird. Early one Sunday morning, I watched the bird as it was finding many insects and worms. Its left wing appeared to be damaged, with the tips of some feathers pointing upward, but I could not tell the severity of the injury. If it had trouble flying, it might not survive later in the year if the ground froze or became covered by snow. Some Virginia Rails overwinter in marshes in our area and will be okay as long as the water does not freeze. I thought the best course of action might be to try to capture the bird and take it either to a rehab center if its wing were structurally damaged or to a marsh if only the feathers were damaged. Damaged feathers molt out, and new ones can grow in.

So the question arose about how to catch an elusive rail. Also, I had to find out where an injured rail could be rehabilitated, if necessary. And most importantly, I had to get permission to go onto Smithsonian property to trap the bird. For the first question, I called Greg Kearns, who did rail-banding studies on the Patuxent River about twenty-five miles from downtown Washington. He was a licensed bird bander and had traps specially designed for rails, and he offered to try to catch the bird. He also recommended a rehab center that could treat the rail if we caught it.

The final step was to get permission to trap the bird. I called the office of the secretary of the Smithsonian, and the receptionist suggested that I call the bird department in the Smithsonian Museum of Natural History. When I called the Natural History Museum, I was told that the bird department would want the rail only if it were shot and skinned (which would defeat the purpose of the exercise). However, I was advised that I might be able to get permission to trap the bird if I called the "Keeper of the Castle," who is responsible for maintaining the Castle building and the grounds around it.

Keeper of the Castle is the best job title I have ever heard, and the person with that title works in the office of the secretary. I called back to that office, and the receptionist, after talking to someone, said I should just go ahead and trap the rail. I said I wanted something in writing, and she said she would send it. As I suspected, the administrators at the Smithsonian had questions about what was going on, so I received a call from the Keeper of the Castle. He asked me questions to make sure I was on the level. I knew that Dillon Ripley, a former secretary of the Smithsonian, was one of the world's foremost authorities on rails, and it helped that I mentioned this. The Keeper of the Castle was very helpful and faxed a permission letter to me. His office also arranged parking passes for me and Greg.

The following day, Greg drove into town with his traps and nets. He brought an assistant who, if you like puns, was named Annette (as in, "He tried to catch the rail with Annette"). They arrived at about 1:20. I had been in the gardens since one o'clock hoping to locate the bird. At about 1:18, I found it on the lawn near the Museum of African Art. When Greg approached the rail, it ran into some shrubbery. He and Annette put what looked like two large butterfly nets on either side of the shrubbery. The rail flew into one of the nets, but bounced out. The bird then flew over a wall and into some low evergreen shrubbery. Catching the rail in there would be difficult. We relocated the bird a few times over the next ninety minutes, sometimes with the help of two small children who could more easily see things that were low to the ground. Once, Greg had the rail netted out of the air, but it somehow managed to slip out. Another time, I waited near a walk-in trap while Greg tried to push the bird toward me. I saw the rail fly up near where I was holding a net, but it escaped. At about 2:50, we stopped trying. The good news was that we saw the rail fly, and its flight appeared normal. Hence, if it needed to depart because of cold weather, it probably would have a chance to get away.

During our attempt to catch the rail, many tourists in the area stopped and asked what we were doing. Standing near popular museums on a sunny summer afternoon with nets and traps provokes curiosity. At least we were the people with the nets rather than the people being pursued by the people with the nets.

70. RAVEN
Birds as Religious Messengers

The sociobiologist Bernd Heinrich published a 1999 book entitled *Mind of the Raven* that contains a story about a woman who saw a raven excitedly fly over her head. It then flew to some nearby rocks where she saw a cougar ready to attack. The woman thought the raven had conveyed a religious message that miraculously saved her life. Heinrich suggests that the raven was more likely trying to alert the *cougar* that potential prey was approaching. A raven would not have been able to kill the woman, but it might have been able to consume the remains of her carcass after the cougar had eaten its fill. Ravens work cooperatively with cougars, hawks, and other predators who are more adept at killing. While ravens are "ravenous," which means rapacious or eating with an overeager appetite, they sometimes share food with each other.

Alexander Skutch's book *The Minds of Birds* contains numerous references about the playfulness and intelligence of ravens. He describes ravens carrying twigs aloft and catching them as they fall. He also mentions the acrobatic feats of flying ravens, such as doing rolls of 180 to 360 degrees. The ornithologist Arthur Cleveland Bent relates an account of ravens playing a game of tag with a "yellow something," passing it from one bird to another. Some have displayed a rudimentary ability to count. Bernd Heinrich cites newspaper stories about ravens damaging roof shingles, parked automobiles, and delicate airplane wings. He suggests that such behavior might be part of a survival mechanism that drives young ravens to explore and understand their world.

Ravens are in the Corvidae family with crows, jays, and magpies. A group of ravens is called an unkindness, which is a bit less harsh than a murder of crows. There are about ten species in the world called ravens, two of whom are found in North America. The Common Raven is about a third larger than the American Crow and has a differently shaped tail (wedge-shaped rather than rounded). The call of the Common Raven sounds like a combination of the caw of a crow with the rolling R sound in the German language. In Australia, there are three species of ravens and three species of crows, and the sizes overlap. The three Australian raven species all look alike and used to be considered one species until research revealed they were distinct populations of different species with different calls. The call of the most common of the three Australian raven species sounds like the laugh of the late Phyllis Diller.

The Common Raven in the United States is the same species found in England at the Tower of London. According to a legend, the tower will fall if the ravens ever leave. Kate Bush alludes to this legend in the title track of her 1978 album *Lionheart* with the line, "Our thumping hearts hold the Ravens in, and keep the tower from tumbling." To prevent the ravens now at the tower from leaving, their wings have been clipped. Someone with the title "Ravenmaster" (one of the Beefeaters) feeds these birds delicacies such as pig livers, sheep hearts, and blood-soaked biscuits. As job titles go, Ravenmaster rates almost as high as Keeper of the Castle.

Ravens have been prominent in literature on both sides of the Atlantic. Geoffrey Chaucer wrote about the "ravenes qualm" in *Troilus and Criseyde* during the 1380s, with a "qualm" being imitative of the cry of a raven. The raven is one of the most famous birds in American literature, thanks to Edgar Allan Poe's 1844 poem about his lost Lenore. Poe liked to get the attention of readers by writing about beautiful women (a ploy that is still popular), but Poe's beautiful women usually were dead. After only forty years of life, the alcoholic Poe joined his beautiful subjects, dying of delirium tremens in a Baltimore hospital in 1849. Baltimore named its professional football team in honor of Poe's Raven poem. In 2001, the Baltimore Ravens became the first team with a bird name to win the Super Bowl. They also are the first team having a player with a correctly spelled bird surname to score in the Super Bowl; in the 2013 game, tight end Dennis Pitta caught a touchdown pass.[21] Avian ravens in Maryland are most common in the mountainous habitat well to the west of the city, although they have been moving eastward and have been seen in the Baltimore area. In 2012, a friend of mine saw a raven within the city of Washington, DC, and I subsequently heard one a few miles from my home in Northern Virginia. There used to be a lot more ravens throughout North America, but their range declined

with the demise of American bison, whose carcasses were a major source of raven food.

A group called ASCAR—the American Society of Crows and Ravens—describes itself on its website as an "international disorganization . . . based on shared attitudes and appetites but markedly diverse interests—appreciative, scientific, aesthetic, literary and mythic—in crows, ravens and their significance both ecological and metaphoric." Ravens have played an important role in many cultures throughout human history. The raven is the first type of bird named in the Bible. In the eighth chapter of Genesis, Noah sent a dove to look for dry land. But right before, he "sent forth a raven, which went forth to and fro, until the waters were dried up from off the earth." According to Ernest Ingersoll's *Birds in Legend, Fable, and Folklore*, the Jews regard the

---

21. Pittas are songbirds found in Asia, Australia, Africa, and the Pacific Islands. They tend to be found on the forest floor. In previous Super Bowls, touchdowns had been scored by Lynn Swann of the Pittsburgh Steelers, but his bird namesake is spelled with only one N at the end rather than two.

raven as unclean because it eats carrion, while the Zoroastrians regard the raven as pure because it removes dead things from the Earth. Ingersoll said the supreme Norse god Odin had two ravens as his ministers. Some American Indian tribes have a raven as their chief god.

In previous eras, the Moors regarded ravens as creatures of Satan. Ravens also might have a link to certain acts in the United States that have been called satanic. Ravens consume carrion and especially like to eat the eyeballs of dead animals. Their taste for eyeballs might explain some of the "satanic ritual" stories based on farm animals found dead with their eyes plucked out.

71. ROADRUNNER
Birds in Cartoons

The United States Postal Service has a rule of not issuing commemorative stamps to honor any individual who is still living. The Postal Service has no similar rule about living birds. The roadrunner has the rare distinction of being honored both as an actual species and as a cartoon character. In 1982, a roadrunner appeared on a sheet of fifty 20-cent stamps that showed all the state birds and flowers—the Greater Roadrunner is the state bird of New Mexico. And in 2000, the cartoon Road Runner appeared on a 33-cent stamp as part of a series featuring Looney Tunes cartoon characters. On this stamp, the Road Runner is delivering a letter to Wile E. Coyote, who appears to have crashed to the ground near the mailbox with a rocket-pack on his back.

Greater Roadrunners are about two feet long. A slightly smaller species called the Lesser Roadrunner lives in Central America. Roadrunners do not run as quickly as the cartoon version. The actual pace of the Greater Roadrunner is about fifteen miles per hour, roughly the same as a world-class miler running a four-minute mile. It moves at a fast stiff-legged trot, but its legs are not capable of the rotary motion shown in the cartoons. Nonetheless, the roadrunner continues to be fast in the public's imagination, which is why IBM used the name of the bird for a $133 million supercomputer that it built at Los Alamos National Laboratory in New Mexico. During the 1970s, Plymouth sold a cheap muscle car called the Road Runner, using the cartoon bird in its marketing material. The horn of the car was the cartoon character's "beep-beep."

Roadrunners are closely related to a half-dozen other species of ground cuckoos found in the New World. Real roadrunners do not say "beep-beep." The song of the Greater Roadrunner is a series of *coo* sounds that more closely resemble a dove than a cuckoo clock. Their omnivorous diet includes such desert delectables as insects, scorpions, spiders (including tarantulas), snakes, and lizards. If a roadrunner catches a lizard that is too long to swallow all at once, it will allow the back part of the lizard to stick out of its bill and wait until the front part is slowly digested, making room for the rest to go down. Roadrunners also eat various types of fruit and are known to eat the eggs and nestlings of other bird species. When Greater Roadrunners are in their preferred hot desert habitat, they are capable of eliminating salt through glands near their eyes, similar to the way some seabirds do.

In the cartoons, the Road Runner never harms the coyote, but roadrunners in the wild can lay a pretty severe beating on critters they catch. I once was at the San Javier del Bac Mission in Tucson around noon on a 115-degree day. While I was standing beneath a canopy near one of the parking areas, I saw a roadrunner with a long lizard in its bill. For the next fifteen minutes, the bird repeatedly whacked the lizard against the ground, never letting go. After each series of whacks, the bird looked at the lifeless lizard, paused a moment, and began whacking again. The bird was trying to tenderize its lunch before swallowing it. The roadrunner did to that lizard what Wile E. Coyote dreamt of doing to the cartoon Road Runner.

72. ROBIN
Violent Birds

Except for the lonely and depressed poet Emily Dickinson, who "dreaded that first robin so," most people are fond of robins. Robins in the United States, Europe, and Australia seem friendly and nonthreatening. The name "robin" conjures up images of gentleness. The Winnie the Pooh stories would not have been as endearing with a character named Christopher Raven or Christopher Turkey.

But not all robins are gentle. In the 1930s, the British ornithologist David Lack performed experiments about the territoriality of the European Robin. He tested what would happen if he placed a stuffed robin in his backyard during nesting season. Most of the real robins savagely attacked the stuffed bird. One female attacked it so violently that she removed its head. After the head flew off, the female stopped for a moment but continued to attack the headless body as violently as before. Lack, being an observant and curious scientist, wondered how much of a stuffed robin had to be present to provoke a real robin to attack, so from the headless specimen he removed the tail. The birds attacked the tail-less specimen. Then Lack removed the wings. Many robins still attacked it. Finally, the whole of the body and back were removed, so all that remained were the red breast feathers and a few white feathers underneath. Half the robins still displayed at it with typical threat postures. Lack theorized that the violent robins literally were seeing red. He then put out a complete stuffed robin with its breast feathers covered with brown ink. The robins ignored the bird without the red breast, even though they had attacked a small clump of red feathers. Lack also reported that one male robin, when confronted with the original complete stuffed bird with the red breast, at first threatened it but then tried to mate with it. When his real mate returned, he ignored her.

The American Robin is widespread and well known. Most North Americans with little knowledge of birds can identify a robin. Its song is pleasant, sometimes translated as *cheerily, cheer-up, cheerio.* American Robins are associated with the coming of spring, although this might be inaccurate depending on where you live. In the Middle Atlantic states, a lot of robins stay throughout the winter, while others are migratory. In the United States, forests are being replaced by lawns, and robins can find food in either. They are not hesitant to look for worms and other food when humans are nearby. Robins like to sunbathe, but this has no connection with the Baskin-Robbins who sell ice cream.

The American Robin got its name from the European Robin, who also has a red breast but is only half the size. Both species used to be included in the thrush family, but more recent research suggests that the European Robin is more closely related to the Old World flycatchers. Australia has robins who are unrelated to the American and European ones. The Australian species are closer in size to the European robin, and some are strikingly beautiful. Among the colors of the breasts of Australian robins are yellow, scarlet, orange, rose, and pink.

The scientific name for the American Robin is *Turdus migratorius,* which does not mean migrating turd. *Turdus* is the Latin word for thrush. In Europe, the Song Thrush and Eurasian Blackbird also are in the *Turdus* genus, and the American Robin resembles them closely in size and behavior. The Pale-vented Thrush, a species found in Central and South America, has the scientific name *Turdus obsoletus.*

There was little mention of robins in ancient cultures, but they have since appeared a great deal in song and verse. Poets such as Geoffrey Chaucer, William Shakespeare, William Blake, Robert Burns, and William Wordsworth have written about robins. More than a quarter of the works in the *Penguin Book of Bird Poetry* feature robins. This collection has a lot of poems from the British oral tradition, including the poem "Who Killed Cock Robin?" that describes many types of birds and beasts playing various roles at a robin's funeral. The collection includes superstitious verses such as: "Kill a robin or a wren, never prosper, boy or man." Some verses involve weather forecasts, such as: "If the robin sings in the bush, Then the weather will be coarse, But if the robin sings on the barn, Then the weather will be warm." And some traditional verses have a turd motif, such as: "Little Robin Redbreast, Sitting on a pole, Niddle noddle went his head, And poop went his hole." Robins also have shown up in American popular song, such as when the "red, red robin comes bob, bob, bobbin' along."

The term "round robin" has nothing to do with the bird. It most likely is related to a process through which citizens petitioned their king or queen, or sailors petitioned their captain. Royalty and ship captains did not like to be petitioned with complaints, so people who initiated such actions often were singled out as the ringleaders and sometimes put to death. To prevent any signature from having to appear first on the document, the petitioners sometimes signed a "round ribbon" so that the names would appear in a circle.

73. SANDPIPER
Birds at the Beach

The birds most closely associated with the beach are gulls and sandpipers. As gulls lazily float through the air, sandpipers run to the wet area where a receding wave has just been and peck in the sand until the wave returns, driving them to higher ground. The speed with which sandpipers run during this game of chase can be comical. If you want to see what they are pecking at, go to an area from which a wave has just receded and dig your hand a few inches into the wet sand. You should see a bunch of small creatures within the clump.

Sandpipers sometimes are called shorebirds or waders, although the latter term also applies to other types of birds in wetlands.[22] Identifying sandpipers is a challenge, because a lot of them look alike, and they often are observed from a considerable distance in poor light. Many of them are whitish underneath and light-brown on the back, with their back color making them more difficult to see on the shore. To complicate the identification problem, most species show significant differences in plumage depending on the time of year and the age of the birds. Michael O'Brien (whose mother is one of my first cousins) is the co-author of an excellent field guide about how to tell them apart.

Many sandpipers are found in wetlands that are devoid of sand, and others prefer fields or other habitats not near a beach. Sandpipers are in the same family as birds called godwits, curlews, stints, phalaropes, knots, yellowlegs, tattlers, turnstones, dowitchers, and other names. The group is diverse in size and shape. Some small sandpipers are about the size of a sparrow, while a large species such as the Long-billed Curlew has a down-curved bill that is longer than the body of some small sandpipers. Godwits are similarly tall large shorebirds, but

---

22. When I was emceeing a bird club dinner, I referred to a female birding friend who likes shorebirds as "the lady in wading."

their long bill curves slightly upward. A friend suggested that the noun of assemblage for these birds should be a "pantheon of godwits."

There are three species of phalaropes. Two of them sometimes venture far from land, sitting in the sea and spinning quickly to create a whirlpool to suck prey up to the surface. Phalaropes engage in the unusual reproductive system of polyandry, in which a female mates with more than one male. After the female lays eggs, the male broods the eggs and raises the young.

Knots are pudgy sandpipers with short legs. Red Knots, some of whom migrate round-trip each year between southern South America and breeding grounds in the northern tundra, have become the center of a major environmental controversy. Knots and other wading birds time their northward migration to coincide with when horseshoe crabs typically lay huge numbers of eggs in coastal areas from New Jersey to Virginia. The birds need to fatten up on the crab eggs to have sufficient energy to fly to the tundra. I have seen before-and-after photos of a migrating knot at its feeding area. The arriving bird looked emaciated after its long journey from South America, but after feeding on the crab eggs, the same knot looked as if it had been blown up with a bicycle pump, having doubled its weight for the remainder of the journey north. To prepare for the long journey, the knots develop larger flight muscles while shrinking their digestive systems, which means that during the migration they cannot digest the snails, clams, and other invertebrates that comprise their typical diet. But they still can digest smaller items such as the crab eggs, which is why the presence of large quantities of these eggs is essential for the survival of the Red Knots.

In recent years, people have harvested the crabs for fertilizer and pig feed. The crabs also are collected for bait to catch eels and conches. The medical profession uses the blood of the crabs to test the purity of certain types of medicines, and the shell has medical uses for promoting blood clotting. The overharvesting of the crabs has reduced the number of eggs available, thereby destroying essential feeding grounds where knots and other shorebirds stop during their long migration. In places where thousands of knots used to converge during migration, there now might be only a few dozen. Such destruction of migratory feeding areas for birds is not unique. Along the California coast, many salt marshes have been drained and developed. For migratory birds who rely on salt marshes, this is equivalent to having a long highway for automobiles with nowhere to refuel.

The current travails of the Red Knot are not the first to afflict this species. They formerly were called Robin Sandpipers (because of their red breasts) and were hunted in large numbers. The ornithologist Arthur Cleveland Bent quotes an 1893 account by George Mackay of a strange manner in which knots were hunted in Massachusetts: "The mode of procedure was for two men to start out after dark at half tide, one of them to carry a lighted lantern, the other to reach and seize the birds, bite their necks, and put them in a bag slung over the shoulder. When near a flock they would approach them on their hands and knees, the birds being almost invariably taken on the flats. This practice continued several years before it was prohibited by law."

Many shorebird species experienced dramatic declines during the twentieth century because of overhunting. Large long-legged shorebirds called Willets were hunted in such great numbers that they were

almost wiped out along the northeast coast of North America. They have made a comeback in some of these areas. The Eskimo Curlew has not been as lucky. The huge population of this species became a target after market hunters had wiped out the Passenger Pigeon. The Eskimo Curlew is now probably extinct.

If you travel to Africa, Asia, or Australia, most of the native song-birds will be different from the ones seen in North America, but you might see some of the same species of shorebirds. Shorebirds tend to migrate great distances, and a lot of them are found on many con-tinents. These distances were an inspiration for the naturalist Peter Matthiessen, who wrote a lyrical book in 1967 called *The Wind Birds* about the shorebirds seen in North America. Matthiessen says, "The restlessness of shorebirds, their kinship with distance and swift sea-sons, the wistful signal of their voices down the long coastlines of the world make them, for me, the most affecting of wild creatures." The distances they sometimes travel are almost inconceivable. In 2010, the biologist Robert Gill discovered that Bar-tailed Godwits with radio transmitters migrated more than 7,000 miles nonstop across the Pacific. Like the Red Knots, they accumulate a considerable amount of fat before starting and then slowly deplete it while flying at a steady speed of about forty miles per hour. Other species of shorebirds have similarly improbable migrations.

Two of my favorite shorebird species are world travelers, and I have seen them in both Australia and North America. The Ruddy Turnstone is a brightly patterned bird who is about the size of an American Robin. My former next-door neighbor, who awakened my interest in birds when I was young, jokingly called them "rusty turnstiles." Michael O'Brien's father Paul, who is an accomplished birder in his own right, calls them "bloody tombstones." An article in the *Wader Study Group Bulletin* said that in 2009, some radio-tracked Ruddy Turnstones were found to have migrated nonstop from Australia to Taiwan, which is about 4,700 miles.

My other favorite shorebird is a small sandpiper called the Sanderling. In nonbreeding plumage, which is how I typically see them, they are whiter than most sandpipers and easy to identify. They are found in coastal areas throughout the world. When I lived for a winter in Ocean City, Maryland, Sanderlings were the most common shorebirds. They are not particularly bothered by people. They seem engrossed with staying just ahead of incoming waves and probing for food in the wet sand. I have spent many enjoyable hours watching them.

74. SHEARWATER
Dreams about Flying Like a Bird

Most birds use their forelimbs for flight, while humans use theirs for manipulating objects. But people have long dreamt about having wings and being able to fly like birds. The ancient Greek myth about Icarus features a lad who flew away from Crete with wings that his dad Daedalus had made out of feathers and wax (and in the process defied the laws of physics). Icarus did not heed his father's warnings not to fly too close to the sun. When the hubristic Icarus soared too high, the wax melted, the feathers fell off, and he plummeted to earth.

Occasionally, I dream at night about being able to fly. My flight dreams, which do not end so violently, feature no wax and no flapping of my arms/wings. Instead, they resemble the gliding of seabirds called shearwaters. Shearwaters use their long wings to glide low over water with their body at an angle. At times, one of their wingtips appears to cut through the waves, which is the basis for the bird's name. Birds who spend a lot of time in the air try to conserve energy by riding wind currents so they can glide without flapping. The gliding of shearwaters is more akin to windsurfing than direct flight. On some boat trips into the ocean, you might see a great many windsurfing shearwaters, which is an arresting spectacle.

There are more than two dozen shearwater species, ranging from ten to twenty-one inches. About ten of the species can be seen off the coast of North America. Shearwaters are in the same family as fulmars, prions, and petrels, but not storm-petrels. They spend most of their lives away from land, and in a way, they breathe both air and water. The salt content of seawater is too high for them to drink without filtering, so they have special glands in their head to filter the salt and excrete it through a tube on top of their bill. Some seabirds drink only saltwater, while others drink fresh water if it is available. Seabirds are one of the groups of birds who have an especially well-developed sense of smell, which helps them to find food. It also can help them to locate their own burrow amid thousands of adjacent ones if they live in a large colony.

In 1995, Graham Pizzey took me to a coastal area in Australia to see a colony of Short-tailed Shearwaters. We arrived shortly before dusk so we could watch thousands of the shearwaters returning from a day at sea to roost for the evening in their burrows in the grass by the dunes. If you stand on the designated path, the shearwaters whiz past your ears on the way to their burrows. Their nickname is muttonbird, because sailors and other people used to hunt and eat them; other species of seabirds share this nickname for the same reason.

A species called the Manx Shearwater (named after the Isle of Man between Great Britain and Ireland) has shown remarkable homing abilities. A 1953 issue of *The Auk* (the journal of the American Ornithologists' Union) talked about an experiment done before World War II involving a pair of Manx Shearwaters who were taken from a colony on the Welsh coast and flown in a plane to Venice, Italy. The species does not normally occur in or visit the area around Venice. In two weeks, the shearwaters were back in their colony in Wales. Then in 1952, two more Manx Shearwaters were put into a box and flown from Wales to Boston. In twelve days, the birds were back in the colony, and they had beaten the trans-Atlantic letter sent by Rosario Mazzeo (who had taken them to Boston) to say that they had safely arrived and had been set loose.

There are two species of fulmars, with one found in northern oceans and the other in southern oceans. If you have seen toy balsa wood airplanes with wings that can be moved forward and back, a fulmar looks like a gull whose wings have been moved into the back position. A fulmar's bill has a salt-filtering tube, which gulls lack. The name "fulmar" comes from two Norse words meaning "foul gull," which might come from their habit of projectile vomiting onto any creature they regard as an intruder. The material that they spew is not food, but a stinking oily substance used specifically for such situations. Northern Fulmars prefer to eat the remains of dead fish rather than catching live fish, so their numbers have increased with the spread of huge fishing ships that clean fish and throw the remains overboard.

Prions are found mostly in the oceans of the Southern Hemisphere. There are six species, and all look pretty much alike. From a distance, they resemble small gulls with gray backs and a black M stretching from wingtip to wingtip. Their name comes from a Greek word meaning "saw," because their bill has serrations and looks like a little saw. The bill is adapted for eating krill, and large flocks of prions congregate where krill is plentiful. Because they eat the same food as whales, one of their nicknames is whalebird. Whalers realize that if they see a flock of feeding prions, whales might be nearby.

I never dream about eating krill or other favorite foods of seabirds. I only dream about being able to fly like a seabird. Considering how relatively few times I have been at sea to watch the flight of these birds, I do not know why their method of flight has become so deeply implanted in my thoughts and dreams. Nonetheless, my puzzlement about why I dream about flying like a shearwater is not going to keep me up at night.

75. SKUA
Bully Birds

Imagine a big, dark, barrel-chested, thug-like gull, and you'll have a good mental picture of a skua. Because skuas are hefty, powerful flyers, they are capable of bullying other birds. They are one of the few types of birds who steal food caught by other birds. Unlike Bald Eagles, who try to force Ospreys to drop fish, skuas fly up to weaker birds such as gulls and terns and force them to disgorge food.

Some species of skuas are called jaegers, which comes from the German word for hunter. There are seven species called skuas or jaegers—the Europeans call them all skuas. They are spread widely over the oceans of the world, but they tend to breed in far northern and far southern latitudes. Their feet are unusual, being webbed as well as having claws. To see skuas, you usually have to visit their nesting areas or take a boat trip into the ocean. Any visitor to their nesting area should be advised that they will attack intruders, sometimes with a force capable of injuring a human. Skuas sometimes fly close to shore, especially when there is a storm. Their name comes from their call. In Britain, the Great Skua is called a Bonxie.

Roger Tory Peterson has described the workings of the skua "protection racket" in his book *Penguins*. Peterson says that skuas hang around penguin colonies to feed on eggs, chicks, and sometimes adult birds. He notes that because skuas are territorial, one pair will patrol an area occupied by about ten thousand penguins. While the skua pair might eat a healthy share of birds and eggs, they prevent the devastation of the colony by driving other skuas away. This system, while brutal, seems to work well for both the skuas and the penguins. Skuas also routinely predate the colonies of other types of seabirds. They become brutal at an early age. A leading cause of death in skua colonies is an older chick pecking and killing a younger nest mate.

Skua

Nonetheless, sometimes skuas get their comeuppance. In 2001, Philip Coetzee found a Subantarctic Skua on a beach in South Africa. The skua appeared to be sick and had a wormlike protuberance coming out of its breast. Coetzee decided to take the bird to an animal rescue center. The skua died shortly after arriving at the center, and it was then taken to Pretoria for examination by a parasitologist. A week later, the parasitologist called Coetzee and said that the creature sticking out of the skua's breast was not a parasite, but rather some type of squid, octopus, or cuttlefish. It had been alive when the skua swallowed it and was trying to eat its way to freedom.

On his 1982 album *Zombie Birdhouse*, the singer Iggy Pop included a song called "Eat or Be Eaten." The incident with the South African skua was an example of eat *and* be eaten.

76. SKYLARK
Bubbly Birds

What John Keats did to immortalize the plain brown nightingale in verse, his friend Percy Bysshe Shelley did to immortalize another small brown bird called the skylark. And just as Keats wrote "Ode to a Nightingale" two years before dying at a young age, Shelley wrote his poem "To a Skylark" in 1820, two years before drowning at age thirty. Shelley began the poem with the famous lines that inspired the title of Noel Coward's 1941 play *Blithe Spirit*:

> Hail to thee, blithe spirit!
> Bird thou never wert,
> That from heaven, or near it,
> Pourest thy full heart
> In profuse strains of unpremeditated art.

The poem goes on for a hundred more lines, including:

> Teach us, Sprite or Bird,
> What sweet thoughts are thine;
> I have never heard
> Praise of love or wine
> That panted forth a flood of rapture so divine.

Why did Shelley become so enraptured with the lighthearted spirit of the skylark? And why did William Wordsworth, Christina Rossetti, and many other poets write so many verses about this seven-inch brown bird who looks like a sparrow? If you are ever around Eurasian Skylarks in the spring, you might understand. Their song is a seemingly unending series of trills and bubbly sounds. It is not so much beautiful as amazingly exuberant and full of energy. The song can carry a great distance, because it often is delivered while the bird is doing a display flight. Skylarks fly high and seem to stall in the air. This behavior, which will attract the attention of anyone nearby, explains why a group of larks is called an exaltation. North America has larks and similar-looking birds called pipits who engage in exuberant courtship flights, but they have not captured the imaginations of American poets as the skylark has inspired British poets.

In addition to being exuberant, the songs of the skylark are extremely complex. They are composed of different consecutive sounds that are analogous to the syllables in human speech. According to a study done in 2009 at Queen Mary, University of London, Eurasian Skylarks can sing three hundred different syllables, and the birds develop distinct dialects in the areas in which they live. The study found that skylarks can use their knowledge of these local dialects to tell the difference between intruders and friendly neighbors. Other species of songbirds seem to share this ability to differentiate songs.

Not everyone enjoys the singing of larks. A species in Africa from the same family as the Eurasian Skylark is named the Monotonous Lark. And the French, who tend to relate to birds more often in a culinary rather than an ornithological context, have immortalized the skylark as a creature to be plucked. The French word for a skylark is *alouette*, and French children, as well as children in the United States and other countries, happily sing a song called "Alouette" in which they verse-by-verse pluck the kind skylark's head, beak, neck, back, wings, feet, and tail. In between each plucking verse, the children are supposed to sing a long *oh-oh-oh-oh*. Had I understood the lyrics I was asked to sing in kindergarten, I never would have joined in. In Montreal, the name of the Canadian Football League franchise is the Alouettes. And in 1962, Canada built and launched a satellite called Alouette—the first satellite put into space by a country other than the United States or the Soviet Union.

The Eurasian Skylark is not native to North America, but a small introduced colony lives in British Columbia. Skylarks are common in parts of Australia, where they were introduced in the 1850s by homesick

British settlers. In Britain, the skylark population has declined significantly, primarily because of changes in agricultural practices. Farmers used to plant cereal crops in the spring and harvest them in the fall. Now, farmers are planting winter wheat crops in the fall and harvesting them the following summer, which creates fields that lack the space for the skylarks to move through when seeking insects during their summer breeding season. The Royal Society for the Protection of Birds is working with farmers to create "skylark plots," which are unseeded areas of up to thirty feet in their fields. These plots help other bird species as well as skylarks.

Percy Bysshe Shelley has a lesser-known connection to the bird world than his skylark poem. Two of his nephews have had bird species named after them. Sir Edward Shelley (1827–1890) is commemorated with Shelley's Francolin, a partridge-like species native to Africa. And Captain George Ernest Shelley (1840–1910) was an ornithologist whose name appears in the common and scientific names of numerous birds.

77. SNIPE
Birds and Practical Jokes

Practical jokers sometimes send their victims on a snipe hunt, asking them to find something that is either nonexistent or very difficult to locate. A snipe hunt is different from a wild goose chase, because the elusive goose is usually chased at breakneck speed, whereas the concealed or nonexistent snipe is usually sought at a less frantic pace.

Snipes are in the same family as sandpipers and are usually found near water. Snipes have long legs, a long bill, and feathers that provide effective camouflage. You might see a snipe through your binoculars and, when you look more closely, realize that there are numerous more you hadn't noticed near the same spot. Other times, you might see where one lands and wonder how it could totally escape detection when you try to find it with your binoculars. Snipes engage in an elaborate courtship flight called winnowing, which in an avian context means to follow a course while flapping one's wings. During the winnowing, snipes fly high in the air and make noises from the wind moving through their tail feathers. Some of the noises sound like troubled laughter.

There are about two dozen species of snipes in the world. There are unrelated birds called seedsnipes and painted-snipes. The only snipe in the United States is called the Wilson's Snipe, who formerly was thought to be the same species as the Common Snipe found on many other continents. In my first Peterson field guide, printed in 1960, the species was called the Wilson's Snipe. Then it was changed to Common Snipe, and now it is back to Wilson's Snipe. Such flip-flops sometimes occur in the bird world. In recent decades, the Green Heron was renamed the Green-backed Heron before being switched back to Green Heron.

Snipes used to be widely hunted in North America, which caused their numbers to seriously decline. They create a challenge for hunters because of their camouflage and erratic flight. Assassins such as Lee

Harvey Oswald are called snipers, because the firing of a rifle from a concealed vantage point is similar to a technique used for hunting snipes. The metaphor has been expanded to include verbal attacks from a distant position.

The name "snipe" probably comes from the snipping motion the bird makes with its bill when feeding. Snipe is a word for a contemptible person; this meaning stays alive with "guttersnipe," which describes an indigent person in the gutter. Snipe also is slang for a cigarette or cigar stub. In the 1800s, snipe was a slang term for a lawyer, especially one who presented a large bill. The large bill itself also was called a snipe, as a pun on the snipe's large bill.

78. SPARROW
Bird Wars

An ugly episode of bird slaughter occurred in China in the 1950s. The Maoist regime declared that Eurasian Tree Sparrows were enemies of the state because they eat grain, and a campaign was initiated to exterminate them. The campaign lasted only a few days and featured millions of people parading through the countryside, beating pans and taking other measures to scare the birds. People also killed the birds by various means, including poison. Unfortunately, many of the people were not selective about the species they killed, and huge numbers of birds other than sparrows perished. A plague of locusts and grasshoppers occurred soon thereafter, because fewer birds were around to eat the insects. Tens of millions of people are thought to have died of starvation from the resulting famine.

Sparrows also have aroused intense passions in the United States. In the early 1850s, House Sparrows, who are close relatives of Eurasian Tree Sparrows, were first taken to North America from England, which is why they sometimes are called English Sparrows. Over the next few decades, they were released in many parts of the continent. By the 1870s, a heated debate—called the sparrow war—developed about the environmental effects of the newly arrived birds. Prominent scientists on both sides of the issue verbally attacked each other. The sparrows paid no attention. By the early 1900s, House Sparrows had become one of the most common species in the United States. In a 1909 book about the birds of Washington, DC, Mrs. L.W. Maynard gave the following advice for dealing with House Sparrows: "Nests should be watched for and destroyed—an iron hook at the end of a long pole is useful in tearing them out. However numerous these Sparrows have become anywhere, they may be driven away by persistent shooting and destroying nests."

In looking at the history of the effects of humans on the environment, two factors have had the greatest negative impact: habitat destruction and the introduction of non-native species. In case after case, especially in closed systems such as islands, the introduction of exotic species has had a devastating effect, even when not accompanied by the destruction of the physical landscape. In the sparrow war debate, those opposing the introduction have proven to be justified. House Sparrows have dramatically and irrevocably changed native North American bird populations for the worse. Ironically, the populations of House Sparrows introduced into North America and many other parts of the world are faring substantially better than the native sparrow populations in Europe.

When people settle on a new continent, they often long for what they left behind. In some instances, they felt more comfortable by calling their new home by the name of their old home—with or without the word "new" in front. But they sometimes went a step further and relocated plants and animals from their old home to their new one. History is full of examples of this disastrous activity, known as acclimatization. The acclimatization movement was not limited to settlers bringing plants and animals with them when they arrived. In the 1800s, both France and England had active acclimatization societies who wanted to introduce "useful" foreign species into their respective countries. The Australian ornithologist Graham Pizzey believed that New Zealand and Australia have suffered more natural disasters from the unforeseen results of acclimatization than anywhere on Earth. Our planet now is on the verge of taking the introduction of invasive species to a new level, with scientists in laboratories creating life forms that have never previously existed. The outcome of introducing these genetically engineered life forms into the natural environment is inevitable; the only question is how long before the disaster occurs.

People who play the tile game called mahjong, which originated in China, have a connection with sparrows. The word "mahjong" comes from the Chinese word for sparrow, because the sound of the tiles was thought to resemble the sound of sparrows. Many people, especially in cities, see few types of songbirds other than House Sparrows, in part because the aggressive, adaptable House Sparrows have driven native species away. The French singer Edith Piaf was nicknamed Kid Sparrow, because she was physically small and sang a song about a sparrow. If you are interested in bird behavior, House Sparrows are an easy species to study, because there are so many of them. Despite all the controversy about House Sparrows, a lot of people like them.

In North America, there is a group of native finches called sparrows who are in a different family than the House Sparrow and Eurasian Tree Sparrow. There are dozens of species of these little brown birds in the United States. Closely related are birds called juncos, longspurs, and towhees. The plumage of North American sparrow species generally lacks bright colors, but some of the patterning of the feathers is lovely when observed at close range. At a distance, the subtlety of the patterns is lost. Many of the species hang out in brushy fields, but they also live in forests, wetlands, and other habitats. They can be difficult to see, because many skulk. Some birders take special trips in June to places such as North Dakota to seek uncommon grassland species of nesting sparrows.

Some of the North American sparrows are talented singers. The Song Sparrow, who is easier to see than most of the other species, likes to sit on open perches and sing the complicated and variable song that is the basis for its name. One of the best-known bird songs in parts of North America is from the White-throated Sparrow, a pretty bird whose male in breeding plumage has a black-and-white-striped crown with a bright-yellow spot near the eye. The song in the United States is thought to sound like *Old Sam Peabody Peabody Peabody*, while in Canada it is represented as *Oh Sweet Canada Canada Canada*. The Grasshopper Sparrow gets its name from its high-pitched insect-like trill. Birders who have lost the ability to hear high-pitched sounds usually cannot hear Grasshopper Sparrows. This is a common affliction as birders get older.

For some reason, many sparrows from Europe and Asia have a penchant for upsetting people. In 2005, a television company in the Netherlands was trying to set a world record for falling dominoes by setting up more than four million. A sparrow entered the building where the dominoes were being set up and knocked over 23,000 of them. The television company created an international uproar by having an exterminator kill the sparrow with an air rifle before more dominoes toppled.

79. SPOONBILL
Charismatic Birds

Some environmentalists use the term "charismatic megafauna" to describe large, popular animals who become symbols for conservation campaigns. The public is more likely to be interested in saving Grizzly Bears and Bald Eagles than endangered small rodents or tiny fish. One of the more charismatic large birds in North America is the Roseate Spoonbill. It is a heron-sized bird with long legs, bright-pink feathers, and a large spoon-shaped bill. It feeds by walking in shallow water with its head down, swinging its bill back and forth. In the United States, it can be found in south Florida and along the Gulf Coast.

In the first half of the twentieth century, Roseate Spoonbills became seriously endangered. Plume hunters killed the spoonbills in large numbers to make pretty pink fans for ladies. Roseate Spoonbills breed in rookeries, so finding a rookery meant that hunters had access to large numbers of birds in the same place. Once the plumes were plucked, their color faded relatively quickly, but that did not deter either the killers of the birds or the buyers of the feathers. Roseate Spoonbills have made somewhat of a comeback, but they still are not plentiful.

There are a half-dozen spoonbill species in the world, and they are in the same family as ibises. The spoonbills in other parts of the world are white and do not have the pink feathers of the species seen in North America. In Australia, you can see the Royal Spoonbill and Yellow-billed Spoonbill. These species can be told apart by bill color— the Royal's is black. Spoonbills often feed nocturnally, which they can do because they seek prey in shallow water primarily by touch rather than sight. The bill shape is the basis for the Spanish name for the bird, *espatula*, and the Italian name, *spatola*.

There are species in other families who have spatulate bills. The Spoon-billed Sandpiper is found mostly in Asia; this species is critically endangered, and there might be only about five hundred left in the wild. A common duck in most of the Northern Hemisphere is the Northern Shoveler. It has a relative in Australia and New Zealand called the Australasian Shoveler. Also, the Pink-eared Duck of Australia has a spatulate bill.

The Pink-eared Duck has only a little spot of pink next to the ear that can be difficult to see in the field. Pink is not a common color for birds. Other than the Roseate Spoonbill, there are no other bright-pink birds in North America, although a couple of water birds have a pink tinge. A lovely species from South Asia called the Pink-headed Duck is probably extinct, having declined because of overhunting and habitat loss. In Australia, there are a couple of pink parrots—the Galah and Major Mitchell's Cockatoo—and a couple of robin species with pink breasts. The Pink-headed Warbler is found in Central America. And of course the most famous pink birds are the ones who gave their name to the popular 1972 John Waters gross-out movie—*Pink Flamingos*.

80. STARLING
Birds and the Bard

In Shakespeare's *Henry IV, Part 1*, Hotspur says, "I'll have a starling shall be taught to speak nothing but 'Mortimer,' and give it him to keep his anger still in motion." Someone named Eugene Schieffelin wanted all the birds mentioned in Shakespeare to be introduced to the United States, so in 1890, he took a cage of European Starlings into New York City's Central Park and set them free. From this cage with about sixty birds (and another sixty the following year) came the hundreds of millions of starlings who plague the United States today. European Starlings have been introduced into many countries, where they have become a serious nuisance.

Problems also have developed throughout the world from the introduction of Common Mynas, who are in the same family as starlings. In my youth, I learned about mynas as cage birds who could talk. The Common Myna is sometimes called the Indian Myna, because its origins are traced to India. It was introduced into Australia, New Zealand, Hawaii, and many other places because it eats a lot of insects. But wherever it has been introduced, it has aggressively competed with native birds, resulting in a decrease in the diversity of birdlife. The Common Myna is larger than the European Starling, and in areas where both have been introduced, the mynas typically dominate.

There are about 120 species of starlings and mynas in the world. Many starling species, especially in Africa, are quite beautiful, with iridescent and/or colorful plumage. When left in their native habitats, starlings are not considered pests. The European Starling, who has caused major problems for North American bird species, does not cause similar problems in Britain. In fact, the number of starlings in Britain has declined in recent years. One reason for the success of European Starlings in the United States is that they are able to discover food in a space by shoving in their bill and opening it with considerable

277

force. Other starling species and members of the American blackbird family also have strong bill-opening muscles.

The European Starling might have gotten its name from the little white star-like spots on its nonbreeding plumage—if not a thousand points of light, certainly a great many. A common starling vocalization sounds like a wolf whistle. When these birds make such whistles at urban street corners, they sound like bullies harassing female passers-by. When huge flocks of starlings congregate, they chatter loudly, which is why a group of starlings is called a murmuration.

Indiana University psychology professor Meredith West gave a lecture at the National Zoo in Washington about the vocal abilities of starlings. European Starlings have the ability to mimic. West had given pet starlings to a number of families and asked people to keep journals of their experiences with the birds. One family had an infant child, and the starling learned to mimic a crying baby after realizing the parents would come when they heard that sound. In another household, a starling mimicked a ringing telephone for the same reason. West said starlings in captivity will eat almost anything and are especially fond of tofu. She added that you should never feed them mealworms; to a captive starling, mealworms are like cocaine, and once such a delicacy is offered, the starling will not want to eat anything else.

One of the most distressing aspects of birds such as European Starlings, Common Mynas, House Sparrows, and Rock Pigeons is the dreary uniformity they bring to the birdlife of cities and suburbs all over the world. You can visit metropolitan areas in virtually any corner of the globe and see the same cast of non-native characters, and sometimes only these non-native birds. The situation is similar to what is happening in the business world, where the same restaurant chains and convenience stores have sprung up in every city, driving out local and more diverse establishments.

In addition to my interest in birds, I am fond of wordplay and anagrams. My favorite bird anagram is for the European Starling. If you rearrange the letters, you can spell "ignorant pleasure."

81. STORK
Birds and Babies

According to DNA analysis, storks may be related to vultures, which means that this group of birds could be connected with both ends of the human life cycle. Vultures dispose of the dead, while storks have been linked to the delivery of babies. The connection between storks and babies comes from Europe. Throughout the continent, huge stork nests are a common sight on top of churches, houses, and other buildings. When small children ask where babies come from, cowardly parents point to a stork nest and say, "The stork brings them." As the human population has increased during the twentieth century, the stork population has declined, but the baby legend remains.

The roughly twenty stork species are among the largest birds in the world. The Marabou Stork has one of the longest wingspans, at twelve feet. Storks walk stiffly, and this "starched" appearance could be the origin of their name. Some stork species are like vultures in that they eat carrion and have bald heads. Storks sometimes soar very high like vultures and have been seen over the Himalayas at around twenty thousand feet.

The Wood Stork is the only stork species who lives in the United States, with the greatest number in Florida. It is also found in Central and South America. It is a large white bird with a large bill and a dark bald head, but it is not a carrion eater. Wood Storks are endangered in the United States, mostly because of habitat loss. They feed in wetlands, seeking water that is six to twenty inches deep. Wetland areas that dry out or become flooded are not acceptable to them, and rising water levels caused by global warming could destroy much of their preferred feeding habitat. The Wood Stork sometimes is called the Wood Ibis, even though it is not related to the ibises.

In Central and South America, one can see a gorgeous stork called the Jabiru, who is almost a third larger than the Wood Stork—fifty-two inches versus forty inches. The Jabiru's body is snow white, and unlike the wings of a Wood Stork, which have a thick black edge, no black can be seen on the adult Jabiru's wings during its slow, stately flight. The Jabiru's head is black, as is its bill, which is huge and curved underneath. A band of feathers across the throat looks like a beautiful crimson turtleneck.

Some stork species nest in large colonies. Outside Bangkok, I visited a temple that had a colony of twenty thousand Asian Openbills. These storks are mostly black and white, although some appear gray or brown. When the birds are in profile with their bill closed, you can see a small bit of light shining through, which is the reason for their name. These storks live in the colony only during the dry season and leave as soon as the rainy season begins. Sometimes, the Openbills soar like vultures in large kettles. (A kettle is a group of soaring birds).

The Black-necked Stork is the only stork species in Australia. The dark feathered head of the adult in bright sunlight looks iridescent green. The female has golden eyes, and the male has dark eyes. I once watched a male who caught a large fish and took it to a patch of grass. This species lacks the ability to rip apart prey and must swallow fish whole. A stork with a large fish does not want to risk dropping it into the water and losing it while trying to flip it into the proper position to swallow, which is why he was flipping his fish over dry land.

Black-necked Storks make huge nests of big sticks, typically at the top of a bare tree. The Australian naturalist John Young has captured wonderful footage at Black-necked Stork nests for two of his videos. In *The Lure of the Daintree*, he shows the elaborate "changing of the guard" ritual that the male and female initiate when one arrives at the nest to relieve the other of incubation duties. The two mates rattle their bills and touch them together before the newly arrived bird assumes a position over the eggs and the other flies off to feed. In *Birds of North Tropical Queensland*, there is footage of storks regurgitating water over their eggs. In the hot climate where the birds live, the water makes the nest steamy and wet, which helps in incubation.

While storks have become symbols for human reproduction, they would not be good symbols for marital closeness. The Israeli ornithologist Yossi Leshem was in charge of a project in which radio transmitters were used to track the migratory routes of birds. Two of the birds fitted with transmitters were a pair of storks who for many years raised their young at the same nest in a village in Germany. The transmitters revealed that when the nesting season was over, the two storks did not spend the winter together: the female flew to South Africa, while the male flew to Spain. Avoiding marital conflict is easy when you are more than five thousand miles apart.

82. STORM-PETREL
Out-of-place Birds

And now, brothers and sisters, today's Bible reading will come from the gospel according to St. Matthew, chapter 14, verses 27 to 29: "But straightaway Jesus spake unto them, saying Be of good cheer; it is I; be not afraid. And Peter answered him and said, Lord, if it be thou, bid me come unto thee on the water. And he said, Come. And when Peter was come down out of the ship, he walked on the water, to go to Jesus."

This Bible passage is the likely basis of the "petrel" part of the name of small seabirds called storm-petrels. They hover just above the surface of the water, pattering their feet in a way that makes them appear to be walking on water as Peter did. The "storm" part is based on a belief by sailors that the birds were an omen for impending bad weather. Storm-petrels often follow boats, regardless of the weather, hoping to get a free meal from waste thrown overboard (such as from the innards of gutted fish). Sailors sometimes call storm-petrels "Mother Carey's chickens," which also has a religious origin. "Mother Carey" is a corruption of the Latin phrase *Mater cara*, a term for the Virgin Mary that means "beloved mother." There are many religious superstitions about these birds, including that they might represent the souls of lost sailors.

There are about two dozen species of storm-petrels in the world. Other seabirds called petrels are not in the same family and usually are considerably larger. Storm-petrels range in size from six to ten inches. Some have bodies the size of a sparrow, but their wingspan can be twice as long. They often flutter in flight as they hunt for tiny sea creatures near the surface of the water. A possible reason for their foot pattering is to stir up prey in the water. Their long legs are not effective for walking on land during the nesting season. Most of them nest underground, which protects them from larger seabirds but not from other creatures who either can get inside the burrows or cause the burrows to collapse.

Storm-Petrel

My most unusual storm-petrel sighting occurred in 2003 within walking distance of my home near the Potomac River in Northern Virginia. I had set aside a tentative date to go birding with a friend, but the week we were supposed to go, Hurricane Isabel was forecast to hit the Washington area. I called my friend and jokingly asked if she wanted to come out and look for storm-petrels after the storm passed through. Isabel hit the Washington area with considerable force and caused major transportation disruptions. The morning after the storm, I picked up my binoculars and walked along a path by the river to see the damage. Some sections of the path were underwater or obstructed by downed trees. Along many stretches, both above and below the path, there was a neat line of plastic bottles, condoms, and brown sludge to mark where the high water line had been. Many road signs and mile markers were knocked down, broken, or tilted.

Across the river from some of Washington's most recognizable monuments, a CNN camera crew was taping Wolf Blitzer talking about the hurricane and Kobe Bryant's rape trial. Near the CNN crew was a birder looking through a telescope. He told me he had seen a lot of birds earlier that morning, including Wilson's Storm-petrels. He had seen one pattering on the river's surface and suggested it might be near the 14th Street Bridge, which was a couple hundred yards downriver. This bridge made national news in 1983 when an Air Florida plane that had not been properly de-iced crashed into it shortly after taking off from nearby National Airport during a snowstorm.

Before Hurricane Isabel, the Wilson's Storm-petrel was not on the list of birds ever seen in the District of Columbia. Wilson's Storm-petrels might have one of the largest populations of any bird species in the world, but because they spend most of their time at sea, relatively few people see them. The closest place for someone from Washington to see any species of storm-petrel usually is hundreds of miles away. You must drive about two hundred miles to Ocean City, Maryland, and then take a boat trip fifty to a hundred miles into an area of the Atlantic where the Gulf Stream passes. You can take a longer drive to southern Virginia or North Carolina, which shortens the boat trip to the Gulf Stream. The likelihood of the combination of factors that would cause this species to be a couple hundred miles inland in Washington are so remote as to not be worth considering, unless there is a certain type of severe storm. Hurricanes such as Isabel that come inland and pass west of an area tend to pull in ocean birds who were trapped within the storm when it formed at sea, while storms that move north along the coast tend to push the birds out to sea.

Around 11 a.m., I saw a storm-petrel swimming near the 14th Street Bridge, a few hundred yards from the Virginia shore. I could not see it with my naked eye and could view it only intermittently through my 10-power binoculars because of its small size (about seven inches) and the choppiness of the water. The bird had a peculiar profile; both the head and tail stuck up, with the body sagging in the middle. I later saw the bird's swallow-like flight near the opposite shore of the river. I also saw it land with its feet down, but it did not patter along the surface. I did not get a close enough look to identify the bird's species; some storm-petrel species look alike and are difficult to tell apart. However, seeing any species of storm-petrel in Washington was exciting enough.

Later that day, I called my friend and told her what I had seen. I also told her that the next time a major hurricane is forecast, I would not make any more dumb jokes about seeing storm-petrels—I would make jokes about seeing albatrosses.

83. SWALLOW
Birds as Seasonal Harbingers

I sometimes wear a small swallow pin that I purchased at the mission at San Juan Capistrano in Southern California. The town has an annual Festival of the Swallows to celebrate the return of Cliff Swallows from their wintering grounds. Most of them used to appear each year around March 19, but now, few of the birds return to nest at the mission, preferring other nearby locations. Where I live in Virginia, swallows rather than robins are the harbingers of spring. Robins can survive throughout the winter by eating berries, but swallows leave as soon as the weather becomes too cold to catch insects.[23]

Swallows are small, agile birds. The size of swallows was an issue in *Monty Python and the Holy Grail* when King Arthur argued with a soldier about the ability of a migratory swallow to carry a coconut to England from the tropics. The soldier argued about the unrealistic weight ratios of a five-ounce bird carrying a one-pound coconut. In fact, the heaviest swallow species weighs a little more than two ounces, and the typical weight is less than one ounce.

Swallows and martins are in the same family, and the names sometimes are interchangeable. The species called the Sand Martin in some parts of the world is called the Bank Swallow in the United States. There are more than eighty species of swallows and martins. Swallows are much beloved because of their colorful plumage, graceful flight, and associations with spring. Their consumption of large numbers of insects adds to their desirability around human habitations. Their back is usually a dark glossy color, and many species have a forked tail. Their bill is small and flat, and it can open wide to catch flying insects. Swallows and martins often perch, but they rarely walk, because their

---

23. There was still debate among American ornithologists near the end of the 1800s whether the disappearance of swallows in the autumn was due to migration or hibernation.

feet are weak. They are not related to swifts, who also fly gracefully through the air in search of insects.

In the spring, I enjoy watching Barn Swallows near a bridge leading onto Theodore Roosevelt Island in Washington. The swallows swoop to pick up mud in their bill and carry it under the bridge to build nests. One spring, I saw some Cliff Swallows mixed in, which is unusual in Washington. Barn Swallows get their name because they often build their mud nests on or in a barn. Tree Swallows, who nest in cavities, often use human-made nest boxes. Bank Swallows nest in banks—the kind made of mud rather than the ones filled with money.

Many people put up multiunit houses for Purple Martins, who are colonial nesters and now have become dependent on humans for housing. I knew a man in Louisiana who manufactured aluminum martin houses with eight, twelve, or sixteen units. These houses had a bright white finish that helped to repel starlings who sometimes try to take over martin nest sites. A friend told me that her father became miffed after he had gone to considerable trouble to build a martin house, but the ungrateful martins chose to nest in the store-bought martin house erected by a neighbor.

84. SWAN
Monochrome Birds

There are seven swan species in the world, and except for their bills, you can enjoy most of them just as much by looking at black-and-white photos rather than color. Five are mostly white, one is mostly black, and one has a white body with a black neck. The ancient Roman writer Juvenal talked about something being as rare as a black swan, meaning something impossibly rare. Europeans did not know about the Black Swans in Australia until more than 1,500 years later. The "black swan theory," which was developed by the financier Nassim Nicholas Taleb, is named after Juvenal's observation and describes events that are very rare but have huge impacts. *Black Swan* is also the title of a 2010 movie for which Natalie Portman won the Oscar for Best Actress.

The Aboriginals in Australia, where the only native swan species is black, have legends about white swans. One such legend, recounted in Charles Mountford's *The First Sunrise*, talks about how in the Dreamtime, all swans were white; Aboriginal people believed that the Dreamtime was a period before the creation when spirits of future life forms were sleeping below the surface of the Earth. The white swans in the legend swam in a lagoon, not knowing it belonged to eagles. The eagles attacked the swans and carried them to the desert, dropping them there after plucking most of their feathers. Hundreds of crows offered their black feathers to cover the naked and nearly dead swans. The only white feathers left were on the tips of the swans' wings. The legend includes white swans as a fictional contrast to the native Black Swans rather than because the Aboriginals knew that swans in other parts of the world are white.

Swans are in the same family as geese and ducks. They are large, heavy birds who spend a lot of time swimming and sticking their long necks into the water to yank up aquatic vegetation. They also feed in fields. A male swan is called a cob, a female a pen, and a baby a cygnet. Like geese, swans can be aggressive, especially when protecting young. They have been known to attack dogs and humans who venture too close. Their vigilance is warranted, because the lives of baby waterfowl can be perilous. Predators can attack young birds from air, land, and sea. A major predator for some swan species is the snapping turtle. The wiggling of the little feet of cygnets at the surface of the water presents a tempting lure for snappers. The turtle grabs a foot and drags the cygnet under.

In Britain, swans have been considered a royal bird for the past thousand years, and nobody can own one unless given permission by the crown. A "swan mark" is cut into the bill of each bird to prove legitimate ownership. Swans likewise have made a deep impression on commoners. Ben Jonson called Shakespeare the "Swan of Avon." The Disney Corporation named one of its Orlando resort hotels after a swan. The United States Postal Service has issued stamps with two swan necks curved to form a heart. On the seventh day of Christmas, my true love gave to me seven swans a-swimming. As symbols, swans are a hot property.

In German mythology, a swan maiden is an elf or fairy capable of becoming a maiden or a swan. The mythologies of other cultures have similar characters. Peter Ilyich Tchaikovsky's ballet *Swan Lake* is based on a German fairy tale in which Prince Siegfried falls in love with the Swan Queen Odette, a woman transformed into a swan by a sorcerer. In Greek mythology, Zeus, the king of the gods, changed into a swan to rape Leda, a minor goddess and the wife of a Spartan king. This myth is the subject of the poem "Leda and the Swan" by William Butler Yeats. Hans Christian Andersen wrote a famous children's story about a swan in 1843. "The Ugly Duckling" is about a mother duck who hatches a clutch of eggs, and one of the offspring is different from the others. The different duckling is ridiculed for being ugly, but it grows into a swan who is more beautiful and majestic than the ducklings.

Unfortunately, the Mute Swan, the species about whom Andersen probably wrote, has become a very ugly duckling in the United States. It is an introduced species and among the largest and heaviest flying birds in the world. Mute Swans eat large amounts of aquatic vegetation on which other birds and animals depend, and their big webbed feet sometimes trample eggs in breeding areas of ground-nesting native species, such as terns. In the Chesapeake Bay region, wildlife officials have tried to control the Mute Swan population by destroying eggs and sometimes shooting the birds.

The United States has two native swan species. The Tundra Swan, formerly called the Whistling Swan before it was lumped with a European species, is about ten percent smaller than a Mute Swan and has less curve to its neck. Around the beginning of spring, I sometimes hear large flocks of Tundra Swans flying over in the evening. They fly in a V-formation and make a high-pitched flight call. Seeing and hearing a hundred swans flying directly overhead in dim moonlight is a memorable experience.

The Trumpeter Swan is the heaviest native bird in North America. Trumpeter Swans, who get their name from their trumpeting call, almost became extinct. In the 1930s, fewer than one hundred remained. They were hunted for food, and their feathers were plucked for hats and made into items such as powder puffs. Before the widespread use

of ballpoint pens, their flight feathers were highly prized for use as quill pens; the word "pen" comes from the Latin word *penna*, which means feather. Trumpeter Swans have made somewhat of a recovery, but in a dramatically reduced area from their former breeding range that stretched from Alaska to eastern Canada. They are being reintroduced into some areas with the help of captive-breeding programs and ultralight aircraft that help young birds learn migration routes.

A famous legend involves the song a swan allegedly sings just before it dies. A "swan song" has come to mean the last great effort of an artist, athlete, or whomever. All swans, including the Mute Swan, can vocalize, but none sing. A somewhat different twist on the legend appears in Frank Muir's *An Irreverent and Thoroughly Incomplete Social History of Almost Everything.* He quotes an epigram by Samuel Taylor Coleridge about a singer: "Swans sing before they die—'twere no bad thing should certain persons die before they sing."

85. SWIFT
Bird Spit

Would you ever eat soup made from bird spit? Would you be more interested in trying it if you knew the bird spit cost thousands of dollars per pound? Edible-nest Swiftlets make their nests from saliva. In some Asian countries, people gather the nests from caves and remove any feathers, excrement, and dirt. The nests then are sold for use in soup and other delicacies. The birds are forced to build replacement nests, sometimes supplemented with sticks. Most bird species have poorly developed salivary glands, but members of the swift family are notable exceptions.

Swifts spend much of their life flitting through the air, hawking insects. Some swift species have bills that are so short that the large opening in the face is like a mouth. I have seen countless swifts, but never a perched one. They spend so much time airborne that some copulate and sleep while flying. Swifts are not songbirds and are thought to be related to hummingbirds. They are found throughout the world, and of the roughly one hundred swift species, four nest in North America.

Swifts are in the family Apodidae, which comes from Greek words meaning "without feet." The family is so named because most swifts have small, weak feet, often with four forward-pointing toes that allow the bird to grasp a vertical surface but not perch on something horizontal. They also have trouble landing and picking up nesting material with their feet, which is why some use saliva to make their nest. A few species of treeswifts, who are in a family closely related to the Apodidae, are capable of perching. A species of swiftlet who lives in the caves of Indonesia has been discovered to use echolocation to navigate, similar to what bats use. The Oilbird, an unrelated cave-dwelling species in the American tropics, also uses echolocation. And as with some of the cave-dwelling swiftlets, Oilbirds have been persecuted by humans; they are so named because the young, who were fat from eating a lot of fruit, were boiled down to make oil. Oilbirds are the only fruit-eating nocturnal birds in the world.

Swifts are indeed swift in the air, and they are the only family of birds in the world named for an adjective that describes an aspect of their behavior. They can be difficult to identify because one rarely gets a prolonged look at them. The only swift species in the eastern United States is the Chimney Swift, so named because flocks of them funnel into chimneys at dusk to roost. These swifts do not have to worry much about predators, because they fly fast enough to avoid most airborne threats, and most land-based predators do not go into chimneys. Information is available on the Internet about how to maintain chimneys to provide adequate nesting habitat for them.

Chimney Swifts look like sooty cigar butts with curved wings. They usually winter in Peru, and each April, I look forward to hearing the first chittering calls of the returning Chimney Swifts, signaling that spring has arrived. One can hear the chittering in all kinds of habitats, including developed areas of cities. The swifts care only about the insects in the air, ignoring what is on the ground.

Swifts might be the most adept flying creatures on Earth. Some swifts in Europe have been seen flying more than nine thousand feet in the air. A species called the White-throated Needletail, found in Asia and Australia, once was purported to achieve speeds of more than two hundred miles per hour, but that number probably is overstated by a factor of two. Still, for a small bird to fly at more than a hundred miles per hour is amazing. This speed makes swifts difficult to study in the field.

In *How Birds Fly*, John Terres quotes an ornithologist named Leonard Wing (an aptronym) who banded a nine-year-old Chimney Swift. Wing estimated that with the migrations to South America and flying on its nesting and wintering grounds, the bird had flown 1,350,000 miles in its life, or 150,000 miles a year, or more than 400 miles a day. That's very impressive for a flying cigar butt.

86. TANAGER
Overwhelming Birds

The only time I have ever felt overwhelmed while birding was when I was on the Blanchisseuse Road in Trinidad. (*Blanchisseuse* means washerwoman in French.) I was looking at a large tree that contained five gorgeous species of tanagers I had never seen before. I wanted to see them all, but I was not sure where to look first or how long to look at each one. It was a bit like being at a buffet table that has five delicious desserts you want to eat. Tanagers are among the most beautiful songbirds in the New World. Many have plumage that features bright colors, a lovely combination of colors, or both. Adjectives in their names such as paradise, golden, emerald, and glistening-green do not represent overstatement.

Besides being overwhelming, seeing five tanager species in a tree offers important information about their behavior. Tanagers are mostly nonaggressive fruit-eating birds, as was indicated by five different species peacefully feeding in a tree without attacking each other. In *Birds of Tropical America*, the ornithologist Steven Hilty says that tanagers have short, strong legs that are effective when the birds are perched in a tree and reaching for fruit. He also says that tanagers have relatively long wings, which allow them to more easily fly long distances in search of fruit; the added speed is at the expense of being able to maneuver quickly in flight. Birds such as flycatchers tend to have short wings, which increase maneuverability and acceleration when they are hawking insects but are not as useful for distance flying.

Not all tanager species are peaceful. In Panama, I saw a group of male White-shouldered Tanagers displaying to try to gain the favors of a female. The males are all black with a white patch on the folded wing. When they raised their wings in the display area, the white patch stood out more. They repeatedly flew at each other, seemingly to gain a more favorable perch position. A couple of the tanagers went into foot-to-foot aerial combat. The female sat placidly on the sidelines while all of this was going on.

Alexander Skutch, who wrote a book about tanagers, noted that in addition to seeing many species of tanagers foraging together, one also might see pairs of each species foraging, because some species form pairs and seem to stay together for the rest of their lives. Skutch also mentions that he has seen some species of tropical tanagers engage in an activity called anting, which involves taking live ants and rubbing them along their feathers. The ants contain formic acid, which supplements the bird's preen oil. One possible reason that tanagers and other bird species engage in anting is that it helps to kill or repel feather parasites. Some birds use items other than ants for the same purpose, including smoldering cigarette butts.

All of the tanagers used to be classified in the same family, but some are now thought to be more closely related to cardinals. Only four tanager species are regularly found in the United States, and another is a casual visitor; all of these are in a genus related to the cardinals. In the eastern United States, the Scarlet Tanager is the most common tanager species. The male is a blood-red bird whose wings and tail are jet black. I once took an ornithologist from California to a woodland area in Maryland, and he screamed in disbelief at the color of a male Scarlet Tanager. The red is deeper and more intense than the red on a male Northern Cardinal. I have seen hundreds of Scarlet Tanagers, and I still must suppress a small scream whenever I see that intense spot of scarlet among green leaves. Sometimes, the feathers of a Scarlet Tanager have an excess of yellow pigment (a condition called xanthochroism). This abnormality usually gives the bird a washed-out orange appearance, but I saw a male Scarlet Tanager in 2005 with bright-orange plumage. For about five minutes, I could not take my eyes off this stunningly beautiful freak as he sat in bright sunlight.

The corresponding species in the western United States is called, appropriately, the Western Tanager. The male is bright yellow, with a red head, black wings, and a black tail. The Summer Tanager, who is slightly larger than the Scarlet, nests in the southern United States. The male is all red (with no black on the wings), but the red is not as intense as the Scarlet's. The Hepatic Tanager is found in a small part of the southwest. Hepatic means liver-colored, and the male is red with liver-colored wings and facial markings. For females of the North American tanager species, the bright coloration of the male is replaced with olive or dull yellow.

If you want to see a lot of tanager species, you should travel to Central and South America. Venezuela, which is less than a tenth the size of the United States, has about a hundred species of tanagers. Panama has more than fifty tanager species, and when I was there, I saw about thirty of them. Fortunately, they were not bunched in the same tree as was the case in Trinidad, because I am not sure I would have been able to handle that.

87. TERN
Birds and Daylight

Seasonal affective disorder is caused by inadequate exposure to light, especially during winter months, resulting in depression, lethargy, and other symptoms that impede normal human functioning. Arctic Terns, who are graceful seabirds, are unlikely to suffer from this condition, because they spend more of their lives in daylight than any bird species on Earth. They breed in high-latitude midnight-sun areas during the Northern Hemisphere spring and summer and spend the remainder of the year in the midnight-sun areas of the Southern Hemisphere, flying as far south as Antarctica for the southern spring and summer. They migrate farther than any other bird species in the world. One bird banded in Russia was found 14,000 miles away in Australia. In 2007, Danish researchers discovered that Arctic Terns equipped with radio transmitters traveled almost fifty thousand miles in a year. The birds can live about thirty years, which means they might travel well over a million miles in their lifetime.

Terns are in the same family as gulls but are distinguished from gulls by their narrow pointed wings and long pointed bill. There are more than forty tern species in the world, and about fifteen can be seen in North America. The smallest tern species in the United States is the Least Tern, at nine inches, while the largest in the United States (and the world) is the Caspian Tern, at twenty-one inches. Terns sometimes are called sea swallows, both because of the way they fly and because of the forked tails of many of the species. When feeding, they hover over the water and then plunge to the surface to snag fish or other sea creatures. The Gull-billed Tern does not feed like the other North American terns, preferring to hawk insects and sometimes capture prey on the ground. Most terns are white, but some species are dark colored.

Skimmers are in the same family as terns and gulls but feed in a very different manner. They are the only birds in the world whose lower mandible is longer than their upper mandible. Skimmers feed by fly-ing low over the water with their lower mandible skimming the sur-face. As soon as the lower mandible comes into contact with a small fish or other creature, the bill snaps shut so the bird can swallow the prey. There are three skimmer species in the world, and all look pretty much alike. Black Skimmers can be seen in the United States along the Atlantic, Pacific, and Gulf coasts. They skim in bays, rivers, and other bodies of water with a calm surface. Because they feed by touch, they do not need much light for catching prey. They prefer to feed at night, because the water tends to be calmer and fish are closer to the surface. Their bill is two-toned, with the half near the base being red and the half toward the tip black. The black portion is the part that skims the water and is less noticeable to prey than the red portion would be. Skimmers are the only birds in the world who have vertical slits for the pupils in their eyes, similar to what cats have.

The feeding habits of terns sometimes can cause controversy. The Caspian Tern, found on every continent except Antarctica, is a large white species with a black cap, black wingtips, and a bright-red bill that gives the appearance that the bird is sucking on a hot poker. The largest concentration of breeding Caspian Terns in the United States is along the Columbia River in the Pacific Northwest. This area also is an important breeding area for endangered salmon, and young salmon sometimes are eaten by terns. Conservationists trying to protect salmon have become involved in a conflict with those trying to protect terns. The controversy shows how the interests of different conserva-tion groups can collide.

Terns often nest in large colonies on beaches. The evolutionary pur-pose of this strategy has to do with safety and protection in numbers, but the strategy evolved without anticipation of plume hunters, egg collectors, and mobs of recreational beach users. Some colonies of nesting terns were virtually wiped out to provide feathers for women's hats in the late 1800s and early 1900s. One of the newest perils is the all-terrain vehicle, which can wipe out most of the well-concealed eggs in a tern colony with a few trips up and down the beach. Tern nests typically are only a scrape in the sand. Conservationists in coastal areas have tried to set aside sections of beach for the exclusive use of terns. Terns will dive-bomb intruders who enter their colonies. They also are known to engage in mass flights, with all the birds in a colony departing in a dense flock.

In 1987, a pair of Least Terns made a rare nesting appearance in Washington. They chose the flat roof of the Kennedy Center for the Performing Arts. The Kennedy Center is a large white box next to the infamous Watergate complex, which is irregular and ugly, with curves and tooth-like decorations. (Some architecture critics have called the Kennedy Center the box the Watergate came in.) While the Least Terns were nesting, I went to the balcony of the Kennedy Center with my binoculars to watch the terns fly back and forth with food for their young. I did not have to buy a ticket, but I was treated to a good show.

88. THICK-KNEE
Birds in Obscure Literary References

Have you ever come across a reference in a novel that is so obscure that probably few people other than you and the author know what it means? I had such an experience while reading Margaret Atwood's 2003 novel *Oryx and Crake*. Atwood, who is an accomplished birder and very active in bird conservation, includes the following passage about the book's two major characters: "Crake had picked the code-names. Jimmy's was Thickney, after a defunct Australian double-jointed bird that used to hang around in cemeteries, and—Jimmy suspected—because Crake liked the sound of it as applied to Jimmy. Crake's codename was Crake, after the Red-necked Crake, another Australian bird—never, said Crake, very numerous."

There are ten species of thick-knees in the world, but none in the United States. When Margaret Atwood wrote *Oryx and Crake,* the two species in Australia were called stone-curlews, but they are not related to the shorebirds called curlews. All ten species are now called thick-knees. They look like large, long-legged plovers and are so named because the joint in the middle of their leg appears to be thick. In fact, this joint is not a knee. Most birds walk on their toes rather than their feet, and the equivalent of a bird's foot reaches all the way up to this joint. As such, the joint is more like the human ankle. A bird's knee, the next joint up, usually is hidden under feathers.

I saw thick-knees in Australia in 1995. I spent the first week of that trip at Cassowary House in a rain forest about half an hour's drive from the city of Cairns. At the time, Cassowary House was owned by John and Rita Squire. One day, John drove me to Cairns, and we stopped at a cemetery. In addition to seeing a sign next to the cemetery that read "Cairns Restoration Center," the highlight of the stop was seeing and hearing eight Bush Thick-knees. These cryptically colored birds blend in with the high grass along the edge of the cemetery, making them difficult to see without binoculars or a telescope. While lurking near the tombstones, they utter banshee-like wails that must be unnerving to nonbirding visitors to the cemetery. Even worse, the thick-knees wail during the night, which could really mess with the heads of people who believe in ghosts. I have not been to the cemetery at night, but in 1999, I arrived at the Cairns airport late in the evening and heard Bush Thick-knees wailing in a nearby field.

In 2001, Atwood was in Australia to promote her novel *The Blind Assassin*. She stayed at Cassowary House, where from a balcony she saw birds called Red-necked Crakes running near the house. The idea for *Oryx and Crake* came to her upon seeing them, and she began writing notes for it that evening. I have stood on that same balcony and seen the crakes but was never inspired to write a best-selling novel. At some point during Atwood's visit, she visited the same cemetery in Cairns, which is a popular destination for birders who want to see and hear the thick-knees.[24]

So unless you knew that Margaret Atwood visited Cairns and Cassowary House before she wrote *Oryx and Crake*, and that Bush Thick-knees (which at the time she wrote the book were known as Bush Stone-curlews) hang around the edges of the cemetery in Cairns, you would have no idea to what she is referring with respect to the code names for Jimmy and Crake. But now you know.

---

24. I wrote to Margaret Atwood about the reference. She graciously replied that she had seen the stone-curlews on her visit to Australia.

89. THRASHER
Birding on a Moonscape

The places where people look for birds sometimes are more memorable than the birds themselves. In 1994, I went to Mono Lake, just east of Yosemite National Park in California. If someone were to drop you off at the edge of Mono Lake in the middle of the night, you would think you were on the moon when morning came. The lunar effect is created by calcium carbonate formations called tufas that stick out of the lake. Around the edge of the lake is scrub habitat where I saw my first of only two Sage Thrashers I have ever seen. A Sage Thrasher is about nine inches, with a grayish back and speckled breast. Its plumage is not nearly as eye-catching as the scenery around Mono Lake.

The word "thrasher" is a variant of thrush, because thrashers look like elongated thrushes even though they are not related to thrushes. Thrashers did not get their name because they thrash things (although some do). This might be a disappointment to Atlanta hockey fans whose National Hockey League franchise was called the Thrashers, but not as big a disappointment as when the team moved to Winnipeg in 2011. *Thrasher* also is the name of a magazine about skateboarding.

There are about fifteen species of thrashers, all in the New World, and half can be found in the United States. The best place to see a variety of thrashers in North America is southeastern Arizona. The Brown Thrasher is the only one found in the eastern United States. It is the state bird of Georgia, which is a reason for the name of the Atlanta hockey team. A Brown Thrasher looks like a large mockingbird with the equivalent of red hair and freckles. It is sleek, with a thin curved bill and evil-looking yellow eyes.

The Brown Thrasher, Northern Mockingbird, and Gray Catbird are the three mimic thrushes found in the eastern United States, and all of them mimic the songs of other bird species. One way to tell apart their vocalizations is by the number of times they sing each phrase.

The thrasher sings each phrase of the bird it is imitating two or three times in succession. The mockingbird sings each phrase four or five times. The catbird sings each phrase only once. In areas where all three species are present, the thrasher often is the hardest to find.

The only other Sage Thrasher I have seen was in 2005 in British Columbia. Vancouver, the province's largest city, receives a lot of rain each year. But if you travel east about 250 miles, you will enter areas that are very dry, including some patches of desert and sagebrush habitat. Not far from the town of Penticton is the Dominion Radio Astrophysical Observatory, a facility that detects and studies radio waves from distant stars. The facility has a radio telescope made of seven large dishes, each of which is about ten feet in diameter. I saw a Sage Thrasher on the lawn in front of a building where the astronomers work. I doubt there is any connection between the fact that this Sage Thrasher was near a place that was monitoring distant celestial bodies, while the other one I saw was in an area that looked like a distant celestial body.

90. THRUSH
Bird Music

Pan was the Greek god of the forests and the pastures. He had the horns and hooves of a goat, and he loved wine, women, and song. The origin of the word "panic" is based on some of his antics. Elizabeth Barrett Browning began her poem "A Musical Instrument" by asking, "What was he doing, the great god Pan, down in the reeds by the river?" The question is more suggestive than interrogatory, based on some of Pan's mythical activities. In one myth, Pan chases a wood nymph named Syrinx, but she wants no part of him. As he is about to catch her, other nymphs change Syrinx into reeds. For oral gratification, Pan has to settle for blowing on the reeds to produce beautiful music. The instrument called the panpipes is named in Pan's honor, while Syrinx has given her name to the organ in a bird's throat that can produce music so beautiful that it puts Pan's efforts to shame.

The voice organ of humans—the larynx—is in the upper part of the windpipe. The syrinx in birds is in the lower part of their windpipe that forks to go to the two lungs, and it is controlled by special muscles that can affect the pitch of a song. An example of the special effects that can be produced by the syrinx is the haunting song of the Veery, a thrush species who nests in the northern part of North America. The Veery sounds as if it is singing in two-part harmony with itself. During nesting season, Veeries are most likely to sing near dawn or dusk. The ornithologist Arthur Cleveland Bent wrote that we "cannot think of it as a song in the sense of its being an expression of joy; it seems to express a calmer, deeper, holier emotion, like a hymn or a prayer." He goes on to quote an 1885 account by Bradford Torrey: "In his own artless way, he does what I have never heard any other bird attempt: he gives to his melody all the force of harmony. How this unique and curious effect, this vocal double-stopping, as a violinist might term it, is produced, is not certainly known; but it would seem that it must be by an arpeggio, struck with such consummate quickness and precision that the ear is unable to follow it, and is conscious of nothing but the resultant chord."

The Veery's singing method does not involve an arpeggio, which is a group of tones produced successively rather than simultaneously. Some songbird species are capable of producing more than one sound at once. One of Richard Walton's *Birding by Ear* recordings features a Veery's song played at half speed so you can hear the separate components. The name "Veery" comes from the bird's call note—a loud *veer*—rather than its beautiful song.

Thrushes are among the most accomplished singers in the bird world. Hearing these songs in April and May when many of these species are returning from their wintering grounds is one of the highlights of birding in the spring. Peter Schickele, best known for his PDQ Bach and Public Radio work, composed a lovely piece of music based on the song of the Wood Thrush. The bird's principal song sounds like *ee-oh-lay*. This and other thrush songs, as well as many other types of beautiful music in the world, have qualities that defy translation into words. Schickele is not the only composer to be inspired by birdsong. *The Birds*, by twentieth-century Italian composer Ottorino Respighi, tries to musically represent the songs of well-known birds. In 1953, the composer Olivier Messiaen composed a symphonic work called *Réveil des oiseaux* (Awakening of the Birds) based on birdsong

heard between midnight and noon in the French mountains, and he used birdsong as the basis for subsequent compositions.

Thomas Hardy wrote a famous poem about "The Darkling Thrush," which means a thrush in the dark. This thirty-two-line poem begins with intense gloom and ends with the hope derived from the beautiful song of the thrush:

> So little cause for carolings
> Of such ecstatic sound
> Was written on terrestrial things
> Afar or nigh around,
>
> That I could think there trembled through
> His happy good-night air
> Some blessed hope, whereof he knew
> And I was unaware.

The thrushes are one of the largest and most diverse groups of birds in the world and are scattered across the Earth. The six North American thrushes who are some of the best singers are about seven inches, brownish on top, light below, and speckled to varying extents on the breast. All but the Wood Thrush are in the genus *Catharus*, which means pure—a possible reference to the purity of their song.

During breeding season, territorial male thrushes sing both to attract females and to repel other males. Research cited in Edward Armstrong's *A Study of Bird Song* says that experiments with recorded songs of some thrush species, including the Veery and Wood Thrush, reveal that males are repelled when hearing songs of rivals at loud intensity but become bold when the songs of rivals are played softly. Thus, if a male wants to protect his territory from males of the same species, he will be more effective the louder he sings. This strategy is fine with me. I would be happy if all Veeries and other thrushes crank their song up to full volume so I can hear it better and enjoy it more.

91. TROPICBIRD
Watching Birds in the Nude

Many birders never go off duty. They notice any bird in their field of view when they ride in a car. They try to identify any birdsong they hear in the background of a movie or television show. When walking down a street, birders notice many birdsongs that will not enter the consciousness of nonbirders. I heard a story about the ornithologist Roger Tory Peterson, who was walking with someone through midtown Manhattan on a busy weekday. The sidewalks were crowded with pedestrians, and the streets were filled with noisy vehicles. Suddenly, Peterson said he heard the call of bluebirds flying over. His companion was amazed and asked how Peterson could hear the bluebirds over the din. Peterson pulled a coin from his pocket and bounced it on the sidewalk. People nearby looked down to the area from which the coin sound had come. Peterson then said, "It all depends what you're listening for."

Occasionally, birders find themselves in situations in which their desire to look at birds can cause problems. In Hana, which is on the rainy side of Maui in the Hawaiian Islands, I visited a beautiful red-sand beach that is clothing optional, and I exercised my option. As I was lying on the sand, a tropicbird flew in and seemed to hang in the air about fifty feet directly over my head. It is a spectral white bird who looks like a large tern, but it has two tail streamers that are about as long as its body. I really wanted to take a close look at this bird, and I had binoculars in my backpack. The problem was that using binoculars on a clothing-optional beach is frowned upon. I tried to think of a way of concealing my binoculars so that I could look through them without anyone noticing—similar to the way alcoholics on the street take drinks from a bottle concealed in a paper bag—but getting caught doing that would be much worse than holding the binoculars in the open. I had to settle for the view of the tropicbird with my naked eyes.

Tropicbird

The three species of tropicbirds in the world are seabirds, and as their name indicates, they are most likely to be found in tropical oceans. They do not seem to have any close living relatives in the bird world. The adults of all the species have two long tail streamers; two species have white streamers, and one species has red streamers. Tropicbirds feed like numerous other types of seabirds, plunging into the water from a considerable height. They are sometimes called "bosun birds," because their long tail feathers are thought to resemble a tool used by a bosun. Bosun is a nautical term and is short for a "boatswain," who was responsible for the maintenance on a merchant ship. One of the land masses in Caroline Island south of Hawaii is called Bosun Bird Islet, named after the Red-tailed Tropicbirds seen there.

You are unlikely to see tropicbirds unless you take a boat trip into the ocean or are near one of their nesting areas. The first ones I saw were Red-billed Tropicbirds off Little Tobago Island—a small uninhabited island near the coast of Tobago in the Caribbean. David Attenborough's *Trials of Life* series used footage of the tropicbirds from this island. They flew so close to the cliffs where I was standing that I could see them well without binoculars. Unlike the situation in Hana, I would not have been embarrassed to use my binoculars to look at these tropicbirds.

92. TURKEY
Birds and Holidays

In the United States, turkeys are closely associated with Thanksgiving, which sometimes is called Turkey Day. The early British colonists enjoyed a feast with native people who brought wildfowl, including Wild Turkeys. But according to John Madson in a 1990 *Smithsonian Magazine* article, the Indians scorned turkey meat and thought turkeys were game fit only for children. Madson wonders whether the Indians brought the turkeys to the feast just to get rid of them.

Wild Turkeys are in the same family as chickens, pheasants, and partridges. Turkeys get their name because the British, who were confused about the country of origin of these imported birds, had bought a similar-looking bird called a guineafowl from Turkish traders. (Neither guineafowl nor guinea pigs come from Guinea.) People from the country of Turkey, as well as France, the Netherlands, and Scandinavia, have given names to the turkey based on the belief that it came from India, while the Greeks call turkey "French chicken." In Swahili, the word for turkey is translated as "great duck."

Domestic turkeys do not have a positive image. Contrary to legend, they do not drown by standing in the rain with their mouths open. Still, "turkey" is a derogatory term to describe a stupid person. Turkey also is a term for a bad theatrical production. The origin of this meaning comes from the habit of theater managers introducing plays of dubious quality around Thanksgiving, because a greater number of uncritical people attend plays during the pre-Christmas theater season.

I once wrote a review of *Wild Turkey Country*, a book by Lovett E. Williams, Jr. It contains a lot of detail, including how to look at turkey excrement and identify the sex of the bird who left it: males have long, straight, or J-shaped droppings, while females have curled or bulbous droppings. Williams explains that Wild Turkeys were domesticated by the early Mexicans and taken to Europe by Spaniards. They were bred in Europe and later carried back to North America by British colonists. A newly hatched turkey imprints on the first large moving object it sees. Williams theorizes that the Mexicans might have been able to domesticate Wild Turkeys by imprinting them on humans. A Central American species called the Ocellated Turkey is more ornate than the North American species. It has never been domesticated.

Before Europeans came to the New World, Wild Turkeys were abundant in about three-quarters of the area that now includes the lower forty-eight states. By the mid-1900s, turkeys had been wiped out by excessive hunting in about a dozen states and were restricted to small ranges in many others. In recent decades, turkeys have been reintroduced into areas from which they had been eliminated. Lovett Williams says that reintroduction programs have been successful, because unlike many other species, Wild Turkeys lack a homing instinct. If you capture and transport turkeys, they will establish a home at the new site rather than trying to return whence they came.

With suburban sprawl, wild turkeys are increasingly being seen in suburban neighborhoods. In 2011, a friend in the Northern Virginia suburbs who put a webcam in her yard for recording the songbirds who visit her pond captured footage of a Wild Turkey coming in for a drink. A 1999 *New York Times* story reported that an animal control officer in Princeton, New Jersey, was called by a woman who claimed to have an endangered species in her yard. The officer went to her house and found a nonendangered turkey. The next day, the woman called again and said she wanted the turkey out of her yard. When the officer asked why, she said, "It's eating the bird seed." The officer replied, "Well, it's a bird!"

Wild Turkeys are wily birds and not easy to find. They are one of the heaviest native species in the United States, along with swans. The males weigh more than twenty pounds, and the females are about half that size. Young turkeys and other young fowl are called poults, which is why the birds raised on farms are called poultry. When giving sexual displays, the male Wild Turkey is quite impressive, puffing out his feathers, fanning his tail, and strutting around. His neck is carunculated, which means it has little bumps on the bare skin. He sprouts strange hair-like feathers from his breast that can be more than a foot long and collectively look like the tassel on a graduation cap. And he has a growth called a snood over his bill, named for the little bag in which some women wear their hair.

While partridges in the wild do not show a strong preference for perching in pear trees (even around Christmas), turkeys sometimes perch in trees. Their willingness to do so makes them more difficult for hunters to pursue than some of the other birds in their family. The chicken-like birds have short, rounded wings adapted for brief bursts of flight to escape from predators. Because the birds have heavy bodies and short wings, they have to flap very hard and fast to become airborne. Some hunters use dogs to chase these birds and flush them repeatedly. For species who prefer to remain on the ground, the repeated flying drains the birds of energy, eventually making them easy for the hunters and dogs to catch.

The Australian Brush-Turkey is unrelated to the American Wild Turkey. It looks like a solid-black turkey with a bald red head. The male has a yellow or lavender wattle around his neck that resembles an Elizabethan collar. Brush-turkeys, who are common and tame in many Australian rain forests, are part of a family called the megapodes, which means "great feet." Male megapodes use their strong feet to kick together large mounds of leaves and plant material in which the female lays her eggs. The heat in the mound allows the eggs to incubate. Although the male is diligent about regulating the heat of the mound to insure hatching, neither he nor the female has anything to do with raising the young. When an egg is ready to hatch, the chick must break out of the shell and dig its way out of the mound. Once the chick finds daylight, it fends totally for itself. From the moment they are born, brush-turkeys and other megapodes are the most independent and self-reliant birds in the world. In general, bird species whose young are better able to function shortly after hatching come from proportionally larger eggs that have a higher percentage of yolk and take longer to hatch, which allows the chicks to grow stronger and take in more nourishment within the egg. Likewise, the more developed the chicks are when they come out of the egg, the larger the number of eggs the female(s) generally will lay, because the young do not need as much care.

When I was a student at the University of Pennsylvania, I wrote a letter to the campus newspaper suggesting that the school change its nickname from the Quakers to the Turkeys. I thought that choosing a religious group as a nickname was insensitive; I could not imagine calling the sports teams the Penn Jews, the Penn Roman Catholics, or the Penn Jehovah's Witnesses. Also, I had gone to a Quaker school for thirteen years before attending Penn, and I thought Penn students should not yell "Fight, Quakers, Fight" during sporting events, considering the peaceful ways of the Quakers. I suggested the new nickname Turkeys, because Benjamin Franklin, Penn's founder, so loved the Wild Turkey that he wrote to his daughter in 1784 that it should be the national symbol instead of the thieving Bald Eagle selected by the Continental Congress in 1782. One wonders whether the United States would have adopted different domestic and foreign policies were its symbol a bird associated with food and plenty rather than a bird with arrows in its talons.

93. VIREO
Monotonous Birds

A challenge of learning birdsong, especially for those of us who are not gifted musically, is to try to translate into words what a bird is singing. Some of these translations are whimsical and differ depending on the translator. The song of the White-eyed Vireo has been portrayed by some as *chick-a-per-weeoo-chick*, while other people think the bird says *pick up the beer check quick!* A nonalcoholic bird is the Eastern Towhee, who sings *drink your tea!*, possibly brewed by a Carolina Wren, who sings *tea-kettle, tea-kettle, tea-kettle.* On the food side of the menu, the Golden Press field guide to North American birds describes the song of the Acadian Flycatcher as "an explosive *peet-suh*" (with no anchovies).

The White-eyed Vireo is part of a family that includes more than fifty vireos and related songbirds in the New World. Some have names such as greenlet and peppershrike. The North American vireos used to sometimes be called greenlets, and the name "vireo" comes from a word meaning green (like the word "verdant"). About fifteen vireo species can be seen in the United States, although not all of them are green. They are mostly five or six inches, and they have a thickish bill. They tend to be a bit larger and more deliberate in their foraging technique than many of the warbler species. Vireos often forage in leafy trees, and some are much easier to hear than see. Where I live, vireos usually visit only from the spring through the autumn.

In the spring, I bird a lot at Monticello Park in a section called Beverly Hills in Alexandria, Virginia. (It is Beverly Hills 22305 rather than Beverly Hills 90210.) This tiny six-and-a-quarter-acre park is on a ridge, which makes it very inviting for migrating songbirds. And because it has a stream running through it, a lot of the songbirds come down to bathe. While many of the warblers go into the water and splash around for a long time, a different technique is used by the

Red-eyed Vireo, the most common vireo species in the eastern United States. The Red-eyes, who are abundant in the park from the last week in April through the end of May, will perch above the stream, quickly dip into the water, and then return immediately to the perch. They often will dip numerous times. Through many years of observation, I have seen them stay in the water only a few times, and then only briefly.

The Red-eyed Vireo is nicknamed the "preacher bird" because of its relentless sing-song vocalizations. Most songbirds sing in the morning and are quiet during the afternoon. Sometimes in the woods in the summer, just after midday, one of the only songbirds singing is the Red-eyed Vireo. Birdsong expert Richard Walton describes the song as *here I am, where are you! here I am, where are you!* In *The Audubon Society Encyclopedia of North American Birds*, John Terres describes the song as having short, preacher-like phrases, such as *you-see-it – you-know it – do you hear me? do you believe it?* While Top-Forty radio stations have been criticized for playing the same songs over and over, the singing of the Red-eyed Vireo pushes monotony to a much higher level.[25] Terres quotes a study claiming that a Red-eyed Vireo might hold the record among birds for singing most frequently, having sung almost 23,000 songs during a ten-hour stretch. At least there is no evidence of payola being involved in the vireo's repeated song.

---

25. A Red-eyed Vireo actually sings many different songs, but most of the differences are difficult for an untrained ear to detect.

94. VULTURE
Birds as Symbols of Death

The C&O Canal towpath along the Potomac River has many excellent segments for birders and hikers to explore. When I was birding there on an April morning, I encountered a woman who saw my binoculars and asked what I was looking for. I took out my field guide and showed her some of the colorful songbirds who were beginning to arrive from their wintering grounds. The woman pointed to some black birds soaring overhead and said, "All I am seeing are these hawks." When I said that the birds were vultures, she gasped as if I had just told her about something that could cause her grave danger. Because this woman looked relatively alive, the vultures had little interest in her as a food source. Vultures have a bad image because they are black and eat dead animals, and people associate them with death and decay. Some communities with vulture roosts have taken action to kill the birds or drive them away, even though vultures perform a valuable ecological function.

Vultures soar on updrafts of warm air called thermals, so they are not usually seen circling overhead until the sun has sufficiently warmed the ground to cause the warm air to rise. If you are a vulture watcher, you can sleep a little later and not miss much. I used to regularly visit a reservoir in Washington during the winter to watch vultures. When the weather became cold, the eels in the reservoir died, providing easy meals for the few dozen vultures who hung around. During the spring, some of the trees along the C&O Canal towpath serve as a roost for either individual vultures or groups of vultures. The name for a group of vultures is a wake, which is consistent with their funereal plumage. The roosting vultures sometimes keep their wings slightly open, causing them to look as if they are wearing a slightly tattered black cape.

There are seven vulture species in the New World. The two common North American species are the Turkey Vulture and Black Vulture.

Vulture

The Turkey Vulture soars with wings forming a V (called a dihedral). Birders call this species by its initials, TV, which in the pre-cable era was a way to remember that the V of the wings was like the V of the antenna on top of some televisions, although with not as sharp an angle. The Black Vulture soars on shorter, rounder wings that have white tips and do not have as pronounced a V shape. Turkey Vultures have a keen sense of smell that they use to find food. Black Vultures have a weaker sense of smell and find food either by sight or by following Turkey Vultures. In 2011 in the German state of Lower Saxony, police experimented with using Turkey Vultures (who are not indigenous to Europe) to search for human corpses on the theory that vultures could cover a larger area than dogs or humans, but the birds were not cooperative.

The only other North American vulture is the California Condor, who became extinct in the wild because of habitat loss and being killed by humans. Ornithologists trapped all the remaining individuals to breed them in captivity. Condors have been reintroduced into the wild in what, to date, has been the most expensive conservation

effort in American history for a single species. The condors are much larger than the Black and Turkey Vultures, with a wingspan of about nine feet. The newly released condors are still under threat, mainly from lead poisoning. When hunters leave behind carcasses of animals who have been killed with lead shot, the condors eating these animals ingest lead, which can be fatal.

The Andean Condor is the most revered bird in South America. It is the national symbol of six South American nations, is the national bird of four, and appears on the flag and coat of arms of Ecuador. In Peru, many villages capture these huge birds to use in annual Yawar fiestas, or blood festivals, to celebrate the nation's independence. One activity during these fiestas is to tether a captured condor to the back of a bull during a bullfight, supposedly combining Spanish colonial culture with traditional Indian culture. This illegal practice sometimes results in serious injury or death to the birds. Like the California Condor, the Andean Condor has come perilously close to extinction. It likewise is still around only because of diligent conservation efforts. Condors are a remnant from a time when large mammals were plentiful in the Americas. As the populations of large mammals have declined, the outlook for the survival of the condors has become bleaker.

Not all of the New World vultures are black. The King Vulture, found in Central and South America, is mostly white with broad black edges on its wings. Its featherless head has multicolored skin. I showed a King Vulture to a British friend on a visit to the National Zoo, and she had trouble accepting my suggestion that the bird is handsome as she watched it rip the viscera out of a carcass in its cage.

The classification of the New World vultures is somewhat confusing. They soar like hawks and have anatomical similarities. They have at various times been thought to be closely related to the storks, to some of the hawk species, or not to any other family of birds. One link between the New World vultures and storks is that species of each group engage in a practice called urohidrosis, which involves defecating on the bare

316

parts of their legs to keep cool and/or to kill the bacteria that accumulate on their legs when devouring a dead meal. In some photos of vultures and storks, parts of the legs appear whitish, which is the result of dried urine and feces from the urohidrosis.

In the Old World, there are more than a dozen birds called vultures who are grouped with the hawks but who have not had as much controversy with their classification. In the United States, "buzzard" is used as a colloquial term for vulture, while in other parts of the world it describes some species of hawks. For instance, the Common Buzzard seen in Europe is a close relative of the Red-tailed Hawk seen in the United States. European settlers who came to North America used "buzzard" to describe the big soaring birds they found here, and the name stuck when referring to vultures.

Each year on March 15, Hinckley, Ohio, which is south of Cleveland, sponsors festivities to observe the return of the buzzards (Turkey Vultures) to their summer roost in town. Hinckley sells caps, mugs, pins, and other memorabilia featuring vultures. In a nonavian context, Americans use the term "buzzard" to describe a contemptible person, usually elderly. The bald wrinkled heads of North American vultures give the birds an elderly appearance, which is why buzzard generally is not used as a derogatory expression for a young person. Many carrion eaters have bald heads, because after sticking their heads into a bloody or putrid corpse, featherless skin can be cleaned more easily than feathered skin. Vultures have remarkable digestive systems that allow them to eat bacteria-laden meat without suffering ill effects.

The term "vulture" has slang meanings that are as negative as "buzzard." It is used to describe a person who greedily or rapaciously preys on others who are weaker, or to describe a person who waits for a relationship between two people to end and then swoops in to date one of them after the breakup. In baseball, a vulture is a relief pitcher who pitches ineffectively when his team is not ahead but gets credit for a victory when his team takes the lead for good in the next half inning.

A vulture is also the name for a revolting mixed drink consisting of red wine and Coca-Cola.

A wake of Turkey Vultures cannot sing dirges, because they lack a syrinx and are capable of emitting only sounds such as grunts and hisses. But vultures have other connections with the arts and culture. One of the earliest known flutes was created tens of thousands of years ago by drilling holes into the wing bone of a vulture. During the second century, the Roman satirist Lucian wrote a fanciful tale about men riding on the backs of huge three-headed "horse vultures" whose quill feathers were longer and thicker than the masts of ships. Vultures also are part of the ancient legend about the founding of Rome. Romulus and Remus quarreled both about the site for the city and about who should be the leader. They decided to settle their disputes by divine augury, which involved looking at the flights of birds. Remus saw six vultures, and then Romulus saw twelve. Romulus said that he saw the greater number of vultures, but Remus claimed to have seen his vultures first. The dispute escalated into a conflict that ultimately resulted in Remus' being killed.

Some arts organizations sell T-shirts with the phrase "culture vulture." While I understand the challenge of finding a clever rhyme for "culture," I wonder if the designers of such shirts have considered the implications of the message. It suggests that the wearer thrives on the cultural equivalent of carrion, which could mean art that is dead and rotting. Perhaps such an interpretation would occur only to a birder.

95. WARBLER
Birds and Espionage

The Prothonotary Warbler, a plump yellow species with blue-gray wings, is one of the only birds who sings *tweet-tweet-tweet-tweet-tweet*. It is named for religious scribes (that's the "notary" part in prothonotary) who wore yellow robes.[26] The species figured in a famous Cold War espionage case in the 1950s. A former spy named Whittaker Chambers accused a State Department official named Alger Hiss of being a communist spy and passing him State Department secrets, but Hiss denied knowing him. Chambers, a birder, tried to prove that the two knew each other by telling what he knew about the personal life of Hiss, including that Hiss too was a birder. Chambers said Hiss had once excitedly told him about seeing a Prothonotary Warbler along the C&O Canal in Maryland. Hiss was convicted and sent to prison.

I too have seen and heard many Prothonotary Warblers along the C&O Canal in Maryland, but I am more interested in the warblers than in spies. In fact, my automobile license plate says WARBLER. Each spring, these small birds put on a fireworks display of yellow, orange, blue, green, chestnut, and other colors. More than fifty warbler species can be seen in the United States, and another sixty or so can be seen only in Central and South America and the Caribbean. With a bit of effort, people in the area where I live can see more than thirty warbler species each year. Some of the species pass through briefly on their way to someplace else, while others remain to nest or spend the winter.

---

26. Pennsylvania (and many of its counties) has an office of the prothonotary, which is responsible for recording documents for many types of civil procedures. The prothonotary office in Philadelphia is thought to be the oldest continuously held legal office in the Western Hemisphere, with the first head of it being appointed by William Penn in 1683. President Harry Truman, when introduced to the prothonotary in Pittsburgh, said it was the most impressive political title he had ever heard. There are also officials called prothonotaries in Delaware, Canada, and Australia.

Most warblers are about five inches, give or take an inch. Warblers have slender, pointed bills, and during migration and the nesting season they eat mostly insects. For many of the species, the female in the spring looks like a dull version of the male. During the summer, many of the colorful males molt into drab traveling plumage for their trip back south. Hence, the most colorful show from the warblers comes in the spring rather than the autumn.

One of the most frustrating aspects of spring warbler watching is that the birds begin to arrive in small numbers when the leaves on the trees are relatively sparse. As the number of warblers increases, the number of leaves does also, so the birds become progressively more difficult to see. On active migration days, many birders develop "warbler neck," a soreness resulting from staring at birds in the tops of trees for long periods. Fortunately, not all warbler species feed in the tops of trees. Some feed toward the middle of trees, some in the lower branches, some on the trunks, some in bushes, and some on the ground. Knowing the feeding preferences of each warbler species can be an aid when looking for them. Knowing the songs helps also, and many skilled birders identify warblers by sound before seeing them. In general, the louder and lower-pitched the song, the lower down a species is likely to be found, because such songs are needed if they are to be heard near the forest floor. High-pitched songs can be used from the treetops, because they can travel a greater distance without interference.

Many migrating warblers and other songbirds in the spring begin their daily flight at dusk and fly all night. Toward dawn, they might decide to land in order to feed and rest. If so, they generally feed through the morning and rest in the afternoon to prepare for another flight at dusk. This is why many birders during the migration try to get into the field as close to first light as possible and stop birding toward midday. Occasionally, birders see a wave or fallout, which is a large group of different warbler species who descend upon a particular area. This could be caused by a storm or other weather event before dawn that causes large numbers of migrant songbirds to suddenly seek protection in trees or on the ground. Sometimes, birds do not stop flying at dawn and continue to fly toward their nesting ground. If food was abundant on their wintering ground, the birds might have fattened up enough so they don't have to stop frequently along the way. If winter food was not abundant, the birds might need to stop often. An ample build-up of fat will make them more likely to complete their migration successfully.

Birders are among the only people in the United States who are seeing the effects of deforestation in the American tropics. Warbler species who return each autumn to the tropics sometimes discover that their habitat from the previous winter is gone. Populations also decline when nesting habitats in North America are destroyed. As a result, the number of warblers now seen in the spring is far lower than the number seen in previous decades, and fallouts of warblers are much less common. Data from bird-banding stations corroborate the declines. Because of the population decline of warblers and other insect-eating species, North American forests might experience significantly more insect infestation and damage in the coming years.

The Yellow-rumped Warbler (nicknamed the Butter-Butt) is one of the most common warbler species in the eastern United States. During some parts of the spring, birders need to sort through a lot of Yellow-rumps to try to find other warblers. The male in breeding plumage is quite handsome and would be appreciated more were he not at times so seemingly ubiquitous. Yellow-rumps are the only species who regularly overwinters in cold eastern climates. Other warbler species return to Central and South America, the Caribbean, and warm-winter areas of the United States. Birders in North America tend to think of warblers as North American birds who winter in more southerly areas. But because these birds spend almost twice as much time on their wintering ground as on their nesting ground, it might be more appropriate to call them southern birds who come north to nest.

The Blackpoll Warbler, named for its black cap, travels farther in a year than virtually any other songbird species in the world. Blackpolls come from South America, nesting in New England, northern Canada, and Alaska. When I see a lot of Blackpolls coming through Washington in the spring, I know migration is winding down. One of the later spring arrivals in Washington is usually the Mourning Warbler, so named because it has a black bib reminiscent of funeral garb (unlike the Mourning Dove, who is named for its mournful song).

Warblers have filled many of my spring mornings with beautiful sights and sounds. My favorite species each spring is the Blackburnian Warbler. This small black-and-white bird has a glare-orange throat. Seeing that throat in bright sunlight is stunning, no matter how often I see it. The male American Redstart is orange, black, and white like a miniature oriole, while the female is yellow, olive, and gray. Cuba, where the redstart is known as *El Candelita* (the little candle flame), issued a postage stamp featuring a male and a female of this species in 1996. The Black-and-white Warbler has striped plumage, looking like a little escaped convict as he hops on tree trunks and branches like a nuthatch. A century ago, this species was sometimes called the Black and White Creeping Warbler.

The Yellow Warbler has canary coloration, and the male's breast is streaked with red. The red streaks are responsible for its scientific species name of *petechia*, a word medical people know as being the red spots on the body caused by broken capillaries. When the parasitic Brown-headed Cowbird lays an egg in the nest of a Yellow Warbler, the warbler often builds a new nest over the top of the old one, thereby abandoning any of its own eggs and the egg of the cowbird; sometimes, the Yellow Warbler will create a stack of more than two nests if the cowbird tries to parasitize the same warbler multiple times. The Yellow Warbler has a pleasant song, characterized as *sweet-sweet-sweet, little more sweet*. Another bright yellow species is the Blue-winged Warbler, whose song is a short whistle, followed by a raspberry. This song is more amusing than pretty.

Warbler

The Yellow-breasted Chat is an atypical warbler. (Some ornithologists believe it should be in a separate family.) It is a hefty seven inches, larger than all other North American warbler species. While this species often skulks and is difficult to find, you can sometimes see one early in the morning in its breeding area, singing from the top of a bare tree. When seen in bright sunlight, the intense yellow on the throat can appear orange. Its song is composed of a variety of chirps, whistles, and strange sounds, reminiscent of a catbird or mockingbird, and you occasionally can see little bulges in its throat with each note it sings. This varied and chattering song is the basis for its name and is the reason the naturalist John Burroughs in the nineteenth century called the chat a "rollicking polyglot" when writing about the ones he encountered in Rock Creek Park in Washington, DC. On other continents, there are birds called chats who are named for their chattering, but they are not related to the warblers in the New World. Among the chat species in Africa are the Familiar Chat and Sombre Chat.

Most warblers in the Americas do not warble. Europeans gave them this name because of a resemblance to small birds in Europe who are much more accomplished singers but not nearly as colorful. There are a great many drab warbler species throughout Europe, Asia, and Africa; some field guides contain pages of these warbler species who look distressingly alike. In fact, a lot of the Old World warblers throughout the year resemble some of the American warbler species in drab fall plumage. These "confusing fall warblers" in the Americas are notoriously difficult to tell apart, and I wonder whether the Europeans called them "warblers" after seeing them in the autumn. A common drab warbler in Europe called the Chiffchaff is named for its slow, mechanical song. In *Springtime in Britain*, Edwin Way Teale says the song "consists of a monotonous repetition of 'chiff-chaff, chiff-chaff,' the whole sounding like a ball being batted back and forth in a game of table tennis."

Australia has species called warblers in a couple of different families, but they are not related to the New World warblers. Before my

1995 trip to Australia, I was amused by a description in Graham Pizzey's field guide that the rarely occurring Great Reed-warbler is probably indistinguishable in the field from the much more common Clamorous Reed-warbler, except that the inside of the mouth of the former is salmon, while the inside of the mouth of the latter is yellow. In 1999, I was standing with Graham in a park in Brisbane watching a Clamorous Reed-warbler singing clamorously from some reeds. The song sounds like a mockingbird's, featuring a lot of variety and repeated phrases. And we could clearly see the color of the inside of his mouth!

My favorite warbler sighting occurred on a trip to the Tidewater area of Virginia. Along a beach was a decomposing whale who smelled very ripe. Flying in and out of a hole in the whale's side was a tiny Magnolia Warbler, feasting on the wriggling treats inside. The Magnolia Warbler got its name because the ornithologist Alexander Wilson shot one in a magnolia tree. While the name is inappropriate because the species does not frequent magnolia trees, it is more likely that you will see one there than inside a whale.

96. WOODCOCK
Birds Who Fly Slowly

A 1981 *NOVA* film called *Animal Olympians* shows footage of animals who are the best at certain physical activities, such as which ones run the fastest or jump the highest. The American Woodcock will never qualify for any animal Olympics. It is thought to be the slowest-flying bird in the world, chugging along at about five miles per hour.

There are seven woodcock species in the world, with the American Woodcock being the only one in the United States. The American Woodcock is eleven inches long, but about a quarter of that length is its bill. Its body is squat and dumpy. Woodcocks are closely related to snipes. They are in the sandpiper family but spend most of their time in moist forests. Woodcock plumage looks like leaf litter. If you unknowingly walk toward a concealed woodcock, it might flush when you are right next to it, scaring the daylights out of you. I have had only a couple of good daytime looks at woodcocks. Once at Magee Marsh on Lake Erie near Toledo, Ohio, I saw a woodcock probing for worms in plain view along the muddy bank of a stream.

Woodcocks have long been a popular game bird for hunters. During the autumn hunting season, hunters in Virginia are allowed to kill up to three woodcocks a day. The "cock" in Cocker Spaniel is based on these dogs being good at retrieving small game such as woodcocks on British hunting expeditions. As for the "spaniel" part, the British thought the droopy, submissive appearance of the dogs resembled the appearance of Spaniards—the *Espagnol*. The American Woodcock is sometimes called a "timberdoodle," originally because some people were reluctant to say the syllable "cock."

Woodcocks are strange birds. Their brain is almost upside down, and their eyes are in the back of their head. The position of the eyes allows woodcocks to peck in the soil for food while watching for predators coming from above or behind. All species of birds have both binocular vision (using both eyes together) and monocular vision (using each eye separately). Binocular vision allows greater depth perception. Predator species such as hawks and owls have their eyes in the front of their head so they can use binocular vision to zero in on prey, and monocular vision tends to make up a smaller range of their total visual field. Prey species tend to have their eyes on the sides of their head so they can see predators coming from multiple directions, and some have binocular vision of less than 20 degrees (compared to 120 degrees in a typical human). These birds are trading depth perception for a greater field of view.

The eye position of woodcocks is extreme compared to most other prey species. They not only can see a full 360 degrees without moving their head, but they also can see with binocular vision above their head, both forward and backward, to watch for a predator coming from above while they are feeding. Woodcocks are thought to determine where to look for earthworms, the primary food in their diet, by soil color. They prefer dark soils to light soils; wet soils, which generally are rich in worms, tend to be dark. Their long soft-tipped bill is specially adapted for finding the food by touch, so their eyes have evolved to use depth perception more for spotting aerial predators than terrestrial worms.

During the mating season, male woodcocks perform an elaborate ritual to impress females. At dusk, the male woodcock starts to make a farty little noise (described as a nasal *peent*) after the sun has set but before total darkness has set in. He points his head in different directions while he calls, so the noise might sound as if it is coming from nearby one moment and far away the next. Shortly after the farty sounds commence, the woodcock begins a slow spiraling ascent to about two hundred feet in the air, making a whistling sound with his wings. After he gets as high as he wants to go, he starts to drop like a sheet of paper wafting in the wind. During the descent, he utters a call that resembles the sound people make when kissing the back of their hand to call a Cocker Spaniel. Upon landing, the male woodcock makes more farty noises and then flies upward again. He typically does this many times in succession. On my numerous visits to woodcock display areas, I have twice seen males mount females in the dim light after landing. Before one of the matings, the male on the ground raised his wings as he approached the female as if he were about to envelop her in a cape. Sometimes, the male woodcock performs the display flight just before sunrise.

I used to work in a building in downtown Washington that is near a church where a couple of Peregrine Falcons occasionally perched. The building engineer, to whom I had shown the falcons, came to my office one morning and said he had found a dead Peregrine on the patio. I asked what he had done with it, and he said he had put it into a Dumpster. We went to the Dumpster, and after he rooted around for a moment, he pulled up a beautiful dead woodcock. After I recovered from the surprise of seeing a bird quite different from a Peregrine, I looked closely at the plumage. Each feather has beautifully subtle patterns that are responsible for the woodcock's effective camouflage in the forest. Not until the following day did I realize the irony of the engineer mistaking the slowest-flying bird in North America for the fastest.

97. WOODPECKER
Headbanger Birds

Our cartoon friend Woody has helped to popularize woodpeckers. Woody was created by Walter Lantz in the 1940s. The inspiration came when a woodpecker in Northern California repeatedly banged on the honeymoon cabin of Lantz and his new wife. The bird probably was an Acorn Woodpecker, one of whose calls sounds like the first part of the Woody Woodpecker laugh.

Woodpeckers are a large, diverse group found on every continent except Australia and Antarctica. There are about 225 species, and they vary widely in size, shape, and color. Some are mostly black and white, while others have colorful plumage that features red, green, or yellow. In Thailand, I saw both a tiny woodpecker called a White-browed Piculet, who is less than four inches long, and the enormous Great-slaty Woodpecker, who is about twenty inches. These species are near the two ends of the size range for the entire family. My favorite Thai woodpecker is the Heart-spotted Woodpecker. It is only six inches long, but it has a large head and nape—it looks like the top of a large woodpecker who has been sawn in half.

The special anatomy of woodpeckers has evolved to suit their headbanger manner of feeding. Their brain is encased for protection from the jarring that occurs when they bang their bill against trees. There are feathers in front of their nostrils to prevent them from inhaling particles of wood while chiseling bark. The feet of most woodpeckers are adapted for grabbing and climbing tree trunks. Woodpeckers have a stiff tail to anchor themselves to trees. They have a long tongue with barbed tips for extracting insects and other food from tree crevices. In 2009, a photo was posted on the Internet showing a Northern Flicker pulling the long tongue of a Red-headed Woodpecker during a fight. The tongues of some woodpecker species can measure half the length of their body, minus the tail.

Some of the twenty or so woodpecker species seen in North America are common backyard and feeder birds. The sexes look similar but usually have a slight difference in markings, such as a small dot on the head of one sex or a different color mustache stripe. Seven species are seen in the Middle Atlantic states, and a birder friend from Maryland has seen all of them in the trees behind her house.

Many woodpecker species have loud calls, drum loudly, and move around a lot, making them easier to locate than birds who sit quietly on branches. The most common is the Downy Woodpecker, who is the smallest of the bunch. It has almost-identical plumage to the Hairy Woodpecker, who is larger and has a longer bill. The Downy Woodpecker was given its name because the white feathers on its back are softer than the similar feathers on the back of the Hairy. These soft feathers are responsible for the Downy's scientific name of *pubescens*, which means soft like the genital fuzz on humans going through puberty. Apparently, a lot of botanists were also hung up on this subject, because there are many living types of flora that have *pubescens* as their species name. Some examples are: *Betula pubescens* (a birch tree); *Cinchona pubescens* (a South American tree whose bark provides quinine for malaria treatments); *Centrosema pubescens* (a South American herb); *Angelica pubescens* (a medicinal root); *Toxicodendron pubescens* (Atlantic Poison-Oak); *Cypripedium pubescens* (a North American yellow lady's slipper orchid); and so on.

The Pileated Woodpecker, who looks a bit like Woody, is the second largest woodpecker species in North America, at seventeen inches. A friend who was in Washington's Rock Creek Park when a Pileated landed on a nearby tree said she saw a woman hustle her children away for fear that a dangerous zoo bird had escaped. The Pileated is mostly brownish black, with white on the neck, throat, and wings. The name comes from the bird's red pileum, which is the top of a bird's head from the bill to the back of the neck. The word "pileum" comes from the Latin word for an old Roman pointed cap that the crest of a Pileated Woodpecker resembles. There is disagreement among birders as to whether the first syllable of the bird's name should be pronounced "pill" or "pile." The first syllable of "pileum" as well as the Latin word from which it is derived is pronounced like "pile," which suggests that the "i" in pileated is long.

The bill of the Pileated Woodpecker is a formidable tool. I once had to try to grab and hold the bill while a bird bander extricated a Pileated from a net. While the bird was trying to peck at us, the bill moved back and forth with surprising slowness. Still, when a Pileated drums on a tree, the sound sometimes can be heard hundreds of yards away. The power of the drumming is distinctive and does not sound like any other woodpecker species I regularly see and hear. Once on a Christmas Bird Count, I heard the loud banging of a Pileated nearby yet could not locate the bird. I put my hand on a tree and realized the banging was coming from inside. Eventually, the bird poked its head from a hole in the tree.

The Pileated looks similar to the slightly larger Ivory-billed Woodpecker. Compared to the smaller Pileated, the Ivory-billed Woodpecker has more white on its wings, a whiter bill, and plumage that is jet black rather than brownish black. It used to be common when the southern United States was covered with large expanses of forest, but as these forests were chopped down, the species lost its habitat. The Ivory-billed Woodpecker was thought to be extinct in the United States during the latter half of the twentieth century. There is a lot of controversy about whether it was rediscovered at the beginning of the twenty-first century in a swamp of about a half-million acres in Arkansas. Nobody was able to take a photograph of the bird or definitively record its call. A brief video of the bird flying has raised questions about whether it was actually a Pileated. I have seen situations where people want to see a bird species so much that they are inclined to make a similar species into the one they want to see. Still, the possibility of the rediscovery highlights that there are still places in the world and the United States that remain unexplored and unknown. Nobody knows what species might be found in some of these inaccessible tracts of forests, which is a compelling reason to not chop them down.

Woodpeckers provide a valuable service for other species of birds and animals by excavating holes. Many non-woodpecker species use these holes for nesting and roosting. The service is not limited to trees. In the Arizona desert, many large cacti contain Gila Woodpecker holes used by other species; the Elf Owl is almost entirely dependent on woodpecker holes for nesting. Woodpeckers do not have unlimited ability to drill holes, and some species will do so only in certain types of trees. The endangered Red-cockaded Woodpecker of the south-eastern United States seeks mature pine trees infected by a particular fungus to excavate a hole in which to nest and roost. This species has become endangered, because modern forestry practices tend not to leave many mature trees standing. In *Helpers at Birds' Nests*, Alexander Skutch describes a special defense the Red-cockaded Woodpecker has developed for its nest cavity. The woodpecker drills many small holes around the nest opening, causing resin to ooze. This keeps away predators such as rat snakes, who are sickened by the resin. A cockade is a small hat ornament, and the bird gets its name from a small red ornament spot on the side of the male's head.

Woodpeckers called sapsuckers also drill holes in trees to cause resin to flow. There are four sapsucker species in North America, with the most common being the Yellow-bellied Sapsucker (a name sometimes said by entertainers for comic effect). You can tell if sapsuckers are in the vicinity if you see rows of sap holes on a tree. The sapsuckers suck the sap and eat insects attracted to the flowing goo; hummingbirds also are sometimes attracted to these sap-oozing holes. Acorn Woodpeckers, common in parts of California, make different types of holes in trees. They get their name from making the trunks of trees look like Swiss cheese and sticking acorns into the holes. Acorn Woodpeckers are noisy, gregarious communists. Groups of up to fifteen birds form communes, in which they feed together, sleep together, and raise their young together.

Woodpeckers sometimes create problems for homeowners. During the spring, male woodpeckers drum loudly on wood or other materials to send a message both to attract eligible females and to warn rival males to stay away. Some woodpeckers drum on houses, which is unsettling to the residents. Much more unsettling is when woodpeckers excavate holes in wood siding and shingles. One explanation for this behavior is that there are insects crawling in the wood. Another is that appliances or wiring in the house are emitting high-frequency noises that woodpeckers mistake for insect sounds. Among the suggested solutions for homeowners are to hang aluminum pie plates on the house or to stuff the holes with rags containing vinegar, bleach, or other repellant substances. The pie plate solution was suggested to newscaster David Brinkley when he sought help from a local Audubon Society. He thanked the Audubon Society but declined to hang the plates, believing the solution to be worse than the problem.

A couple of familiar words might have derivations related to woodpeckers. "Yokel" might be derived from an old English dialect word for the Green Woodpecker, because the person so described might be like the stupid bird who banged its head against a tree. And "jinx" might be related to an Old World woodpecker called the Eurasian Wryneck, who is named for its ability to turn its neck in either direction almost twice as far as a human. Wrynecks are in the genus *Jynx,* which comes from the name the ancient Greeks had given to them. According to some sources, witches would invoke the name of these mysterious twisty-necked woodpeckers when casting spells and would put a "jynx" on someone. But in *A Browser's Dictionary,* John Ciardi says that there is no conclusive evidence to support this explanation and that the origin of jinx is unknown.

Woodpeckers are in a family called the Picadae. It was named after the mythological figure Picus, whose father Saturn was the god of agriculture. Circe, the enchantress who turned some of Odysseus' men into swine, had the hots for Picus, but the feeling was not mutual. Using her magical powers, she gained revenge by turning Picus into a woodpecker. Not many people think about Circe these days, but lots of people think about woodpeckers, so you could say Woody and company have had the last laugh.

98. WREN
Girl Birds and Boy Birds

The Wren features prominently in British folklore. It is often called a "Jenny Wren," with Jenny denoting a female. The chattering, scolding character of these diminutive birds earned them a female label from male poets and writers, even though the most vocal and prominent wrens are males. Jenny Wren often is portrayed doing things with her male friend Cock Robin. Wrens and robins do not mate in real life, but the *Penguin Book of Bird Poetry* includes verses such as:

> Says Robin to Jenny, 'If you will be mine,
> We'll have cherry tart, and drink currant wine.'
> So Jenny consented—the day was named,
> The joyful news the cock proclaimed.

On a 1957 album, Oscar Brand sings a bawdy English sea ballad called "Jinny Wren Bride." The lyrics, told from the perspective of the groom, describe the bride's strange and disreputable friends and relatives. The groom suggests that his bride is not, as Madonna might say, like a virgin.

The wren of British folklore is the only wren species found in Europe and Asia. It used to be considered the same species as the Winter Wren in North America, but it was split off in 2010. It is a skulky little bird who sometimes disappears into holes when humans approach. This behavior is the basis for the scientific name of the wren family: the Troglodytidae. A troglodyte is a person who lives in a cave or a hole.

For pure musical ability, wrens are among the best singers in the bird world. There are about eighty species, all but one of whom live in the New World, with the greatest number in Central and South America. Some have names such as Flutist Wren and Musician Wren. The Rock Wren should not be included in this list, because it is named for its habit of hopping on rocks rather than for its musical tastes. Likewise, the Band-backed Wren is named for its plumage rather than because it has musical accompaniment. Some wren music strays into the avant-garde. For instance, the Song Wren, found in Central and South America, is described in *The Birds of Panama* by George Angehr and Robert Dean as sounding like a "haywire cuckoo clock."

Wrens are mostly small brown birds with black, white, or gray markings. There are nine species in North America who range in size from four inches for the Winter Wren to more than eight inches for the Cactus Wren. Wrens often act animated and feisty, frequently cocking their tail. While some are handsome, none are drop-dead gorgeous, because they don't have much of a palette of colors with which to work. But what they lack in color, they more than make up for in singing ability. Wren songs can be wonderfully melodious, very complex, highly energetic, and extremely loud. Where I live, the Carolina Wren has one of the loudest songs of any resident songbird. The volume is surprising considering that the Carolina Wren measures only five or six inches. One of my favorite songsters is the Canyon Wren, found in the western half of North America. Its song moves straight down the musical scale. Because it hangs around in canyons, its loud song resonates against the rocks, which heightens the effect. Not all wrens are great songsters. Some can manage only a harsh chatter.

Some wren species build complex nests, and sometimes a male wren will build numerous nests during the breeding season. Many of the bird houses that Americans put in their yards are designed to attract House Wrens, whose name is based on the fact that the wrens frequently live near human houses rather than because humans provide houses for the wrens. According to Hal Harrison's *A Field Guide to Western Birds' Nests*, House Wrens have built nests in the radiator of an unused automobile, the top of a pump, an empty cow skull, an old boot hanging on the side of a cabin, the leg of workpants hanging on a clothesline, a flowerpot, the pocket of a scarecrow, and the crevice of a hawk's nest. The book contains a photo of House Wrens nesting in a pair of swim trunks hanging on a clothesline.

Not all birds called wrens are related to the Eurasian or American wrens. Some New Zealand wrens are strange-looking birds who look as if their tail has been chopped off. The Bush Wren is one of the New Zealand wren species now thought to be extinct. Another believed to be extinct is the Stephens Island Wren, who lived only on a small island off the north coast of New Zealand's south island. Peter Greenaway's *The Falls*, an obscure film that has more ornithology references crammed into its three-plus hours than any other film ever made, refers to the Stephens Island Wren "whose entire species population was slaughtered by a lighthouse keeper's cat in the first four months of 1894." While this account of the wren's demise is apocryphal, free-roaming cats as well as introduced rats on the island certainly contributed to the demise of this small, defenseless bird.

99. YELLOWTHROAT
The Poetry of Birds

A friend who was taking a poetry class asked me for help with an assignment involving "found poetry." She needed to find an example of prose that when read aloud sounded poetic. I suggested a passage about the Common Yellowthroat from *The Audubon Society Encyclopedia of American Birds*: ". . . he scolds intruder with chirps, chattering notes— *chack!*—darts about wrenlike, disappears in dense cover, reappears to scold again, occasionally rises to sing in thicket in full view, loud, clear *witchity, witchity, witchity, witchity* or *witch-a-we-o, witch-a-we-o*."

Of the roughly 110 warbler species in the New World, nine are called yellowthroats. The Common Yellowthroat is the only one who regularly visits North America, and it is common throughout much of the United States and Canada during breeding season. The newsletter of the Maryland Ornithological Society is called *The Maryland Yellowthroat*, which is the name by which the species was called early in the twentieth century.

The Common Yellowthroat measures about five inches. The male has an olive back, a yellow throat, and a bandit-like black mask. The female looks similar, but lacks the bandit mask. In May 2005, I found a dead female yellowthroat on a bike path. She did not appear to have been dead for long. I picked her up and took her to a nature center about a quarter-mile away. When you handle a live bird, you need to have a secure grip so it does not fly away until you want it to. Dead birds might make you feel sad, but you can view them in a more relaxed manner.

Having a lifeless female yellowthroat in my palm made me wonder how a creature so beautiful and complex could weigh virtually nothing. Common Yellowthroats weigh between a quarter and a half ounce, so two or three in an envelope would be under the maximum weight for a first-class letter. Because I found her in the spring, her fat reserves might have been depleted after making the long migration from her wintering ground in Central America or the West Indies. Depending on how much she had fattened up beforehand, the trip from her wintering ground to the park where she died might have taken about as long as the typical time to deliver a letter from Central America to Washington.

During the spring, seeing a Common Yellowthroat would not be deemed unusual or noteworthy by most serious birders. In fact, were you to say excitedly, "I found a Common Yellowthroat," other birders might wonder about your level of field experience. Were you to excitedly exclaim, "I found poetry!" after hearing a yellowthroat sing, other birders might question your sanity.

Such attitudes will not discourage me from seeking more poetry rising from the thickets.

About the Author

William Young is a writer who lives in Arlington, Virginia. His long-time interest in birds developed when he was growing up in suburban Philadelphia. He has traveled around the world to study birds and is especially interested in bird behavior and bird conservation. His travels have taken him to Australia, Asia, Europe, South America, Central America, and the Caribbean, as well as throughout the United States. He is also interested in recreational linguistics, and his articles have appeared in publications such as *Word Ways* and *Verbatim*. In 2004, he wrote a novel entitled *Cuma's Voice: An Environmental Utopia*, in which he imagines an existence that might have evolved had society not developed along technological lines.